THE CERTAINTY TRAP

THE CERTAINTY
TRAP

*Why We Need to Question Ourselves More
—and How We Can Judge Others Less*

Ilana Redstone

Foreword by Joe Walsh

PITCHSTONE PUBLISHING
DURHAM, NORTH CAROLINA

Pitchstone Publishing
Durham, North Carolina
www.pitchstonebooks.com

Library of Congress Cataloging in Publication Control Number: 2024024543

ISBN (hardcover): 9781634312561
ISBN (ebook): 9781634312578

The Certainty Trap *is dedicated to my three amazing children: Ezra, Oren, and Zachary. I hope they continue to move through the world with a little open space in their hearts and minds.*

Contents

Foreword

I come from the world of politics. And today in America, this world is one of daily, really hourly, hand-to-hand combat over all kinds of policy issues, political reforms, Donald Trump, culture war issues like race and gender, and, heck, the future of democracy altogether. The battlefronts in this war are the streets, TV, radio, the internet, and social media. I've been on this political battlefield for the past thirteen years. It's exhausting. And not a week goes by that I don't wearily say to myself, "I'm done, I can't do this anymore, I gotta go relax under a willow tree for the rest of my life." I was at this end point one more final time in June of 2023 when I met Ilana Redstone. I invited this college professor on my political podcast to discuss a new book she was writing, and what was supposed to be a straightforward ten-minute chit-chat turned into an hour-long-plus conversation. I would have kept going, but my producer (who had to edit the conversation) was pleading with me to stop.

I couldn't stop listening to Ilana Redstone because, for the first time maybe ever, I was being given a roadmap for how to reasonably work through and overcome the heated and divisive hand-to-hand political battles. For the first time, I was being given real hope for a country I've always assumed is irreparably divided. Meeting her for the first time, listening to her describe how the problem of "certainty" is driving this polarized country off a cliff was, to put it mildly, a real "wow" moment to this former Congressman and right-wing media star.

This book, *The Certainty Trap*, comes at a time when trust in institutions has cratered, political polarization is off the charts, and Americans are all too ready to dismiss, as stupid, horrible, or evil, people who disagree with them. As Redstone says, our minds are closed, but she doesn't just call for open minds, as necessary as that is. Rather, she explains *why* our minds are closed and what we need to do to change that. While everyone has been calling for civil discourse these past few years, she goes well beyond that and gets to the heart of the problem: transforming how we think and how we see the world and each other. What Redstone puts forth here goes well beyond impacting the world of politics; it impacts *all* places and spaces where people gather and communicate. Because, trust me here, EVERYTHING in America is politicized at this point, so understanding why we think as we do, why we are so certain in how we think, and why we choose our version of reality over others will build trust and reduce resentment.

Look, what's so cool about this book and what Redstone is saying is she isn't pushing any particular political agenda. She has no political agenda here other than helping to talk this country off the ledge. I really appreciate this. Right now, in America, people have their backs up and are ready to punch back at any perceived slight. Redstone isn't asking anyone to change their minds or change their political or policy stances. She's asking us to change the *way* we think—to be clear about our principles and goals, acknowledge the way our assumptions about the world shape how we view one another, and think about and pay attention to the questions we don't ask, but need to.

She's not making a moral argument. She's not saying that any opinion is as good as any other. She's simply saying we need to understand the fundamental uncertainty in the world and, when we communicate with one another, to use words and concepts in a way that the other person would agree with. If we're going to disagree with someone, do so in a way that doesn't rely on assumptions about the other person's motives, intent, or character. Her example of someone who believes that women shouldn't have the right to drive makes this point. You could call that person a misogynist or you could discuss why you believe all people should have equal rights under the law. And you can allow someone to hold the opinion that women shouldn't be allowed to drive while believing the exact opposite. All ideas are subject to questioning. Respectful questioning. And we need to open our minds to this.

This is heady stuff. The thrust of *The Certainty Trap* is like dropping a bomb of stunning insight onto our bloodied political battlefield. And I can think of no one better suited to do this than Ilana Redstone. She's the perfect meeting of a thinker/problem solver and a moment, the moment being the unraveling of our body politic. She's been writing and speaking on this topic for years, giving her a unique insight into the problems of political polarization, the coarsening of civil discourse, the waning of public trust in institutions, and the lack of diversity in the media and on our college campuses. What I find when I speak with her and what I find when I read this book is that she has a perspective so unique in this field. I learn something new and insightful from her in every discussion, which is all of immense value to me in my world of politics. She sees our dangerous political divisions as fundamentally a problem in how we think and, by extension. talk. Put simply, each of us is way too certain in what we believe, and we lack precision in how we communicate. In other words, it's fixable; we just need to change the way we think, which in turn will change how we relate to one another. We don't have to change our beliefs, principles, or political views.

Here's the thing: We are a nation at each other's throats. We are a nation in crisis. We are a nation dangerously divided. We are a nation, many people believe (myself included), on the verge of a national divorce. Avoiding the Certainty Trap is the way out; it's the way for this nation to heal. The lessons in this book are lessons for all of us. They are lessons for all of us who have ever felt that the answers are simple, the causes are obvious, the people who disagree with us are racists, libtards, idiots, and just not even worth engaging. Avoiding the Certainty Trap doesn't mean there aren't bad actors. It just means we're willing to try to understand who's who, what's what, and what's the cost of getting it wrong.

Democracy depends upon us avoiding the Certainty Trap. Democracy depends upon our changing the way we think. Because our democracy cannot survive when there's no communication across divides and when one side wholly dismisses or writes off the other side. Redstone gives us a roadmap here in how to avoid the Certainty Trap. And, as someone committed to trying to defend democracy until I drop, I intend to carry Redstone's roadmap with me every day I'm out there doing battle.

Joe Walsh

Preface

This book is the culmination of long and sprawling conversations, discussions, and disagreements with many people over several years. I'm thrilled to be able to share it with you now. It would be bold of me to talk about our need to change how we think without first saying something about how I got to this point.

I'm a sociology professor. I have a joint PhD in sociology and demography from the University of Pennsylvania. I've been at the University of Illinois since the start of my career in 2005. The first decade or so of my academic career was spent writing academic and peer-reviewed papers on US immigration. I had no real public-facing side to my work. But I've long been interested in contentious topics and, more specifically, moral and ethical complexity. So, when I observed our political discourse becoming more hostile, more strained, and more heated, of course it caught my attention.

I developed and have been teaching a course called "Bigots and Snowflakes" since 2019.[1] I've been writing about topics related to how we think and communicate about polarizing issues since at least 2018. I've worked with various organizations—both public and private—who struggle to build a culture where contentious topics can be discussed openly. I've written extensively on related topics for outlets including the *Washington Post*, the *Hill*, the *Chicago Tribune*, and *Tablet*.

My journey to understanding the negative role of certainty in our discourse—and toward growing comfortable with, if not embracing, uncertainty when discussing important issues—extends much further back in my personal and educational history. I spent a lot of time living overseas when I was younger. During my junior year in college, I lived in southern Spain. After graduation, I lived in Mexico and then in South Korea, both times teaching English. I spent a few months in the Dominican Republic with something called Crisis Corps, which came after living for just over two years in northern Togo as a Peace Corps volunteer. Sometimes I lived with host families and sometimes I lived alone. One of the simple yet profound lessons I took from these experiences is that the world is full of decent and good people just trying to make their way through life. But there was something else I learned too: The problems we care the most about are often morally and ethically complicated.

This lesson became especially salient during my time in the Peace Corps, when my mind often raced with questions about the work we were doing. I was 24 years old when I was posted as a Peace Corps volunteer in northern Togo. Togo is one of a small number of sliver countries in West Africa. It sits between Ghana to the west and Benin to the east. Land-locked Burkina Faso lies to the north. Togo has a mere 32 miles of coastline on the Gulf of Guinea at its southern edge. I joined the Peace Corps for many of the same reasons other people do. As an idealistic young person, I wanted to do some good in the world. I figured I couldn't do much better than spending two years volunteering in a developing country.

Now, it probably goes without saying that people have a wide range of experiences living overseas in general and in the Peace Corps in particular. But it's almost always life-changing in some way. My experience made me realize that even something that seemed to be unambiguously good wasn't necessarily as simple as I'd originally thought. And seeing that complexity led to questions I didn't have before.

The government of Togo was dysfunctional. The primary school teacher in the village I lived in hadn't been paid in months. I wondered whether we, as volunteers, were playing a role in enabling this. Was our presence serving to prop up a corrupt regime? Were we helping lull people into a sense of complacency when they would otherwise be demanding accountability?

One day, in the village I lived in, a man came to my door and asked me to help him understand why his tomatoes were rotting on the vine. There must have been at least a hundred people in that village who could have answered his question better than I could. So why was he asking me? Was I unwittingly fostering dependency on foreigners?

And how should I think about these potential costs? Were they real? Did they matter? Were they outweighed by the benefits of us being there? And who should decide?

I wasn't alone in struggling with these kinds of ethical questions. These were things that many volunteers grappled with. I just know I never shook them off.

I couldn't stop thinking: If the *Peace Corps* had potential costs to it, did that then mean that everything I once thought could neatly be divided into good and bad might also be more complicated? I felt confused, but by simply asking these questions, I better understood why some volunteers had chosen to leave.

To be clear, I didn't (and still don't) have answers to my questions about the Peace Corps. And I wasn't prepared to conclude that we should all get up and leave Togo forever. Indeed, I decided to stay. I simply realized that something I thought so clearly had only benefits with no costs was, in fact, complicated. If that was true in this case, was it true in other situations, too?

The challenge before us is to continually find the doubt, name the uncertainty, and interrogate and clarify our thinking—each and every time we think the solution to a complex problem is obvious or easy. What we're describing goes beyond simple intellectual humility. After all, it's often the things for which we don't realize we *lack* humility that do the most damage to our thinking. These tend to be the values, beliefs, and principles we take so for granted that we don't even think to say them out loud.

In this book, we will see the ways in which we think without depth, take our assumptions for granted, and understand the consequences of both. We'll know we're doing it right not because we're all in agreement (we won't be), but because we're willing to live with the disagreement.

We'll start by talking through the scope of the problem of certainty and we'll continue with a discussion of the Settled Question Fallacy, which underpins the Certainty Trap. We'll then talk about the cost of doing nothing to change our thinking, what the world looks like from inside and outside of the trap, the challenges associated with leaving certainty behind, the move from certainty to confidence, the Certainty Trap in our institutions, the forces at play that make uncertainty difficult, and how the path forward requires vigilance. At the end of each chapter, you'll find a short summary with key ideas. And I've highlighted a few points (noted in text boxes) that are important to bear in mind as you read.

With that, I throw down the gauntlet.

THE CERTAINTY TRAP

Introduction

"Where two principles really do meet which cannot be reconciled with one another, then each man declares the other a fool and a heretic."

LUDWIG WITTGENSTEIN, *ON CERTAINTY*

If you look at any news website or social media feed, it seems clear that our societies are being torn apart politically. Too many of us have come to see our ideological opponents—whether they're online, across from us at the dinner table, or in the break room at our workplace—as little more than bigots, snowflakes, or just plain idiots. Many of us are asking, whether quietly in our own minds or loudly for others to hear: how will we end this rancor and stop being at each other's throats?

The short answer is that we need to be less certain—or, put another way, we need to avoid what I refer to as the Certainty Trap. This is true whether you're fearful of the prospect of a right-wing takeover or a woke revolution, concerned about climate change or government overregulation, or alarmed by a growing wave of white identitarianism or a surge of migrants at the border. I don't expect you to believe me just yet. Indeed, sometimes when discussing the pitfalls and dangers of certainty, people tell me that avoiding the Certainty Trap by questioning ourselves more and judging others less might be an interesting intellectual exercise, but it will not help solve real problems in the real world—as though there's a dividing line between the two goals.

If you're wondering how common this trap is, here's one way to think about it: If you've ever felt that the answers to complex problems are simple and obvious and that anyone who disagrees must be ignorant or hateful, you've been trapped. Rest assured, even if you have been doing this, you're in excellent company. We wouldn't be where we are today unless pretty much all of us have done, or still do, the same.

We are most prone to falling into the Certainty Trap when we are confronted with something that we find objectionable from a moral or ethical standpoint. But even then, we can and should avoid it. For example, when Uganda passed one of the world's strictest laws in the world against homosexuality, I wrote a piece called "The Problem with Calling the Ugandan Law Homophobic." In it, I argued that calling the law homophobic was a way of giving yourself permission to simply dismiss its supporters with a wave of the hand. I said that instead of calling it "homophobic," an opponent could be more specific. I might say I oppose the law because "I believe we shouldn't criminalize the sexual behavior or preferences of consenting adults." In this sense, my condemnation doesn't require any assumption about what's in the hearts of people on the other side of the issue. The first comes from within the Certainty Trap; the second doesn't. A friend immediately commented on the article, chastising me for making what he viewed as a semantic argument when the lives of the homosexual population of Uganda were on the line. To him, I said, "It's *because* it's important that I want to make sure I'm being clear in my thinking and am ready and able to engage."

A sense of moral superiority, a feeling made up of anger laced with contempt, fuels righteous indignation. And it gives us permission to disengage. As good as it feels, it's played a large role in getting us to the point we're at now. It's done this by alienating us from one another—by leading us to believe that, especially when it comes to complex social problems, the world can be neatly divided into people who are good and bad, right and wrong, evil and virtuous. This can be done because the good people know who's on which list and what got them there.

So, we're at a crossroads, with a decision to make.

One option is to lean into our righteous indignation. We can admit that we like feeling morally superior more than we like figuring out how to get along with people we disagree with. Such a confession would probably come as little surprise, given we've built a culture where the same moral outrage that pushes people to extremes can get you more likes on X or, if you're lucky, even make you a star. If that's the world we want to inhabit, then more power to us. Damn the torpedoes and full speed ahead. But, if this is the case, it might make sense to stop griping about the fallout that comes from this culture we've created.

For those of us who don't think this is such a great option, this book offers an alternative—one that requires us to be willing and ready to both challenge and clarify our thinking. Some people will read this book out of a deep and abiding sense of altruism. Others will read it simply because they wish to understand, as best they can, what's true about the world. And others still will read it because they are looking for pragmatic solutions to some particularly concerning social problem. No matter your particular reason for picking up this book, it offers a roadmap for people ready to do their part when it comes to correcting our current course. Not because you've changed your mind on the issues that matter to you—as you'll see, you don't have to—but because you want to be part of something bigger. This book is for people who fear where we're headed more than they fear questioning their own sense of moral superiority.

In that regard, this book is not an instruction manual for morality. Throughout its pages, I make no claims about moral truths or absolutes or any lack thereof. In part, that's because I have no secret information on the right way to live in the world. But mostly it's because we can observe that a failure to question our thinking drives our judgments of one another and understand that labeling something as good or bad only makes sense if we're clear and precise about our goals and values all without making a single moral claim. It is for those who want to strengthen society by having a more robust understanding of the world around them and perhaps even of themselves.

THERE'S NOTHING ABOUT AVOIDING CERTAINTY THAT MEANS
WE CAN'T SAY "THIS IS RIGHT" AND "THIS IS WRONG." IT JUST MEANS
THAT WE NEED TO DO THAT FOLLOWING A SET OF GUIDELINES
WE HAVE MADE CLEAR.

I recently gave a talk to a group of Harvard alumni. There was a woman present—let's call her Jane—who, only a few days prior to the talk, had the traumatic experience of being assaulted in the New York City subway. She was, understandably, still upset, although she was physically fine. She was angry at the woman who assaulted her and indignant about the slow response time on the part of the police. And yet, at the end of our discussion, she let out a slow exhale and remarked how much better and more relaxed she felt.

Without in any way minimizing what she had been through, thinking about uncertainty gave her space to consider whether the woman who assaulted her might not be a horrible person. Maybe she herself had been traumatized. Or maybe she needed help that she hadn't been able to get. Jane was able to wonder whether the police might have a reason for their delayed response. Perhaps they were woefully understaffed. Or in the middle of an emergency. Maybe it wasn't abject indifference or laziness after all.

None of this meant Jane's initial conclusions were necessarily wrong—and yet, opening the door to the possibility of a different explanation changed how she viewed the people involved. At the end of the talk, she thanked me, saying she felt happier than when we started. In Jane's case, uncertainty was a bit like empathy, but without the moral baggage. As important as empathy can be, it doesn't answer the question of who we should empathize with. Ultimately, mine is not a moral argument. It's about understanding the ways that certainty distorts how we see the world and one another.

Avoiding the Certainty Trap won't solve all the world's problems. But undermining moral outrage is a necessary first step toward having the conversations we so desperately need. It's how we can move toward seeing each other as fellow citizens rather than enemies to destroy— something that democracy itself requires us to do. What's more, just like Jane, it might even make you happier. There's something rather freeing about knowing there's always a chance you're wrong. Perhaps that's because it means there's always a chance the other person is wrong, too.

One way to think about the challenge we face when it comes to breaking out of the Certainty Trap is to imagine ourselves in Ancient Greece. It turns out we can learn a few things about certainty from Socrates.

According to history books, Socrates regularly challenged the people of Athens by pressing them on what they thought they knew about the world. Regardless of the topic, he is said to have asked, "But why . . . ?," pushing his conversation partner until they realized that what they thought they knew for sure was actually based on a series of assumptions. We are told that he would often keep pressing until there were no questions left to ask.

Socrates is also remembered for linking the concept of wisdom to a deep and abiding sense of the limitations of our own knowledge, yielding the quote, "The only true wisdom is in knowing you know nothing."

While there's a way to hear his words as a simple declaration of the value of humility, they also point to something deeper. Perhaps Socrates knew, even then, the powerful implications of forgetting to question what we know. Maybe he saw that it could lead to unparalleled divisions and resentment in a society. In this sense, maybe his words are a warning. Just imagine a society cleaving in such a way that dueling groups lay conflicting claims to what's real and neither acknowledges their fallibility. Sound familiar?

1

Laying the Foundation for Challenging and Clarifying Our Thinking

"To teach how to live without certainty, and yet without being paralyzed by hesitation, is perhaps the chief thing that philosophy, in our age, can still do for those who study it."

BERTRAND RUSSELL, *A HISTORY OF WESTERN PHILOSOPHY*

In a 2005 commencement address at Kenyon College, the writer David Foster Wallace described what might be one of the highest hurdles to clear when it comes to questioning how we think: certainty. He told a story of two men, drinking together at a bar in a remote corner of Alaska. He described one of the men as religious, the other as an atheist. They were arguing over the existence of God. In Wallace's story, the atheist says:

> Look, it's not like I don't have actual reasons for not believing in God. It's not like I haven't ever experimented with the whole God and prayer thing. Just last month I got caught away from the camp in that terrible blizzard, and I was totally lost and I couldn't see a thing, and it was 50 below, and so I tried it: I fell to my knees in the snow and cried out, "Oh, God, if there is a God, I'm lost in this blizzard, and I'm gonna die if you don't help me."

The religious man looks at the atheist, and says, "Well, then, you must believe now. . . After all, here you are, alive." The atheist responds, "No, man, all that was, was a couple Eskimos happened to come wandering by and showed me the way back to camp."

Wallace told his audience that an easy lesson to take away from this is that it is narrow minded to call one man right and the other man wrong. Then he explained that the "religious dogmatists' problem is exactly the same as the story's unbeliever: blind certainty, a close-mindedness that amounts to an imprisonment so total that the prisoner doesn't even know he's locked up." Each man in Wallace's Alaskan story behaves as though his position deserves to be held with unshakable confidence. Of course, that is unwarranted both for the atheist and for the person of faith.

And yet, this kind of thinking is pervasive. In fact, the problem Wallace put his finger on is relevant for how we understand the world more generally. When we hold our beliefs in a way that leaves no room for doubt, this leads to *an unwillingness—whether conscious or not—to question what we think we know about the world and one another.* And that has other knock-on effects.

One is that it leads us to stop asking questions. After all, there's no need to ask questions when we already have the answers.

Another is that it leads us to behave as though there are no questions that can be asked. So, we see anyone who does as stupid or hateful.

Still another effect, as with the example of the Ugandan anti-homosexuality law mentioned in the introduction, is that certainty gives us permission to be sloppy in our thinking. It leads us to forget that labeling one thing right and another wrong only makes sense when that thinking is made clear.

What counts as a heated or contentious issue can change over time and place. We're probably not arguing over exactly the same things Socrates did. But for the past several decades, they have included subjects that touch ideas around identity, fairness, intent, racism, inequality, freedom, or harm. For many of us, our thoughts and opinions on these issues are rooted in core beliefs about the world—beliefs that the Certainty Trap prevents us from naming, criticizing, examining, and holding up to the light.

Failing to do this tends to lead us to focus on the wrong things. For instance, many of us have probably heard that, when it comes to talking with people across divides on heated topics, we should focus on the mechanics of better communication. We are reminded not to raise our voices or roll our eyes. We are to be active listeners. And we're supposed to take turns speaking.

These skills are important—but they are ultimately the aesthetics of how we interact. If a conversation on a contentious topic is like a house, remembering not to raise your voice is the shiny coat of paint on the outside. Not rolling your eyes is a new set of shutters, and remembering to take turns speaking is a fancy door knocker. As any realtor will tell you, while these things increase "curb appeal," the structure of the house matters more. The studs, joists, and rafters represent how we think about the issue at hand, what we assume to be the underlying truth about the world.

When we neglect our house's structure, focusing only on the outside, we wind up stuck. What's more, we often don't even realize this is the case. It's like I'm standing in the front yard of a house with rotting rafters, tapping my finger to my chin, mystified by the fact that the roof is caving in. I'm telling myself: The paint is flawless, the windows are clean, the yard is raked, so what's the problem? But you don't have a to be a professional builder to understand that a fresh coat of paint won't fix rotting timbers.

The consequences of *not* questioning our thinking vary widely, depending on the topic and the context. And while the list of heated subjects given above may seem short—it's only seven items long—these subjects are so broad and the world is so complex that almost no realm of life is untouched by them. This is why a conversation about sports can turn into an argument about whether it's fair that a trans woman athlete competes on the women's sports team. Or a lunchtime discussion about a pregnant co-worker turns into a clash about abortion. Or a comment about someone's promotion becomes a heated debate about affirmative action.

Of course, there are times when the consequences of not questioning our thinking are negligible. I am sitting here in a comfy chair, my feet tucked under me, with my water bottle on the end table. I'm pretty sure it's a water bottle. I can hold it. It's tall, light blue, metallic, it has a black lid, and it has water in it. I can take a sip to confirm the contents. Is there a chance I'm wrong—that my certainty is misplaced? Could this be nothing more than an elaborate hallucination? Perhaps someone slipped a high dose of LSD into my oatmeal this morning. It's possible, though highly unlikely. More importantly, there are probably no consequences if I choose not to engage with these questions. But heated moral issues aren't water bottles.

NOT ALL CERTAINTY IS A TRAP. THE TRAP IS WHEN CERTAINTY LEADS US TO DISMISS, DEMONIZE, AND JUDGE OTHERS HARSHLY, ESPECIALLY ON HEATED POLITICAL ISSUES.

When we're righteous, we feel morally virtuous and justified. And when we feel morally virtuous and justified, we see the person who doesn't agree as inherently morally *flawed* and *un*justified. We find the other person's positions threatening and in need of a swift, strong, and unambiguous condemnation. But when we're busy being outraged, we're often ignoring the importance of understanding or being clear about where that outrage is coming from.

Ultimately, our sense of righteous indignation creates, inflames, and sustains the conditions we say we want to avoid—conditions where politics are bitterly polarized. As a result, relationships between people on opposite sides of the political aisle can feel impossible to sustain.

Why Do Clarity and Precision
in Our Thinking Matter So Much?

Let's say I observe someone on the street getting into a car. And let's assume, for the sake of this thought experiment, that I have good reason to believe that the car isn't theirs and that they don't have permission to use it. Setting aside for the moment the question of whether I decide to try to intervene ("Stop thief!"), my inclination will probably be to judge that person for this action. And when I do, that judgment will be coming from a principle. In this case, it's probably my sense that stealing is wrong. Now, that particular principle happens to be one that is shared by much or most of society—so much so that it's enshrined in our laws, but what if it weren't? Say it's my principle, but not yours.

Imagine that you and I are standing next to one another while the car theft is happening and that I look at you, nod with a frown in the car thief's direction, and say, "Can you believe that guy?!" But let's say you don't share my principle about stealing being wrong. You might be confused by my gesture and my words. That will remain the case until or unless I share with you my thinking and make *explicit* what was going on *implicitly* in my head. That doesn't mean I can't hold onto the idea that stealing is wrong. It just means I have to be clear in my thinking for our interaction to make sense.

Let's think in terms of an example that takes a step closer to a heated issue. Assume I think, as I do, that women should have the right to drive. Does my commitment to avoiding the Certainty Trap mean I can no longer hold that opinion? No, it means I am committed to being clear and explicit about what value or values I'm drawing off—and to having those questioned. In this case, my value might be something like, *I think all people—women included—should have equal rights under the law.*

So far, we've been circling like vultures around an important point that we haven't yet stated. It is this. Naming out loud our principles or values accomplishes two important goals. One is that it allows someone else to challenge them. In the car thief example, if someone wants to disagree with me, it's hard for them to do so until I've named my claim that stealing is wrong. To see why this matters, imagine that I said instead that I objected because "I don't think that people wearing green jackets should be allowed to drive." As unlikely as it is that I'd think that, if I did, we'd have a fundamentally different conversation.

The other benefit of stating our principles clearly is that doing so reveals where we're using words in a way that the other person doesn't understand or doesn't agree with. Imagine if, in the women being allowed to drive example, instead of declaring my commitment to people having equal rights under the law, I said, "I'm trying to keep evil out of the world." Someone listening to me would rightly wonder, what in the world does she mean by "evil"? They might even think, "That's' not what *I* mean by 'evil.'"

Notice that the key focus here is on precision—not on making claims about morality. Here's one way to think about it. If I am standing before a work of art, I can talk about its colors and the composition in a way that's separate from whether I think the work is good or not. It's not that I (or someone else) can't make that determination. It's that the determination itself would be subject to examination and challenge. *Why* do I think it's good/bad? While immigration, policing, gun control, abortion, and discrimination aren't works of art, the principle is essentially the same.

Failing to question our beliefs and assumptions distorts our understanding of the world. When we watch social interactions and events unfold, we tend to behave as if we're looking out a window. And windows have certain properties. Perhaps most importantly, if I'm looking through a window out at a bird on the fence in my yard, I assume that if you stand next to me and look where I'm looking (assuming we're both wearing our corrective lenses), you'll see what I see. You'll see the same bird on the same fence, and it'll look to you more or less as it does to me.

But a more apt comparison would be that we're seeing the world in a mirror. Not because we're seeing our own reflection, although mirrors do that too, but because of another property of mirrors. Let me back up for a minute.

When I was little, sometimes my dad would take my siblings and me to the local county fair. We'd walk around, past the prize pigs and the fried Oreo vendors. I remember throwing darts at balloons in a desperate attempt to win a cheaply made yet impossibly colorful stuffed animal that, if I actually got it, was all but guaranteed to split at the seam within the first 24 hours. I also remember playing Skee-Ball and only rarely getting the darn ball to land in one of the prized inner circles.

And then there was the fun house. In the fun house, you could wander through one pathway after another lined with mirrors that made you look fatter, thinner, weirder, scarier, funnier, and all kinds of bizarre. People must have liked those mirrors because it seemed like there was a fun house every time I went. (For the younger generation—like my teenagers—who didn't grow up with county fairs, fun house mirrors have an effect similar to Snapchat filters.)

Distorted reflections are the result of curvature in the plane of glass that the mirror is made of. That curvature can be concave or convex and it can be subtle or severe. But all curvature distorts the image being reflected. Here's one way of thinking about the problem we face: Certainty curves in the glass, and it does so while leading us to believe we're looking out a window.

It's worth noting that certainty in our beliefs isn't the only thing that can bend that glass in the mirror. Psychotropic drugs (back to the LSD in my oatmeal) probably do it, too. But certainty might be the most insidious because we generally don't realize it's happening. Worse still,

---

CERTAINTY CURVES THE GLASS IN THE MIRROR REFLECTING THE WORLD TO US, ALL WHILE LEADING US TO BELIEVE WE'RE LOOKING OUT A WINDOW.

---

we think it's only happening to other people—not to us. When we think we're seeing the world through a window, we're ready to be righteously indignant. Because without even thinking about it, we're sure that we're seeing the world as anyone with eyes would.

Earlier, I mentioned the example about women and driving. But let's make the importance of uncertainty even more concrete. When I assume that anyone who supports gun control doesn't care about freedom and wants to live in a nanny state, my failure to interrogate and clarify my own assumptions makes me feel justified in my judgment of others. In this case, that might mean that I see wanting to live in a nanny state as the only possible reason someone might support restrictions on guns. We could make a similar claim about anyone assuming that people who support expansive gun rights are callously indifferent to the children who have lost their lives in school shootings.

Avoiding The Certainty Trap might mean getting to the point where each person sees that, while their ideological opponent might indeed hate freedom or not care about the lives of innocent children, there are other possible motives and explanations for each of those positions.

There's a well-known saying that there are three sides to every story: my side, your side, and the truth. Someone could reasonably point out that questioning our thinking is just another way of trying to under-stand truth or reality. And while there's overlap, the comparison is too simplistic. For these two things to be the same, our definition of "truth" would have to be more expansive than it currently is. A more accurate description would be to say that being willing to question our thinking simply gives us a better reflection of what is—even if "what is" remains uncertain or, in the language of truth, isn't or can't be known. Sometimes I think of the search for truth as asymptotic. We can get closer and closer to it, without ever getting there. We can't eliminate every last shred of doubt.

Both the subtlety and pervasiveness of the problem of certainty make its effects difficult to overstate. If we want to understand the many ways it affects our lives, we might look at a related topic: the culture wars. Culture wars are fought with words over contentious, morally laden issues that cause deep divisions within a society, where each side attempts to win dominance over the other. The righteousness and harsh judgments—which happen when we fail to question our thinking—are part of what make the culture wars so vicious and protracted.

The culture wars are so vicious that a 2021 Ipsos poll showed that fully 57 percent—*well over half*—of Americans think these wars divide the country.[1] According to the report, out of all 28 countries surveyed, the United States was at the top for "perceived tension between different ethnicities" and close to the top for "perceived tension between political parties and those with different values." And, yet, while the United States may stand out on this issue, we're not alone. Nations as varied as Great Britain, Australia, Turkey, and India all had percentages of around one-third or higher saying that culture wars were dividing their own countries. This concerning picture is reinforced by what we observe at the highest levels of our national discourse and across both political parties.

Speaking at a White House event back in 2019, President Donald Trump declared that four women lawmakers "hate our country."[2] This was proclaimed as though hatred was the only possible explanation for why someone might disagree with his positions or, for that matter, criticize the United States. Do you see the similarity between this and the gun control/gun rights example? In both cases, there's only one possible explanation for the opposing position.

Trump isn't alone in this kind of thinking. Looking back to 2022, President Joe Biden signed an executive order "confirming that gender-affirming care is trauma-informed care" as though anyone who disagrees or has concerns wants to traumatize children.[3] From one president to the next, from one political party to the next, we're awash in our convictions. A cursory look at recent years will reveal many similar examples.

These consequences are visible in virtually all domains of society and have affected topics from abortion to transgender rights to Covid-19 and beyond. We see them play out in bitter fights over cancel culture, arguments over free speech, debates about book bans, and misguided legislative attempts to control how and what people think. If there's any doubt as to how real these threats can become, we need look no further than the 2022 attack on author Salman Rushdie or the 2023 attacks in Israel. In an extreme form, certainty can lead to the justification of precisely this kind of ideologically motivated violence. Although incidents reaching such levels of brutality are thankfully rare, other insidious consequences are not. And one of the most alarming might be the way this trap contributes to the deterioration of public trust.

Societies need a baseline level of trust, in one another and in institutions, to function. That trust underpins a sense of shared goals and a belief that people are mostly working toward a common good. In a democracy, social trust also allows us to live with people with whom we disagree. However, the heavily moral nature of the kinds of topics where we're least likely to question our own thinking, combined with the negative judgments of those who disagree, eat away at this. After all, it's hard to trust someone when we feel we're being demonized for holding an opinion we see as justified. Similarly, it's hard to trust people we think are morally corrupt.

Perhaps it'll come as little surprise that questioning our thinking on one topic might be easy while, on another, it might feel impossible. For instance, I'm not particularly attached to which cat food brand I buy. Being challenged on my choice probably won't faze me. But setting aside feelings of certainty can feel especially daunting when the issue feels personal and when it touches deeply held beliefs. Maybe instead of cat food brands, we're talking about whether euthanasia should be legalized or whether the police department should have a bigger budget.

This all means that even getting to the point where we're open to challenging and questioning our thinking is often no small feat. What's more, it's not always triggered in a predictable way. For Floyd Cochran, it was the birth of his son. In 1992, at the age of 35, Cochran had recently left the white supremacist group Aryan Nations. He had spent much of his life up to that point working with and expanding the reach of the group, rising to become its chief spokesman and executive strategist.[4] Cochran's transformative moment came after his son was born with a cleft palate. He realized there was no way to reconcile his objection to the way his community viewed his son with his own hatred of other groups.[5] In his words, Cochran tells the story:

> I had been told by the leadership, the people above me at Aryan Nations, when they found out that my son was born with a cleft palate and cleft lip, that he was a genetic defect and that he would have to be euthanized, which is a polite word for murdered or killed because he was a genetic defect. I don't want to tell you . . . that at that very instant I stopped being a racist. It took me two months from that point to build up the courage to leave the compound and also to examine is this what I want to do? But I couldn't get beyond that stumbling block. . . . (A)fter that was said about my son, and I had time to reflect, think, examine how I felt, I couldn't get past that wall that what was said about my son was wrong. But then how was it all right for me to say the same thing about people who were born different than I was. Because of their skin color, because of their faith, without being hypocritical.

Floyd Cochran couldn't live with what his beliefs meant for his love for his son. In this case, his paternal love didn't just challenge them, it upended them. While we might not be able to conjure moments as dramatic as what Floyd experienced, we can use what we know about certainty to reshape our own thinking and how we interact with others. And we can sustain this by not losing sight of some of the costs of continuing to do nothing.

I said earlier that, when we're sure about something, we stop asking questions and we stop looking for new or innovative solutions. Some of the problems that we suffer as a result are concrete and tangible. Take economic inequality, for instance. It's a topic that regularly makes an appearance on polls asking Americans for their views of the biggest challenges facing the country. Making inroads when it comes to reducing inequality is much less likely when we have people discussing it as though the best solutions are obvious, and anyone who disagrees is either a horrible person or a moron.

Other affected problems sit more in the realm of ideas. For instance, by the early 2020s, several states were being torn apart over how to teach topics related to gender or the history of slavery in K–12 schools.[6] To avoid or to move the needle on these challenges, as well as a long list of others, we need problem solvers who are committed to clear thinking.

I also said that certainty tells us that *there are no questions to be asked.* Because almost any issue can become heated, the ability to engage matters any time or place people get together. This is true even when no policy decisions are being made, like in our workplaces, at our dinner tables, in our schools, and our places of worship.

And I said that certainty leads us to be sloppy in our own thinking in a way that justifies righteous indignation—particularly around culture war issues. So, another way to think about the costs of doing nothing is: What are the potential risks associated with unchecked culture wars? At least one scholar has noted that, while not every culture war leads to a shooting war, shooting wars are always preceded by culture wars.[7] It's hard to know if this is true in every case, but a 2021 national survey showed some alarming results. A plurality (46 percent) of Americans responding to this survey believed "a future civil war was likely."[8] The way to avoid such a dire outcome is with thoughtful, deliberate, and open thinking and conversations.

To be sure, being willing to interrogate our thinking doesn't confer special insight into complicated social problems. No rabbits will be pulled out of hats and no magic will save us. And yet, it can understanding and recognizing how this works can make us less susceptible to distorted conclusions, whether they come through the media and social media, through people in our communities, or from anywhere else. This matters because not being aware of what we're missing doesn't mean we aren't missing something important.

Part of why avoiding the Certainty Trap matters so much is that an increasing number of people have had the experience of losing contact with friends or family over heated political issues. A commitment to clarifying our thinking can help rebuild many of those relationships and even create new ones. I'll talk about some specific ways to do this elsewhere in the book, but here's the big one: *When you find yourself judging someone who doesn't agree with you on a contentious and heated topic, recognize that your judgment is coming from some principle you probably have neither named nor questioned. Find that certainty. Identify it and name it. In so doing, you can clarify your own thinking, while also serving as a model for others to do the same.*

Last, it's worth a note on asymmetry before we dive in further. The failure to be clear about or question our thinking is not a problem that belongs to one side of the political spectrum or the other. It knows no bounds in that regard. And yet, readers may note that, while I pull examples from the political left and the political right, I make no claim of symmetry. In many ways, the examples I point to are more critical of the left. This does not mean that the right isn't awash in its own convictions. We need only point to the certainty of election deniers or in, as we saw, the willingness to condemn as anti-patriotic anyone who kneels during the national anthem. The reason for any tilt here is fairly simple. The left has adopted an approach that has eroded trust in a way that can be more difficult to pin down than the right. In other words, figuring out how the January 6 riots went off the rails tends to be a little easier than figuring out what's wrong with the trend toward gender-affirming care or the anti-racism movement.

We could have a good faith discussion about which side bears more responsibility for the current polarized state of our society. And I genuinely do not know where I come down on that question. But by bearing the lessons in this book in mind, you will take an important step away from the Certainty Trap.

Chapter Summary

- David Foster Wallace's parable about the religious man and the atheist shows us that blind certainty is a form of intellectual imprisonment. Both sides of an argument can suffer from closed-mindedness.
- Holding beliefs without room for doubt can prevent us from asking questions, make us dismissive of others, and foster sloppy thinking.
- Society's debates around identity, fairness, racism, and similar topics are often distorted by certainty.
- Articulating our underlying principles allows others to challenge our views and fosters a clearer understanding of disagreements.
- The certainties held in culture wars can be dangerous and divisive, and they may even foreshadow more serious conflicts.

Practice Uncertainty

Identify a deeply held belief you have, particularly one related to a contentious issue (such as gun control, abortion, etc.). Write down the reasons for your belief and then challenge each point, considering alternative perspectives. This exercise is about understanding the roots of your certainty and opening your mind to other viewpoints.

2

Certainty and the Settled Question Fallacy

"I tore myself away from the safe comfort of certainties through my love for truth—and truth rewarded me."

SIMONE DE BEAUVOIR, *ALL SAID AND DONE*

At the root of our distorted thinking is a willingness to treat our knowledge as definitive. I call this the Settled Question Fallacy. If I know without a doubt that I'm right, particularly about an issue that's social or political, I am going to automatically view opposing views as misguided and maybe even as an existential risk. And I wouldn't be alone in that. An October 2022 poll showed that over three-fourths of Democrats and Republicans say that the other "party's agenda poses a threat that if not stopped will destroy America as we know it."[1] It's difficult to see how that number would have declined since then. If your response to reading that is to double down on your conviction that the other side *is* an existential threat, this is an invitation for you to interrogate and clarify your thinking in a way that you may not have before.

What drives us to see the other side's views as a danger of this magnitude? While there are likely multiple factors at play, one of them is the sense that the concerns they voice are both groundless and unjustified. Because the underlying certainty driving this is the same conviction that gives us license to judge others, it should come as little surprise that polling reflects this, too. And indeed, an August 2022 survey showed that 72 percent of Republicans and 63 percent of Democrats view the other side as immoral.[2]

Imagine seeing half the people in your country as mindless sheep, hateful bigots, ignorant morons, or some combination of the two. For some readers, this may be more of a stretch than for others. Regardless, many people would likely feel angry in this position. They might think that the folks on the other side have everything backward and are standing in the way of a truly better world. They might even wish they could somehow, magically—with a Thanos-style snap for the Marvel fans— get rid of their opponents. At the same time, it's easy to imagine that being on the other end of this—living in a country where half the people see you as a mindless sheep, a hateful bigot, an ignorant moron, or some combination thereof—is also not appealing. And it, too, would likely foster resentment.

But what if your assessment isn't quite right? What if you're wrong about (at least some of) the people who are on the other side? While the Settled Question Fallacy can take several forms, each has the effect of shutting down our thinking and, by extension, closing off inquiry and dialog. And, as in the gun control/gun rights example, this tends to happen on the most difficult and heated questions we face. After all, those are the ones where we feel most threatened by disagreement. Paradoxically, those are also the ones where we most need to be able to talk to one another.

Why Is It a Fallacy?

Let's start with a basic question: What makes the Settled Question Fallacy a fallacy? A fallacy usually refers to an error in reasoning or argumentation. Much of the time, we aren't aware that we're falling into fallacies or, if we are, we convince ourselves that doing so is justified. In

---

WE SPEND A LOT OF TIME IN THIS BOOK TALKING ABOUT THE
IMPORTANCE OF QUESTIONING OUR KNOWLEDGE. BUT THIS
DOESN'T MEAN THAT ALL EXPLANATIONS SUDDENLY HAVE AN
EQUAL PROBABILITY OF BEING TRUE.

---

some cases, these fallacies are named and widely recognized.

The Ad Hominem Fallacy is where we attack the character of the person giving voice to an idea or position rather than the substance of the idea itself. This can lead to statements like *"We don't have to listen to Jane's opinion on abortion because Jane used to be addicted to drugs."* We might try to justify this by telling ourselves that only people with bad judgment become addicted to drugs. Since Jane used to be addicted to drugs, she must then have bad judgment, and we shouldn't listen to what she thinks about anything, including abortion. The error in this case lies in the substitution of engagement with what Jane is saying about abortion with dismissal of Jane as a person. It also lies in the leaps required to link one claim to the next.

We clarify those leaps by finding underlying questions. For instance, is it reasonable to assume that drug addiction is associated with a lack of good judgment? What about someone who was addicted years ago and isn't anymore? What does it mean to have good (or bad) judgment, who decides which is which, based on what criteria, and why? And what exactly is or should be the connection between the quality of a person's judgment and the determination of whether their opinion on abortion or any other topic is worth hearing?

The Red Herring Fallacy, sometimes called the Fallacy of Misdirection, is another example. A simple case of this might be if 25-year-old Javier says it's difficult to make a living on his salary, and Javier's 73-year-old grandfather responds by saying that, when *he* was 25, he made only $50 a week.[3] The error in reasoning is the failure to recognize that the grandfather's wage at age 25 is irrelevant to Javier's claim about not making enough money today.

To put these in context, the Ad Hominem and Red Herring are just two examples of well-known fallacies. Some sources put a fuller list of the total number of named logical fallacies at more than a hundred.

These kinds of errors tend to undermine the reasoning behind whatever position we're trying to advocate for. Because of this, *reducing* our tendency to fall into logical fallacies is generally seen as a way both to reason better and to make stronger arguments. With that in mind, I'm going to use the term fallacy a little differently. While the Settled Question Fallacy *is* an error in how we think, the main reason to avoid it *isn't* to make a stronger argument; it's to correct a fundamental misunderstanding in how we see the world. This means that avoiding the Certainty Trap isn't about winning an argument or getting people to agree.

With the Settled Question Fallacy, our error is in treating as conclusive the grounds for our positions and judgments on heated issues. This includes treating open questions as though they have definitive and clear answers. The public conversation around the relationship between gender and biology provides an easy example. Definitive claims are often made either that gender is entirely a social construct or that certain traits are clearly biologically determined.

Treating a question as settled is more than just an intellectual blunder where someone overstates their case. Our desire to treat claims as settled is sometimes tied to the fact that the consequences of allowing for something to be *un*settled can feel and be tangible. When it comes to gender and biology, at the heart of at least part of the disagreement is the relative importance of nature and nurture.

And because any character trait that occurs naturally in men more than in women—or vice versa—can be used to explain away differences in outcomes between the two groups, biological explanations can feel perilous. After all, if something is genetic or heritable (nature), our general conclusion is that we can't do anything to change it. What's more, we have a collective history of using biological arguments to justify odious actions. Conversely, however, if the traits that drive differences in outcomes are the result of social norms (nurture), we *should* be able to eliminate them. We should be able to socially deconstruct anything that was socially constructed in the first place.

Because no idea, belief, or value is exempt from examination or questioning—a principle that's central to avoiding getting stuck in our thinking—we can make this observation about the relative risks of nature and nurture arguments without taking a position on which explanation we think is right. We can make this more specific.

Many people recognize that women tend to be more nurturing, on average, than men, particularly when it comes to behavior we can observe and measure. However, understanding *why* this is the case has been the source of much debate. And it isn't one that can be easily passed off to science because empirical research can be found supporting both biological *and* cultural influences on nurturing tendencies. This reflects a limitation of social science research we'll talk about in detail later on.

For some people, it makes intuitive sense to see the difference in nurturing behavior between men and women as being primarily due to societal gender norms. This explanation is consistent with the observation that girls are more often encouraged to take on caretaking roles and the higher likelihood that boys who are drawn to such roles will be teased for liking "girl" things. However, it's also possible that the difference in nurturing behavior is, at least in part, rooted in biology and evolution. We can follow a short chain of thinking from women carrying, birthing, and nursing offspring to a conclusion that they might be naturally more inclined to take care of young more generally. And, of course, we don't have to choose all nurture or all nature—both can play a role.

Here's where things get tricky: The difference in the tendency to be nurturing could be used to try to explain part or all of the inequality in, for example, earnings between men and women. The thinking might go something like this: Because of their greater disposition toward being nurturers, women are willing (or even prefer) to work fewer hours and, as a result, advance less in the workplace than men do. Therefore, the difference in nurturing behavior—and not, for instance, gender discrimination in the labor market—explains why women earn less on average.[4] Or so goes the argument. Now, all of a sudden, whether we think about the tendency of women to be more nurturing than men as a difference that's genetically driven or socially constructed takes on new weight. If it's societal, we fight for change. If it's genetic, we do nothing.

If the stakes were already high on this topic—inequality between men and women in labor market outcomes—they just got higher.

Viewing the relationship between biological sex and gender as unsettled opens up a different kind of conversation—one that requires us to think and talk through difficult aspects of this topic. For instance, if gender is entirely a social construct, we should know we're successful in eliminating the influence of gender norms when we have an even split of men and women up and down the occupational hierarchy. We're there when 50 percent of nurses are men and 50 percent of construction workers are women. However, if gender is *not* entirely a social construct, we're faced with a different set of questions and a different way of thinking about what the successful elimination of those norms might look like. In other words, if some of the difference has a biological basis, we probably shouldn't expect a 50/50 split in every occupation, but what *should* we expect? 60/40? 65/35? 70/30? If the differences aren't all socially constructed, how will we know when we've eliminated the socially constructed barriers?

To take a more extreme—and non-labor market related—example, we could step away from nurturing tendencies and look at gendered patterns of aggression and violence. If we could snap our fingers and get rid of all gender norms, roles, and expectations, would we expect to see the same number of men and women sitting on death row, having committed capital offenses (and gotten caught) at similar rates? If we think that levels of aggression are innately different between men and women, the answer is probably no. In other words, we'd expect differences even in the absence of gender norms and roles. And if we think differences in aggression levels are entirely the result of social norms, the answer is most likely yes. We'd expect parity.

To be clear, I don't know the answers to these questions. And while we may one day know precisely how to characterize the interplay between nature and nurture when it comes to gender and biology, we are not there now.

Perhaps this particular topic hasn't come up recently in your casual conversations. If that's the case, rest assured that gender and biology is an example of one form of the Settled Question Fallacy. Others include treating the path forward or the solution to a problem as though it's obvious; behaving as though the right decision when the interests of different groups conflict or when values conflict is clear; or failing to recognize that, when it comes to heated issues and problems we care about, pretty much any solution has a combination of costs and benefits.

EXAMPLES: COVID-19, IMMIGRATION, AND GUN CONTROL

At the start of the Covid-19 pandemic in early 2020, much of the media coverage of and the public conversation about shutdowns had a particular tone. Often, that tone was that either you favored closing businesses to "flatten the curve," or you were indifferent to the deaths that might result from keeping things open. Flattening the curve meant supporting shutdowns to slow transmission and prevent hospitals and healthcare facilities from being overwhelmed by an influx of patients. In this case, many people treated the costs of this decision as so obviously negligible that anyone who brought them up as a concern was to be condemned.

And yet an uncertain response might have led us to a different set of questions: How *should* we think about the economic and human costs of closing businesses? What's the *right* way to evaluate the mental health consequences that might come from the social isolation of being housebound?

It might even have forced us to contend directly with distasteful questions. For example, is there a certain number of deaths related to Covid that, as a society, we're willing to tolerate in exchange for *not* paying the price of shutting things down? While that feels callous to even write, the question can push us to think about how we tolerate the risk of death all the time. After all, if the preservation of life were always our only or highest priority, wouldn't cars built like army tanks be the safest things to drive on the highway? Given we're not all driving reinforced tanks, does that mean we've decided that certain risks are acceptable, even if those decisions are not said out loud? Without treating the right solution to Covid as obvious, we might have broadened the public conversation to include even bigger questions, such as what level of risk is tolerable for a society, under what conditions, and who should make these decisions?

To be clear, I'm not necessarily suggesting we should all drive tanks. Nor am I trying to argue that the Covid shutdowns were necessarily the wrong choice. By contrast, maybe they were the right choice, given the alternatives. But those choices came with tradeoffs, and the evaluation of those tradeoffs was based on our values, principles, and the information we had at the time. A commitment to questioning our thinking—to avoiding certainty—could have given us permission to ask *out loud* the kinds of questions I suggested.

But maybe Covid is an exception. A strange and idiosyncratic phenomenon. Can we apply this thinking to other issues? US immigration policy is another fiery topic where we tend to see the path forward as obvious. Depending on who you ask, the "right" immigration policy might be to build a wall or to open our borders. And if you disagree with someone taking one position or the other, that person may see you as either not caring about this country or as a racist xenophobe.

Let's dig into this example a little more. The current immigration policy in the United States prioritizes family reunification. Is this emphasis the "right" or "best" policy? How do we answer that when how we think about "right" or "best" itself depends on our values and beliefs? For starters, is there an ideal level of annual immigration? Is it 1,000,000 people per year? 500,000? 10,000,000? Unlimited, with no restrictions? What makes *that* number, whatever it is, ideal?

For now, let's assume we could agree on a number, or at least one that could serve as a starting point. As long as the number of people who want to immigrate to this country is greater than the number we set as our annual cap, we will have to make decisions about which people are admitted and which aren't. So, how should *that* decision be made?

Maybe it should be a random draw. We could throw all the hopeful migrants' names in a hat and pull some out. We could assume there would be enough pieces of paper so that replacement doesn't matter (in other words, the resulting change in selection probability is tiny when I don't toss back in each piece of paper that I pulled out). Let's also imagine that all the little pieces of paper are indistinguishable from one another meaning everyone would have a more or less equal chance of being chosen. Do we use this method?

Of course, using a random draw—an approach where no single group is prioritized—would need to be justified. But then again, so would using anything other than a random draw.

In this sense, making one decision leads us to *more* questions and *more* decisions, not fewer. If we're trying to figure out which migrants to admit, we might consider questions like: What is the primary purpose of immigration? By that I mean, who is supposed to benefit the most from it? Is it the people currently living in the country? Or is it the people seeking to escape less desirable situations elsewhere? We can try to prioritize both, but the two goals might end up pulling us in opposite di-

---

OUR USE OF TERMS LIKE "RIGHT" AND "BEST" REQUIRES CLARITY ABOUT OUR ASSUMPTIONS, GOALS, VALUES, AND PRIORITIES.

---

rections. And frankly, even optimizing for both is a decision that should ultimately be justified.

Let's say we think immigration should primarily benefit the people currently in the country. What's the best way to ensure that? Does it mean putting into place an immigration system that prioritizes the admission of educated and skilled workers? And if we think immigration should primarily serve the purpose of providing opportunities for a new life to people coming from bad circumstances, how should we do that? Should we craft a policy that somehow measures the adversity someone faces? And how would we do that?

The "right" immigration policy is rooted in value- and principle-laden questions that reasonable people can disagree on. Recognizing this doesn't provide answers, but it can move the conversation away from a simple choice between racist xenophobes and unpatriotic monsters.

Earlier we touched on the example of gun control. Now let's take it a little further. What's being treated as settled on this topic? In other words, what kinds of questions might come up?

Let's start with what many people would see as an uncontroversial assertion: *Having fewer gun-related deaths is better than having more.* If that is, in fact, a widely accepted statement, then a reasonable conclusion might be that we need to reduce the number of guns. After all, it seems reasonable to assume that, at some point, fewer guns would mean fewer gun deaths.

So, let's try a thought experiment. Let's jump from reducing the number of guns to eliminating them entirely. Thinking this through doesn't mean we're saying this is a viable solution or even that it's something even the most ardent gun restrictionists are advocating for. The purpose is to push at the boundaries of our thinking.

If we could wave a magic wand and make all guns in the United States disappear, should we wave that wand? We might think about this in a couple of ways. In one scenario, we might be talking about eliminating only civilian-held guns. In another, we might be talking about *all* guns, regardless of who holds them. Since we're waving a magic wand, we can add another layer of complexity to our thought experiment and declare that there is (poof!) no black market for guns either.

On the one hand, it seems crazy to hesitate or to think for even a second that we might not wave that magic wand. Eliminating guns would almost certainly mean more lives saved, and that has to be an unambiguously good thing. But are there costs we should consider? For instance, would a world without guns be *better* than the one we're in now? How we think about that question depends on how we answer at least two others: How do we define "better"? And what comes to mind when we imagine what a world without guns looks like?

Without guns, do we have a world where people find ways to come together and protect themselves, perhaps unifying and strengthening communities? Does public or social trust increase, as people know (since we waved our magic wand) that whoever they come into contact with won't be armed with a gun?

Or do we have a world where, in every conflictual interaction, the youngest, toughest, strongest, or most aggressive person always emerges as the victor, predetermining the outcome of essentially every physical confrontation?

Let's say that, in our world with no guns, we could create social systems and networks that functionally served a protective role, minimizing or eradicating the need some individuals feel to have a gun for self-defense. Even with such a system in place, someone could reasonably point out that the best system and network can't protect every person all the time.

In other words, there are values that come into tension. How do or should we trade-off the risk of violence that guns clearly bring and the importance of individuals' rights to protect and defend themselves? Although the values being traded in this case are tied to straightforward ideas about harm and freedom, even more fundamental questions lie just beneath the surface. When we wonder how conflictual the world would be without guns, we're getting at our core beliefs about human nature. Are human beings by nature peaceful and egalitarian, or are they by nature competitive and hierarchical? We don't have to be thinking about these questions explicitly for them to be generating assumptions that run unspoken in the back of our minds.

Let's not forget the simple statement we started with: *Having fewer gun-related deaths is better than having more.* This question that at first seemed to have an obvious answer maybe wasn't as straightforward as we thought. I bring this up not to answer it, to debate it, or even to take a position on it. I bring it up to demonstrate that, as with the immigration issue, finding the underlying questions can make it easier to see how people of reasonable minds could come to different answers.

Recall that finding the questions on this or any other issue doesn't require you to change your mind. Even when you're allowing for uncertainty, your initial intuition about gender and biology, immigration policy, or gun control/rights may remain the same as it was before. But finding them can make the "right" choice a little less clear than it seemed at first.

WHAT DO WE MEAN BY "SETTLED"?

So far, we've been talking about how the Settled Question Fallacy keeps people from questioning or challenging their thinking. But let's step back and think through what we mean by *settled*. One way to do that is by turning the concept on its head. In other words, what does it mean to say that a question *isn't* settled? Does it mean the answer isn't known? Does it mean there is no answer? Does the difference between those two types of questions matter?

We might imagine that some kinds of questions have answers, even though those answers aren't known to us right now. Perhaps the link between gender and biology falls into this category. In this kind of scenario, the answer—whatever it is—exists independent of our awareness of it.

Consider, for example, that water probably turned to ice when the temperature dropped below 32 degrees Fahrenheit even before humankind understood the physics involved. The same line of thinking applies to things we don't know today but learn tomorrow, including the relationship between gender and biology. They are no more or less accurate just because we don't know enough about them now.

But we might also look at an example of a question whose answer is, in theory, knowable but that we will probably never know due to the constraints inherent to being human. For instance, let's say we want to know how many lizards there are in the world at a given point in time. If we lined up all the world's lizards and counted them, presumably we could arrive at an answer. We would also need to agree on when and whether we've counted them all and done so correctly (no double-counting and no skipping any lizards).

Why does agreement about what counts as a lizard matter? Part of living in a society with other people means being able to talk about and communicate on aspects of that society and its place in the world. This is one reason a commitment to challenging our thinking is so important—it forces us to make that thinking explicit. When we fail to use words in the same way as the people we're interacting with, particularly when those words are tied to complex social problems, communication becomes heavily strained. This means that we probably also need to be on the same page about what makes a lizard a lizard and what doesn't.

Although our intuition tells us that an answer to the question of how many lizards there are exists, there are practical reasons why it would be difficult to get a precise count. For instance, how would we find each lizard? Would we send teams to every corner of the earth where we think lizards might live? Might there be lizard habitats we're not aware of? What about people's pet lizards? How would we count those? Could we develop sensing equipment that could detect lizards and only lizards with no false positives (identifying things as lizards that aren't lizards) and no false negatives (failing to identify actual lizards as lizards)? How would we know if or when we found them all?

When it comes to the Settled Question Fallacy, the point is to recognize that all answers have uncertainty, and all knowledge is subject to being challenged. While reasonable minds can disagree about how much confidence to have in our provisional answers, a commitment to interrogating our thinking means treating assertions that are presented as definitive with a heavy dose of skepticism.[5]

While the importance of challenging and clarifying our thinking may seem fairly straightforward, in practice, it's consistently overlooked or brushed aside. Our deep need to simplify and have clarity often preclude us from a more complete understanding of the world we live in and the interactions in which we engage.

When it comes to contentious issues where the stakes feel high, understanding when we're not using words the same way and recognizing unknown and unknowable answers become even more important. After all, it's one thing if I'm using a narrow scientific definition of a lizard and you're basing your use of the term on an animal's physical appearance alone, possibly leading us to different conclusions. It's quite another if I consider something *unfair* or *racist*, and you don't.

With that in mind, let's compare the question of how many lizards are there with this one: How many racist police officers are there in the United States? Or this one: What percent of men are sexist? To say these are hard questions probably doesn't do justice to just how vexing they are. And yet, we tend to spend little time trying to understand *why* they are so hard.

For starters, we'd first have to agree on how to define the relevant terms. And, in this case, we'd have to agree on what the words *racist* and

WHEN WE VIEW THE ANSWERS TO HEATED AND CONTENTIOUS QUESTIONS AS DEFINITIVE AND OBVIOUS, IT'S EASY TO CONDEMN OR DISMISS PEOPLE WHO DISAGREE.

sexist mean, not on what makes a lizard a lizard. That also means coming to an understanding of what makes someone deserving of one label or the other. And even if we could come to such an understanding, we'd still be left trying to figure out how to actually assign those labels.

Would we assign them based on people's behavior? In other words, based on whether a person *acts* in a racist or sexist manner or *says* racist and sexist things? And if we did that, we'd likely end up with some statements on which people would disagree. For instance, is asking a non-white person where they're from racist? What about calling a woman "sweetie"? Is that sexist? What if it's coming from someone of an older generation when that term was more commonly used? Where's the line between poor (or outdated) taste and racism/sexism and, what's more, who decides and why?

Alternatively, would we assign labels of racist and sexist based on people's attitudes and how they *think* about people of different races or the opposite sex? And not on what they do or say? If we think racism and sexism, to stay with this example, are best measured with people's attitudes, we'd have to figure out how to extract reliable information from people on what their thoughts are on these topics. After all, if we can't get the truth from people about what they think, then our measure won't be useful, and our labels won't have meaning.

Ultimately, these questions—how many racist police officers are there? and how many men are sexist?—are difficult to answer. As we've seen, the answers depend on, among other things, how the words themselves are defined. And yet, many of us behave as though we know the answers in a definitive sense, as though they're settled. To paint this in the extreme, if I think that all police officers are racist, I'm probably going to draw a particular conclusion about interactions between police officers and civilians, especially of different races, that go wrong. I'll assume that racism is one of the causes, if not the singular one. Alternatively, if I think that *no* or few police officers are racist, I'm going to draw a different conclusion—that racism isn't likely to have been a factor.

I am making no claim that the answer always lies in the middle or that the solution to all our problems is to just split the difference. I'm simply pointing to how our failure to realize that these questions matter shapes our thinking in ways we don't always realize.

Other ways we treat knowledge as settled matter, too. Like how we think about tradeoffs. We saw this with the deep dives into the gun control example, but the thinking applies more broadly.

One morning, I was in the car taking my kids to school. They were joking around and being smartasses, as kids tend to do. And for some reason, one of them said "#MeToo" (he actually said the word "hashtag"). He wasn't intentionally referencing the movement to speak out against sexual violence against women; he was trying to make a joke about agreeing with something one of his brothers had said. But his older brother seized the opportunity to point out that he didn't know it had this broader meaning. This led to a lengthy conversation about the #MeToo movement, #BelieveAllWomen, and, well, tradeoffs. So, I asked them, "Do you know what #BelieveAllWomen refers to? Do you know why it's important?" Silence was the response.

Since we were all in the car, I had both a captive audience and a golden opportunity. I pressed on. "Believing women is important so we don't retraumatize victims of sexual assault by treating them as though they're lying." And then, I asked them why this approach might have a downside. My oldest replied, staring straight ahead and looking a little bored, "Because sometimes people lie." We talked about the perils of convicting, even if it's just in the court of public opinion, someone who's innocent. We jointly acknowledged the tension between the two values: not wanting to revictimize women while also not wanting to blame an innocent person.

We talked a little about what we might want to know about both the definition and frequency of false allegations and how and whether that might be assessed meaningfully. And, assuming it could be assessed meaningfully, we wondered whether there's a percentage of false allegations below which #BelieveAllWomen would continue to be seen as justifiable. In other words, if we knew with a high degree of confidence that 40 percent of allegations of sexual assault are false, #BelieveAllWomen would, to many people at least, seem hard to justify. After all, 40 percent of the people being accused would be innocent. (I'm in no way suggesting the actual percentage is that high.) But what if it were 10 percent? What about 2 percent? Less?

I don't have the answers and I don't know what percentage would or should be "low enough" to eliminate real concerns for most people. Fortunately, however, when it comes to challenging and clarifying our thinking, the answers aren't the point—the questions are.

Ultimately, I hope my kids came away from that conversation with a sense that it's complicated. And that it's important to recognize the limits of our knowledge even or especially when it comes to questions on which we desperately want clarity.

Naming and examining our beliefs, values, and principles doesn't come easily to many of us. Perhaps this is simply because we're not in the habit of doing so. However, when the questioning and challenging of ideas is done with honesty and sincerity—what some people refer to as "good faith"—we can both transform conversations and build trust. What's more, there can be a sense of balance in knowing that, in a battle of ideas, the process of questioning values, beliefs, and principles applies to everyone equally.

Being able to name our values and allow them to be challenged while understanding we do not need to let them go is an important skill. It's why a commitment to questioning and challenging our thinking doesn't mean we can't declare right or wrong. Let's take a deeper dive.

Unsettled Questions and Morals

Avoiding the Certainty Trap means questioning the grounds for our judgments. That is not the same thing as saying that no judgment can be made. They can be, provided we understand that they, too, are subject to questioning and examination. That means that those passing them have an obligation to be clear about the set of values their judgments are based on.

I made this point earlier when I used the women and driving example and when I discussed the Ugandan anti-homosexuality law. In the first case, I pointed out that saying, "I believe all people should have equal rights under the law," and letting that statement be challenged doesn't mean I have to let it go. This ability is what makes the challenge to leave certainty behind an intellectual and philosophical one rather than a moral one.

In other words, this distinction is why this book is neither a declaration about moral truths nor about moral relativism. Moral relativism is the idea that no one can condemn any practice or belief, no matter how abhorrent, because even the most horrific tradition is culturally and contextually specific and can't/shouldn't be judged from the outside. As in, female circumcision isn't necessarily wrong because it's a cultural practice. In contrast, the idea of moral absolutes is that there are particular principles, universal to all human beings, by which people can be judged. As in, stealing is always wrong.

Let's use the female circumcision example as it's one that most people in Western countries find barbaric, so it doesn't often break along standard left-right political lines. Imagine you're talking to someone who believes that women should undergo female circumcision. And let's assume you don't think this is such a great idea. There's nothing about being willing to question and clarify your thinking that suggests you have to change your position or back down. You just have to be willing to name and have the other person challenge what you're taking as given, and vice versa.

We might start with a few questions. And while they might sound ridiculous to readers, being clear about the answers matters. Those questions include: *Why* don't you think female circumcision is such a great idea? Maybe you feel that women have the right to a full life that includes sexual health and sexual pleasure. Someone on the other side of this issue might be driven by an entirely different set of concerns.

That person might think women *shouldn't* have the right to a full life that includes sexual pleasure. It's also possible that he is worried that the ability of women to experience sexual pleasure will lead to unchecked adultery, which will then lead to the decay of society and the breakdown of families. And controlling women's sexuality to avoid the decay of society, to that person, is a price worth paying.

The conversation wouldn't necessarily have to stop there. For instance, what other rights do you, the person opposed to female circumcision, believe are non-negotiable (other than the right to a life that includes sexual fulfillment), and why? What does the other person mean by "the decay of society"? And what is it about women's sexuality that would lead there? Are there other things that might lead there, too?

Of course, not everyone would be comfortable having a calm and measured conversation on the topic of female circumcision. In some ways, the fact that it's an extreme example is precisely the point. We're taking a topic for which it seems impossible to understand where the other person is coming from and pulling it apart by naming our principles.

Again, when it comes to how we describe our values and concerns, clarity and precision matter enormously. We saw this earlier with the meaning of terms like "evil," but it applies here, too. People may have a shared understanding of what the terms "sexual health" and "sexual pleasure" mean. Although there's probably less consensus about what is meant by the term "decay of society." A commitment to being clear and explicit in our thinking can reveal these kinds of differences. At that point, we can decide whether to ignore them or to resolve them, but if we're committed to being clear in our thinking, we can no longer pretend they don't exist (or, to go back to our earlier metaphor, pretend that we're looking out a window).

ATTEMPTS AT SOLUTIONS

The magnitude and scale of the problems that can be traced to settled thinking have led to various attempts to look for corrective measures. However, those solutions, while well-intentioned and not entirely without merit, really can't lead to the kind of transformation we need. That's largely because they focus on the symptoms rather than on the underlying problem.

For instance, one strategy that is sometimes proposed is to focus on promoting norms of civil discourse. While the term "civil discourse" is used somewhat inconsistently, most definitions share a few core norms. For instance, the American University Project on Civil Discourse describes it as "truthful," "productive," and "audience-based" "listening and talking" for which each speaker takes responsibility."[6] The idea is that setting expectations for how people should interact, especially when it comes to contentious topics, will show people how to model and practice engagement with people who disagree. The problem is that these behaviors operate at a surface level. It's like adding a fresh coat of paint to the drywall while termites gnaw away at the studs underneath. On the outside, it looks slick, but it's probably going to crumble eventually.

Our problem is not simply that we have forgotten that conversations on heated topics require respect, a calm tone of voice, and active listening. To be sure, those are crucial skills to have. But the real challenge is the thinking that drives the judgments and demonization in the first place. And without addressing this problem at its source, without changing how we think, moving past it will remain out of reach. One way of understanding the limits of civil discourse as a remedy is that a person can be practicing all of its best norms and still be mired in certainty.

Debating is in a similar situation when it comes to its capacity to bring about the kind of meaningful change we're talking about here. On the positive side, there's good reason to believe that the movement toward debate-centered instruction in schools has been beneficial for

---

A PERSON CAN BE PRACTICING ALL THE NORMS OF CIVIL
DISCOURSE AND STILL BE STUCK IN THE CERTAINTY TRAP.

---

many young people. Debating can build confidence and promote leadership in ways that many students clearly benefit from. It can also teach the art of persuasion and how to anticipate an argument.

At the same time, we need leaders and thinkers who can name and interrogate their *own* thinking and their *own* assumptions, at least as much as (if not more than) they examine and question those of people who are on the other side of an issue. While a skilled debater may be able to do both, it's still with an eye to winning an argument. We're talking about a change that runs deeper.

Yet another proposed solution to the challenges we face is to battle mis- and disinformation. The difference between the two terms is largely one of intent—both involve the presentation of inaccurate or false information, but disinformation does so with the intent to deceive.

Some people see the broader battle waged against mis- and disinformation as tied to a reconnection with ground truth—what's really real about the world. In this framing, our social and political problems mainly come from too much false information being put out into the world and too many people's inability or unwillingness to separate fact from fiction.

Unfortunately, the fight against mis- and disinformation is fraught. This is partly because identifying it can be challenging. Consider an easy example. Let's say someone tweets, "The shelter at 200 Main Street is giving away sleeping bags," when no such giveaway is occurring. This is relatively cut-and-dried when it comes to verification. Go to the address specified and see if sleeping bags are being handed out. Of course, many cases of mis- or disinformation are not that straightforward.

One popular story around the highly tense 2016 and 2020 presidential elections was that Donald Trump's father was a supporter of the Ku

Klux Klan. Further investigation suggests that Fred Trump was arrested at a KKK parade in 1927, but it doesn't confirm that he was an actual member.[7] If you're a Trump supporter, you may see the lack of support for the assertion that he belonged to the KKK as exonerating. If you're opposed to Trump, knowing that his father was at a KKK parade in the first place may be reason enough for condemnation, regardless of whether he formally joined the organization.

If we assume that the purpose of the story's circulation was to condemn Donald Trump through allegations made about his father, an additional question arises. That is, is the condemnable piece his alleged membership in the KKK, or is the condemnable piece the fact that he was present at the parade at all? If you're a Trump advocate, you might think it's the membership, labeling the calling of Fred Trump a KKK supporter as disinformation. You might reason that we can't be sure why he was at the parade or, even if we could, we can't draw conclusions about the son's values from those of the father. If you're opposed to Trump, you may be more likely to think the condemnable piece is Fred Trump's presence at the parade at all and, moreover, that it confirms everything you already suspected about Trump's deeply held racism. In this case, the story barely meets the requirements of being called disinformation.

Here's another way to think about how slippery terms like misinformation, disinformation, fake news, or, in this case, even "myth" can be. Let's start with the following statement: "The side effects of the Covid-19 vaccine are dangerous." According to the Johns Hopkins Medicine website, this was classified as a myth.[8] At the same time, the Mayo Clinic website stated, "The risk of myocarditis or pericarditis after a COVID-19 vaccine is rare. These conditions have been reported after COVID-19 vaccination with any of the vaccines offered in the United States. Most cases have been reported in males ages 12 to 39."[9] As Mayo noted, those reports are rare. But does their being rare make the possibility of dangerous side effects a "myth"?

Ultimately, neither the Fred Trump example nor the vaccine case is as straightforward as the sleeping bag giveaway example. When we label something as mis- or disinformation, we're doing so having removed all the questions and doubt. In other words, we're using definitive language to talk about things that aren't, in fact, definitive.

If we could limit the identification of mis- and disinformation to things like sleeping bag giveaways, perhaps there'd be little cause for concern. But when one political party sees a claim as demonstrably false (Trump's father supported the KKK) or true (Covid vaccines have no serious side effects) and another sees it as not nearly as clear, using these labels creates new problems. Under these conditions, someone in the former group might reasonably think: If the media, news outlets, etc., are going to use labels indicating falseness in ways that seem indefensible to me, why should I trust anything they say at all? Reasonable people could disagree over whether that's a side effect worth tolerating.

What's more, this isn't the only problem with the mis- and disinformation labels. Let's say we could agree on what counts as one or the other. And let's assume we could wave our magic wand again, getting rid of it all. Even if we could do that, we'd be just as stuck in our thinking as we are today. Because we wouldn't have changed the way we understand the world. In other words, failing to question our thinking and acknowledge doubt in what we know could persist even after the wand had been waived.

Perhaps the most promising approach to our problems of political polarization and a loss of social trust is grounded in the idea that we need to see the humanity in people that we disagree with. By doing this, the thinking goes, we will judge them less harshly.

This approach is largely the model behind organizations that bring politically red and blue folks together for workshops, conversations, or shared meals. And to be sure, this unity can have powerful effects. However, it seems entirely plausible, likely even, that people might come out of such workshops having had a transformative experience that doesn't scale. In other words, if I am blue and I do a workshop where I'm exposed to a couple of people who are red, maybe that exposure is successful in changing my impression of the handful of people that I met and spoke with. But will I be able to take what I got from that initial experience and apply it more broadly the next time I cross paths with someone who's red?

Hidden Questions

One of the most difficult aspects of leaving certainty behind is that the settled questions we're aware of are only a small fraction of the problem. In other words, it can be extraordinarily difficult to see what exactly it is that we're taking as given. This is why the Certainty Trap isn't just something that affects those people over there—it affects all of us.

Take a heated topic like the Israeli-Palestinian conflict. Framing this issue in a way that suggests that Israel is a colonial power, that it's an apartheid state, or that all Israelis are racist, all come from a place of certainty. As does framing the conflict as though Israel has done nothing wrong and has an unblemished record. Neither perspective engages with the underlying questions. For example, can a particular group be both aggressor *and* victim? What does that mean and how should we think about that? If two groups claim victim status, is there a way to determine whose claim matters more? How? What's the right way to compensate people who have been wronged? What's the difference between self-defense and unprovoked aggression? And, for all of these questions, who should decide and why?

Getting a handle on the questions we're *not* asking can be so tricky and counterintuitive that I see it as an ongoing learning process. And it's one where I learn new things all the time.

In most of the undergraduate classes I have taught, we spend a lot of time talking about inequality. What are its causes and solutions, how much inequality is acceptable, why do outcomes differ systematically across groups, and so on. Sometimes, discussions about inequality can get so difficult to sort through that it's helpful to consider an extreme thought experiment. When this happens, I'll often turn to "Harrison Bergeron," a short story by Kurt Vonnegut Jr. The story opens with this description:

> THE YEAR WAS 2081, and everybody was finally equal. They weren't only equal before God and the law. They were equal every which way. Nobody was smarter than anybody else. Nobody was better looking than anybody else. Nobody was stronger or quicker than anybody else. All this equality was due to the 211th, 212th, and 213th Amendments to the Constitution, and to the unceasing vigilance of agents of the United States Handicapper General.

While various events occur over the course of the story, I try to direct students' attention to the world Vonnegut imagined. It was a world where equality in every dimension was socially engineered and achieved. If a person was smarter than average, they were forced to wear a contraption that disrupted their thoughts so they couldn't string ideas together.[10] If a person was too graceful, they were forced to wear weights. If a person was too attractive, they were forced to make themselves appear uglier. And so on and so forth.

Usually, the story is a jumping-off point for a conversation that starts with the acknowledgment that the society described in Harrison Bergeron isn't one that most of us would want to live in. This generally leads to a lively conversation about what the "right" level of inequality is, who should decide, and how we should think about it. However, one day, when we were discussing Bergeron's world as I'd done many times before, a student in the front row raised her hand. She asked a question that challenged an even deeper assumption.

She said, "Maybe Bergeron's world is not such a bad way to live after all. Maybe it's the son [in Vonnegut's story] who's out of line for trying to go against a system that most people don't seem to be complaining about." I thought for a moment and smiled. In all the times I'd discussed this story in class, no one had raised this question. Of course, the characters in the story aren't exactly able to express dissatisfaction with the world they're in—those who might have objected have their thoughts interrupted constantly. And yet, I found the student's question interesting, nonetheless.

It was interesting because almost everyone, myself included, who reads the story takes as given that the world Vonnegut created is a dystopian vision. But we rarely put words to *why*. With her question, the student was pushing us all to think more deeply about our own assumptions, even though she ultimately agreed with them. I nodded and said to the class, "She's 100 percent right to ask this."

Even in a context as depressing as the one that Vonnegut created, we should be committed to exploring, understanding, and naming *why* the world of Harrison Bergeron is so bad. What is the principle, value, or belief that drives that judgment? Once again, we can ask that question without condemning (or, for that matter, endorsing) the principle itself. As the conversation progressed, we came to an understanding that our judgment, in this case, is driven by a core belief in the importance of the sovereignty of the individual and the individual's right to pursue their human potential. Because we can name and examine that value without letting it go, we can also think about what it might be like to have a different one.

There's no shortcut to learning to find these kinds of questions. But our clue to look for them is the harsh judgment, demonization, or dismissal of someone who disagrees or a sense that a contentious issue has a simple cause or solution. In some ways, these reactions are the metaphorical smoke, and your commitment is to find the fire. And while there's no trick to it, here are a few questions that can be a useful starting point:

Are there any other (non-hateful) reasons why someone might think _____?

Is _____ the only possible explanation for _____?

Is there agreement, especially across political divides, on the meaning of the terms being used?

What would a person have to be treating as given in order to come to that conclusion?

The goal of each of these questions isn't to change your or anyone else's mind. These are just questions you might start with as you look for complexity. These questions can also be useful to bear in mind when you're trying to think through different perspectives on a contentious topic.

Before we start talking about the costs of staying trapped, I'll make one more point. Leaving certainty behind isn't a how-to guide on how to arrive at the "best" solution. This is because the idea of "best" itself depends on values and assumptions, all of which are subject to examination. But it *is* a way to get to a place where potential solutions can be more openly discussed.

Chapter Summary

- The Settled Question Fallacy lies in treating our knowledge as definitive rather than provisional, which can lead us to view opposing views as born of ignorance or hate.
- A fallacy indicates an error in reasoning. Just like Ad Hominem and Red Herring fallacies, the Settled Question Fallacy prevents us from engaging with opposing ideas. Avoiding it can help correct fundamental misunderstandings of the world.
- Identifying unasked questions and naming underlying assumptions is challenging but also essential to avoid the certainty trap.
- Solutions like promoting civil discourse or combating misinforma-

tion address symptoms rather than the underlying problem of certainty.

Practice Uncertainty

Go to the social media or regular media site of your choosing. Look through the headlines and select an article or two to read on a heated issue. Look for instances of the Settled Question Fallacy and think through how they might be corrected.

3

The Price of Doing Nothing

*"If I am a fool, it is, at least, a doubting one; and I envy no one
the certainty of his self-approved wisdom."*

LORD BYRON, *JOURNAL FOR SATURDAY*

Earlier, I said that failing to question our thinking is like insisting we're seeing the world through a window rather than in a mirror. And just as curved glass distorts the image of what's being reflected, certainty distorts what we're seeing. It turns out that this has far-reaching implications. While we scratched the surface of these earlier, here we'll linger and take them one at a time.

WE STOP ASKING QUESTIONS
AND THERE ARE NO QUESTIONS TO BE ASKED

A failure to interrogate our thinking is linked to a sense that we already know everything we need to know. And, if that's the case, there's no reason to continue asking questions. This has some pretty clear downsides. The most obvious is that it arrests our understanding of the world around us by limiting the creation of knowledge. And because we *can't* actually know everything there is to know *and* because what we do know

50

isn't fixed (to take a simple example, remember how eggs were bad for us one minute and the next they weren't?), certainty closes us off.

Understanding the hypothetical costs of questions that don't get asked requires us to jump with both feet into the unknown. It's a place where the best we can do is wonder, "What would have happened if. . .?" For instance, what would have happened if Edward Jenner, the scientist and surgeon credited by many as being the father of the modern vaccine, hadn't asked the question he asked in 1796? That was the year Jenner was inspired to use a sample of cowpox to inoculate a child against smallpox, making this a what-would-have-happened-if question that quite literally changed the course of history.

While we don't get to know ahead of time which questions are going to lead where, the example about Jenner and vaccines is at least tangible. That means that, because we know he asked the question he asked, we can try to imagine a world where he hadn't. It's much harder to get a handle on the price of questions that haven't even been asked, as it requires us to step past counterfactuals like the one about Jenner into a world of unknown unknowns. More simply put: We don't know what we don't know. The good news is that we don't need to agree on what that world would look like; we just have to agree that it would look different than the one we're in now.

When it comes to the accumulation of knowledge, there is no moment when the final whistle blows, when we pack our equipment and go home, never to return to the field. Much of the time, at some point, we become sure *enough* about what we have learned to treat it as though it is certain. This is why there are some questions we don't endlessly ask over and over. For instance, I don't know that anyone, for instance, is still testing whether water comes to a boil at 100 degrees Celsius and 212 degrees Fahrenheit. But treating things as certain isn't the same thing as them actually being certain. We all too easily forget that what we're doing is ignoring the micro space of doubt that never actually went away.

When we're referring to the way certainty leads us to behave as though there are no questions that can be asked—we're talking about a different kind of cost. This is the thinking that leads us to: treat the path forward or the solution to a problem as though it's obvious; behave as though the right decision when the interests of different groups or different values come into conflict is clear; fail to acknowledge that pretty much any solution has both costs and benefits; or simply neglect to make our assumptions clear.

And yet, a person might question either the substantive conclusion (e.g., you say gender is entirely a social construct and the other person disagrees), or they might disagree with the conclusion that that assertion can't be challenged (e.g., the person agrees with you that gender is entirely a social construct, but you think there are questions to be asked and the other person doesn't).

The certainty that leads us to condemn someone's character shapes how we view the world in ways that aren't always obvious. Failing to question or clarify our thinking leads us, without even realizing it, to take our principles for granted and assume that they're shared broadly. Sometimes, as with the car thief example, this works just fine. When it does, it's because the principle—like, stealing is bad—is widely shared *and* because we are using words in the same way. It's probably safe to assume that most people are operating from within the same definition of theft.

But what about situations where the principle—or the words—are more ambiguous? My son was telling me recently about a paper he was writing for school on free speech on Twitter (now X). In the paper, he took the position that Twitter should follow John Stuart Mill's harm principle. The harm principle is essentially the idea that people should generally be free to act as—and presumably say what—they want unless their actions harm somebody else. So, I asked him what he (my son, not Mill) meant by "harm." He replied with, "Well, you know, obvious harm." The natural follow-up question was, "Well, what counts as "obvious harm" and who decides?"

Sometimes when I talk about the ways in which certainty traps our thinking, people nod and draw comparisons with things like critical thinking, intellectual humility, and curiosity. In fact, because of the overlap between these concepts and certainty, at one point I even referred to this work simply as "critical thinking." The name seemed to fit in the sense that I was trying to solve a problem in how people think, and I was also trying to get people to see the importance of criticizing ideas.

However, I quickly learned that there are at least two downsides to this framing. One is that there seems to be no shared understanding of what it means to think critically. Does it have something to do with objectivity? Rationality? Evidence? Logic? Analyzing facts and forming a judgment? Or maybe it's about determining what we gain from learning about other people's lived experiences? The absence of a clear and consistent definition made it difficult to know if, when I used that term, the person I was talking with had the same thing in mind that I did.

The other, more intractable, problem with the concept of critical thinking is that it's difficult to get people to pay attention to something they think they are already doing. In other words, few people think they *aren't* thinking critically. For instance, if you ask educators and instructors, they will almost universally say they value this skill. Many will say they promote critical thinking in their classrooms. And to be fair, they might be doing just that—given how many different definitions of it there are.

But something must be breaking down somewhere. Otherwise, how would we be in a critical thinking crisis?[1] Somehow, we are failing to foster the thing that most of us agree is valuable. This tells me that, at the very least, we don't always have a good sense of what we are and are not doing well. And that brings us to intellectual humility.

The concept of intellectual humility does important work by making us aware of the value of understanding that we might be wrong. As with critical thinking, it has considerable overlap with the idea of certainty. But intellectual humility requires the ability to recognize what it is that you're *not* being intellectually humble about.

Similar to how it's difficult to get a handle on where we're falling short when it comes to critical thinking, it's hard to know when we're not being intellectually humble. Think of it this way: If you stood on a street corner on any college campus and asked people if they thought intellectual humility is important, I imagine the vast majority would say yes. Most people are more than willing to verbalize the importance of being willing to see the world in a different way.

But intellectual humility and, for that matter, curiosity require the ability to recognize when we're falling short. As in, oh, I need to be curious/humble now. And, for many people, that turns out to be far from straightforward. To explain how important this is, it might help to back up a minute.

Let's say that I recognize that the question of whether immigration is "good" for this country has multiple possible answers. I might think it could depend on how you define "good" ("good" for whom?) and which measure you're looking at. But am I also willing to have humility when it comes to my conclusion that people who advocate for immigration restrictions are racist xenophobes? Many of us struggle to recognize that the second example requires humility in a manner similar to the first.

Here's the paradox: By the time you can name the thing you need to have intellectual humility about, you're already allowing for doubt. The same is true for curiosity. This leaves us trying to tackle a problem we can't observe.

HARSH JUDGMENT AND DEMONIZATION ARE YOUR CLUES

When we're committed to interrogating our own thinking, as well as that of other people, we need a way to know when we're *not* doing it or not doing it adequately. I've said that one of the telltale signs that you need to interrogate your thinking is the harsh judgment, demonization, or dismissal of someone who disagrees. But that assertion might understandably raise questions. As in, does that mean there's never cause to judge people harshly or to demonize them? Am I saying that there really aren't horrible people in the world?

As far as I can tell, the short answer to the question of whether there are truly horrible people in the world is this: I don't know. My hesitation might be easier to think through with an example. So, let's look at this using an extreme case.

On July 31, 1966, Charles Whitman went to his mother's home and stabbed and shot her, before he returned to his own home and stabbed his wife to death. The next day, Whitman went to the University of Texas at Austin tower and killed the receptionist and two tourists before taking out his rifle and firing into the campus below. By the time Whitman was shot and killed by a patrolman, he'd killed 14 people and injured more than 30 others.

During the autopsy of Whitman's body the following day, a brain tumor was found. At first, the medical examiner said it was unlikely to have impacted Whitman's behavior. Three days later, however, on August 5, this finding was called into question. Further examination led the medical experts to state that the tumor could have indeed impacted Whitman's actions, perhaps by pressing on his amygdala.

Let's assume for the moment that the tumor *was*, in fact, pressing on his amygdala in a way that could have interfered with his ability to control his behavior. What might such a finding mean for how we think about Whitman?

It's not likely to change our view of the horror of what he did, nor will it diminish the suffering that he caused. And it doesn't have to change our sense that, had he survived, it would have been right to remove him from society. Might such a finding, however, raise doubts about what we can conclude about Whitman as a human being?

Here's another way, using a different example, to think about the question I'm posing. If we knew that the notorious serial killer Jack the Ripper had a chemical imbalance in his brain that made it virtually impossible for him to do anything other than live a life of violence, would we be less inclined to condemn him as evil? Should we be? In thinking that through, it might be useful to remember that, as with Whitman, there's no reason we can't believe his actions should have consequences, while not necessarily condemning who he was as a person.

Why does any of this matter? Is it simply an intellectual exercise with no practical application? Why should I or anyone else question the conclusions we draw about people who committed some of the vilest acts in history?

We question them because doing so reminds us of the importance of recognizing what we don't know. And because it helps us understand that not knowing something doesn't always mean that the thing we don't know doesn't matter. In the previous two examples, I chose cases where people had committed heinous crimes. But we could apply the same reasoning to any situation where our inclination is to demonize.

When I try to get students to recognize the importance of uncertainty, I often start with a question. And since, in sociology, we spend a lot of time talking about inequality and race, sometimes I'll pick a topic that touches both of those issues. For instance, I could ask: Why might someone object to the use of race in college admissions decisions?

When I first pose this question, a few hands usually go up right away. Racism is generally one of the first answers given. When that answer is offered, my response is, "Yes, that makes sense." Sometimes I'll write it down on the board as I start to make a list of the students' suggestions. Then I'll press on: "Are there any other reasons someone might oppose the use of race in college admissions?" After a minute or two, usually another couple of hands will go up. "Someone might think it's unfair?" Or "Maybe someone could worry that it makes people question whether members of minority groups really earned their place?" Those answers get written on the board, too.

The goal of the exercise isn't to answer the question of whether using race in college admissions is or isn't fair or to try to figure out what the right solution is. The point is to generate possible reasons for the position and to realize that not all of them require hateful motives or ignorance. I do these kinds of exercises to get us to a place where we can say, "Well, given what we've just said, if all I know about someone is that they're opposed to the use of race in college admissions, can I tell which of these reasons [pointing to the multiple written on the board] is driving them?" The realization that the answer to that question is "no" opens up a conversation that can go in new directions—without the judgment that comes from oversimplification.

Here's one place such a conversation could go: "We know someone could, in fact, be opposed to using race in college admissions for reasons that most people would understand as racist. After all, that's one of the motivating reasons on our list. But there are other things on the list as well. So how do we know who's who and what's what?" Another way to put it might be: "Given that you don't know what's motivating the person, if you find the position objectionable, what is the *right* way to respond?"

We can push this example even further. After all, we might recognize that there is a subset of people who would say that even the reasons we're calling "non-racist" are, in fact, driven by racial resentment. In other words, people who express concerns about fairness are really just hiding a deeper racial hostility. But that response itself is nested inside yet another principle, belief, or value that can be challenged. That could be the conviction that either a person's intent can be assumed or that it doesn't matter. Or the conviction driving that response could be that all inequality—in this case, in college admissions—is due to discrimination. In other words, if I think all inequality has discrimination as its cause, it stands to reason that I'm more likely to use the very same traits used to exclude people, in this case, that would be race, to give them a leg up.

To be sure, I could do a parallel exercise on a different topic going in the other political direction. I could ask a room full of students why someone might think that people should kneel during the national anthem. And if the default answer is "they hate this country," we could push through that certainty in a similar manner.

This exercise with race in college admissions is different than the way conversations around critical thinking or intellectual humility are usually framed. By slowing down, making our assumptions explicit, and challenging our thinking at each step, we get at something deeper. This tendency to make assumptions we don't realize we're making is why the power of certainty is not to be underestimated.

CERTAINTY AND DEMONIZATION

The consequences of certainty include social ills like extremism, the erosion of trust, and political polarization. Before we go deeper into these consequences, however, let's step back and look again at the link between certainty and demonization. We might start with two of the premises we've already laid out. One is that judgment, the kind that condemns someone's character, always comes from some principle, belief, or value that we hold as inviolable. Another is that the world is fundamentally uncertain.[2] The combination of these two statements can lead us to interesting places.

If I am judging someone's character, that judgment is, by its very nature, based in the belief that I know everything I need to know to condemn him. The statement "I misjudged you" actually demonstrates this. It suggests that I judged you based on some information that I had. I then found out new information or a new way to interpret the existing information, and I changed my mind. And while it's good that I was willing to change my mind, understanding that we never have full knowledge in the first place makes demonization difficult to ever justify fully.

So, if there is no justification to demonize someone or condemn their character, does that mean that there is no right and wrong? Is every decision about how to behave and how to treat other people simply a coin toss? Fortunately, as I'll continue to say in different contexts, not having justification to condemn someone's character doesn't require either of these scary statements. The establishment of right and wrong is fundamentally a different question.

To see how these questions are different, we might recall the classroom Harrison Bergeron example from the previous chapter. Asking why most people see Bergeron's world of socially engineered equality as dystopian doesn't mean that it isn't one. Of course, it also doesn't mean that it is. We can separate the curiosity-driven question of *why* we see it as dystopian from the evaluative question of whether it *is* dystopian.

In some cases, ceasing to wonder what we know about the world makes enormous practical sense. We can't realistically move through our days questioning everything all of the time. It hardly seems efficient for me to walk into my house every afternoon and wonder if someone switched out my cat for a duplicate that looks just like her. Although, setting aside for a second the paranoid tendencies that this would suggest on my part, it *is* theoretically possible. It is likely? Nope. Is it possible? Yes.

When I walk into the house each afternoon, give the cat a scratch behind the ears, and tell her hello, I am assuming that she's the same cat I left that morning. My assumption doesn't eliminate the remote possibility that I'm wrong. Of course, the question of whether my cat has been switched out for a doppelganger isn't a contentious one. In fact, arguably no one really cares about this question other than me. So, it's not likely to raise anyone's hackles. While this example is obviously silly, it's a short step from here to a situation where the illusion of certainty isn't costless.

CERTAINTY AND EXTREMIST POSITIONS

One of the, sometimes less intuitive, effects of certainty is the way it can push people to adopt extreme positions. Imagine the following scenario. Jim and Sara work together. One day the subject of affirmative action comes up in the context of how hiring decisions get made. Jim says he's opposed to it. Sara finds Jim's position objectionable. Sara sees no reason why any non-hateful person would hold such a view. Sara then concludes Jim is hateful. Jim knows Sara thinks he's a bad person for holding this opinion on affirmative action. He is resentful of being judged by her and feels this label is unfair. In response, Jim seeks the company of Sheila, who shares Jim's position on affirmative action.

But what if Sheila is more than just a fellow traveler who shares Jim's view on affirmative action? If Jim is feeling judged by Sara for his position, he might not be in a big hurry to shout his view from a rooftop. He might assume that doing so will open him up to more criticism. So, how does Jim find Sheila? The easiest way to imagine this happening is that Sheila is open and public about her views—and, therefore, easy for Jim to identify.

Here's where our hypothetical with Jim, Sara, and Sheila gets even more complicated. In a social and cultural climate where Jim's position is stigmatized, only a subset of people will be willing to bear the social cost of that stigma and let their views be known publicly like Sheila did. And those will tend to be people who either aren't aware of or don't care about those costs.

And as those social costs become common, it becomes less likely that people don't know about them, meaning it's probably the people who don't care about them who are making their views known. Why does this matter? Because a climate where relatively commonly held views lead to the condemnation of someone's character tends to set up a perverse selection mechanism. Among people who hold a particular stigmatized view—in this case, opposition to affirmative action, those who are public about it are likely different from those who keep it to themselves. And the way in which they might be different matters.

For instance, it's entirely possible that, in this context, a significant fraction of those who are willing to let their views be known publicly (Sheila, in this example) are more likely to have other, more extreme views than those who hold that view secretly. This could be the case if the desire to take your views public increases the further away from the "acceptable" view you are or the more you view it with disdain.[3]

If this is the case, Jim may quickly find himself in the company of people who hold more extreme positions than he did when he first spoke with Sara. For instance, maybe Sheila also feels strongly that white people are actively discriminated against. That might be a thought Jim didn't seriously entertain before. If, through exposure to Sheila, Jim adopts some of her views as his own, Jim now has a more extreme position than he did before he was negatively judged by Sara.

Nothing here is meant to suggest that Jim's views, whatever they are, are Sara's fault. They are not. I'm simply using this example to point to the way certainty creates the social conditions where such a shift can happen.

CERTAINTY AND THE EROSION OF SOCIAL TRUST

Certainty can push people toward extreme positions, but its effects don't end there. Another consequence is the erosion of trust. If I come to a different conclusion than you on a heated issue, and you condemn my character for it, I'm likely to feel resentment or frustration toward you. Resentment and frustration do not foster trust. Not only that, but our one-time sour interaction is likely to shape future interactions you and I have. And unresolved tension now breeds more tension later. Our interaction is also likely to affect how I see other people that I perceive to have views similar to yours—as in, I assume they will judge me, too. In other words, my deteriorating trust in you isn't limited to our narrow interaction.

To be sure, I'm not suggesting that certainty is the *only* thing that erodes trust. Other factors do as well. For instance, corruption, nepotism, straight-up lying—all of these would have a similar effect. Ultimately, societies can manage when a relatively small subset of people lives off the grid—disconnecting themselves from the broader social network, but they can only function when a critical mass is invested and participating.

The difference, and what makes certainty in many ways more insidious, is that people often aren't aware that they've stumbled into it. By contrast, people generally know when they're taking bribes, embezzling money, only hiring their family members, and telling bald-faced lies. In those instances, the corrective measure might be a criminal investigation, a public outing, or even an appeal to the person's sense of integrity. With certainty, however, none of these will matter.

In a later chapter, we'll talk in detail about the consequences of institutions failing to question their assumptions in a way that leads them away from neutrality. For now, however, let's consider the example of a loss of trust between students and teachers at the level of the individual interaction.

We can start by imagining two classrooms, both with an instructor teaching high school biology. In each classroom, they're covering the topic of evolution. In one, the teacher makes it clear that students' questions that challenge the theory of evolution aren't welcome. In another, the teacher encourages or initiates such discussion.

If I'm a student in the first class and I have doubts about the theory of evolution—perhaps my family is devoutly religious—the fact that the teacher closes off discussion to my questions probably isn't going to eliminate those doubts. But I might have any number of emotional responses to the fact that I can't voice them. I can imagine feeling resentful, angry, or even contemptuous. What's more, the teacher's unwillingness to acknowledge the uncertainty, however minor it may be, could lead me to conclude that their own ideology has clouded their judgment. Taken together, it seems unlikely that I'm going to trust this teacher going forward.

What if, the following week, in the same classroom, that teacher is talking about the importance of vaccines? Am I now even less inclined to trust what she's saying, given her approach to evolution? The answer is probably yes. And this will likely be compounded every time information that isn't definitive is presented in a way that implies that it is.

We'll go into questions of science and evidence in considerably more detail when we talk about moving from certainty to confidence, but here's one way to think about the evolution example. Scientific theories are inherently probabilistic in nature. In other words, despite all the evidence we currently have, there's some chance that evolution is *not* the right way to understand human history. This is the case whether we choose to recognize it or not.

It is also accurate to say that most scientists place that chance quite low. But low, even minuscule, isn't the same as *zero*. This is apparent in the assertion, often attributed to biologist J. B. S. Haldane, that the presence of rabbits in the Precambrian would be enough to unravel his belief in evolution. After all, our current understanding of the timeline of history places the first mammals far later than the Precambrian period. In making this declaration, Haldane is indicating that, should such an unlikely discovery be made, he would be forced to reevaluate the theory. By contrast, if he were instead to insist that there's *nothing* that would change his view, he would be refusing to challenge or question his thinking.

When it comes to a classroom setting, fielding questions about evolution *does not* change the underlying probability that it's correct, but it *does* foster trust.

Now, someone might reasonably worry that opening the door to doubt in this manner understates the stability of the theory—that it makes it sound more provisional than it is. In an extreme version of this concern, the fear is that a discussion of evolution gets reduced to a shrug of the shoulders on the part of the teacher. As in, "Eh, maybe it's right, maybe it's not." But there's nothing about allowing for questions that re-

---

IN EDUCATIONAL SETTINGS IN PARTICULAR, ALLOWING FOR UNCERTAINTY CAN FOSTER TRUST AND CURIOSITY.

---

quires that to be the case. Allowing for questions, whether on evolution or anything else, is fully compatible with a broader conversation about what leads us to the conclusions we draw and why.

To be sure, teachers have a balancing act to do. Biology classes, as with all classes, are allotted a finite amount of time. And a teacher may not feel comfortable siphoning away significant chunks of that time to explore alternative possibilities that have a small probability of being right. While this is a valid concern, it's one that probably warrants a different response than shutting down questions altogether. There may be no need to dedicate a month of the school year to discussing why people doubt evolution, but might it warrant one class period? Thirty minutes? Five minutes?

When we began with this example, we had two classrooms. One where the teacher didn't allow questions on evolution and one where she did. We've talked through the first case and it's time to imagine the second. If I'm, once again, playing the role of the skeptical student, what if this time I'm in the class where questions are welcome? Perhaps I come away feeling heard and understood. Maybe I have learned something about how science works. It's even conceivable that I'm more open to the theory of evolution than I was before. And maybe that teacher has earned a little more of my trust. So, next week, when they talk about something else, I might be a little more likely to listen.

The scenario I've just described has another layer of complexity as well. After all, when we're talking about secondary or high school education, we're talking not just about a loss in trust on the part of the students but also a parallel loss among the parents.

We can take the situation just described and imagine that the topic isn't evolution. Let's say instead that it relates to one of the heated themes we mentioned at the outset of this book: identity, fairness, intent, racism, inequality, freedom, or harm. Maybe the topic is gender and biology. Or maybe it's about how we understand US history. The importance of removing certainty, of finding the underlying assumptions, is at least as important as it was in the evolution example.

When assumptions about the world break along political lines, it can lead members of those political parties to be defined by different realities and governed by different norms. Because of its inherent divisiveness, it's a phenomenon tied closely to political polarization.

CERTAINTY AND POLITICAL POLARIZATION

Political polarization can admittedly be an annoyingly vague concept. One way to think about it is as a spectrum where there's an increase in the distance between the average voter preferences on the left and the average voter preferences on the right.[4] This increase is seen as a move toward extremes, by one or both sides. But we can also just think of it in terms of how we're feeling toward the "other" side and the vitriol of our discourse.

Increases in animosity can show up in different ways, including in the tendency to express disdain not just for the position one doesn't agree with but also for the character of the person who holds it—another way of referring to the demonization we've been talking about. Political polarization can also show up in the exasperation many people feel when communicating across divides about difficult social problems. Because it feels impossible to do, the easiest thing is often to avoid those conversations.

The chasm between dominant political parties matters. It has downstream effects that include ideological segregation in our communities, a more antagonistic and adversarial political culture, and gridlock in our government. This chasm widens in a climate where the version of the world you see is largely a function of your political ideology. Cartoonist Scott Adams, years before making comments on race relations that many people found objectionable, made an interesting observation. He described this two-version-of-the-world in the following manner:

I have been saying since Trump's election that the world has split into two realities—or as I prefer to say, two movies on one screen—and most of us don't realize it. We're all looking at the same events and interpreting them wildly differently. That's how cognitive dissonance and confirmation bias work. They work together to create a spontaneous hallucination that gets reinforced over time. That hallucination becomes your reality until something changes. This phenomenon has nothing to do with natural intelligence. We like to think that the people on the other side of the political debate are dumb, under-informed, or just plain evil.[5]

This may be more than pure speculation. In one study, psychologists Anthony Washburn and Linda Skitka found empirical evidence suggesting support for the idea that we have two incompatible versions of the world.[6] In their paper, participants were "randomly assigned to read about a study with correct results that were either consistent or inconsistent with their attitude about one of several issues (e.g., carbon emissions)." The authors found that "[b]oth liberals and conservatives engaged in motivated interpretation of study results and denied the correct interpretation of those results when that interpretation conflicted with their attitudes."

Psychologists have studied motivated reasoning for a long time. It's the idea that we search out results that support our prior convictions. It's the explanation for why, in an experimental setting, subjects led to believe they have an unfavorable medical result based on a saliva test will take longer to determine the test is complete, are more likely to retest the result, and cite more life irregularities that might have influenced the test than people who received more favorable diagnoses.[7]

The demonization that results from certainty partly affects political polarization through resentment, as in people who feel unfairly judged might, not unreasonably, choose to surround themselves with people who *don't* judge them in this manner. We saw this with our earlier example of Jim and Sara. But demonization has multiple potential consequences, one of which puts us squarely within what, in psychology, is referred to as "group polarization."[8] Group polarization is the name for the way decision-making among like-minded folks tends to yield more extreme outcomes than individual-level decisions.

This phenomenon was famously shown in a study of mock juries.[9] When juries were leaning toward a low award to a plaintiff in their pre-deliberation, group discussion made their decision even more lenient to the defendant. When they were leaning toward a harsh penalty for the defendant in their pre-deliberation, group discussion made their decision harsher. Research that is specifically on the intensification of political attitudes rather than jury deliberations has shown similar results.[10]

Political polarization is seen as a significant enough problem that concerns about it come from across the political spectrum. A January 2022 report from the Carnegie Endowment for International Peace bears the following subtitle: "The United States' Democracy Is Being Threatened by Increasingly Polarized Politics. Other Countries' Histories Offer Warnings and Suggest Possible Solutions."[11] A February 2022 article in the politically left *Jacobin* journal stated, "US Politics Have Become Hyperpolarized along Partisan Lines."[12] A January 2022 center-left Brookings publication bore the title "Reducing Extreme Polarization Is Key to Stabilizing Democracy."[13] The libertarian Cato Institute released a December 2021 podcast episode titled "Partisanship, Polarization, and Political Hatred."[14] And a December 2021 article from the conservative *National Review* was titled "The Irony of Our Polarized Age," where one line reads, "The sense of apocalyptic panic that drives our politics now persuades partisans that it's impossible to work with the other party."[15] This problem belongs to all of us.

Perhaps because it affects all of us, people often want to know which side shoulders a greater share of the blame. Is it the "dogmatic left"? Is it the "authoritarian right"? But this way of framing things is a distraction.

It pulls us to look at the issues themselves rather than the meta-challenge that unites them. Certainty and the failure to question our thinking form a root problem, regardless of which side it's coming from. We don't need to establish blame or to make a claim of symmetry to recognize that.

Particularly when it comes to contentious issues, the more assertions any side makes from a place of certainty, the more it fosters resentment and confusion. It's true if it's that the results of the 2020 presidential election were falsified, it's true if it's a claim about gender and biology, it's true in how we think about the "right" Covid policies, and it's true in how we think about the causes of and solutions to racial and gender inequality.

Some people have observed that politics seem more vicious and vitriolic now than in the past. Politics are bitter in large part because we're no longer disagreeing about the best way to solve the problems we face. We can't get to that conversation because we haven't been able to come an understanding of what "best" means.

Instead, we disagree both about what's real and what's morally justifiable. Words have become politically charged in a way that makes it difficult to know what people mean. For instance, some people view terms like "law and order" as a racist dog whistle, while others see it as the reflection of a legitimate concern about reducing crime and chaos in communities. What's more, as we saw in the Washburn and Skitka study, people on different sides see evidence differently, depending on whether it goes against their preferred beliefs. Ultimately, we're looking into separate fun house mirrors, all the while insisting we're looking out a window.

There is a separate book to be written about how we got here. And while that's not our task here, one entry point to thinking about this question is to consider the factors that have made our polarization worse.

Several items repeatedly appear on lists of the top causes of political polarization.[16] They include things like the end of the Cold War, the rise of identity politics, new rules for Congress, and the decline of journalistic responsibility. But while these may be proximate causes, they are each largely driven by a shared underlying problem.

If we think of a model of all the different factors that link to political polarization, the mechanism through which each of them works is by shaping how we think about our opponents. Let's take the factors we listed one at a time. While the end of the Cold War had clear geopolitical implications, one additional thing it did was remove the common threat that America faced.

Whether we're talking about Congress in particular or the American populace in general, people tend to unify in the face of a common enemy. And when people with opposing views are brought together, one of the most common side effects is that they start to see each other differently. They often begin to see the monsters they previously felt only hostility toward as three-dimensional people with families, worries, and values. It turns out it's much more difficult to demonize or hate someone you see as a flawed person just like yourself. One way of putting this is that the conversations and interactions that come from the unification against an outside threat create a micro space (or more) of doubt when it comes to disdain for our political opponents. In this line of thinking, the end of the Cold War and its unifying effect led to an increase in polarization.

We can also look at identity politics. Among other things, identity politics is a way of thinking about who we are that treats, for instance, race, ethnicity, and gender as the most important elements that define our experience in the world. In an extreme form, it communicates that, for members of minority groups in particular, our experiences are so unique that no one can understand them except other members of our group. Similarly, identity politics often tacitly assumes that there's enough common to the experience of all members of a particular group to talk about, for instance, a female experience, a black experience, or a Latino experience. My point is not to say that these are good or bad assumptions or to label them as true or false in a broader sense. It is to reveal that they *are* assumptions, and they usually go unstated.

When it comes to our social identities, it would be hard to make a convincing argument that they play *no* role in shaping how we experience the world. There's a reason, for instance, that most women have close friends who are other women. When it comes to how we interact with the world, there are probably some experiences that women share simply by being the same sex.

And yet certainty often prevents us from asking ourselves whether it's possible to lean too far into this claim. When we lean more and more without thinking through the possible downsides, walls tend to go up between groups that minimize or ignore any human experience that might transcend them. Failing to interrogate how we do and should think about identity prevents us from asking the kinds of questions that would open our own thinking on this topic. Identity clearly matters when it comes to how we experience the world, but what does it mean to lean into it too much? And who decides what's too much?

When it comes to new norms among members of Congress, another item on our list of polarization's causes, one of the changes people have pointed to in recent decades is the decline of fraternization across political parties. Members are less likely to cross the aisle than they once were. A study of C-SPAN videos confirmed this in the literal sense.[17] Further, starting in the 1990s, members of Congress were encouraged to spend less time in DC and more time in their home states. What is the predictable consequence when people on different sides of complex political issues stop socializing with one another? They become more entrenched and more certain in their own thinking and their judgments of the people they disagree with.

Let's look at one more cause that's commonly cited: a loss of journalistic integrity. Sometimes, when I find myself in conversation on this topic, I'll hear people say things like, "The worst thing journalists and the media do is take an activist role." My response is always the same. Regardless of whether you think journalists should be activists or not, that's *not* the worst that can happen. Take, just as an example, this headline from the *Washington Post*, "No Systemic Racism? Look at Student

Achievement Gaps in Reading."[18] A reporter's own convictions might lead her to unintentionally blur the delicate line between reporting and interpreting the news. What's more, when faced with the question of which it is, the writer herself might be unsure.

WHY NOW?

While one important question is how did we get here, another is why now? It would be foolish—and more than a little hypocritical in a book talking about the problem of oversimplification and a failure to see complexity—to suggest that there's a singular cause or that we have a full understanding of the answer. With that in mind, and at the risk of sounding frighteningly old, one of the contributing factors is likely our online lives.

People have long suggested that the Internet in general and social media in particular have made us more polarized. For several years, this has been thought to be the result of the way social media siloes people into groups where they only come into contact with people who think as they do. Similar to the Congress example, the idea is that the lack of cross-party contact makes it easier to dehumanize and demonize people on the other side of contentious issues. However, the mechanism behind this link isn't fully understood, and at least one study has suggested that it might work differently.[19] That study found that it's, in fact, contact with people with different views (rather than isolation from them) that leads to the kind of sorting that increases polarization.

These theories share the belief that the primary factor at play is the ideas of the people to whom we're exposed. And while this makes sense, perhaps there's something else too. What if we're not just affected by *who* we're exposed to but also *how much* we're exposed to? In this line of thinking, the increase in certainty might be, in part, a response to the staggering increase in the volume of information we're faced with via our online lives. Such a link seems plausible given what we believe about how human beings process information.

While the link between an increase in the quantity of information and an increase in political polarization is theoretical, the increase in data exposure has empirical support. A 2009 study showed the amount of information we take in per day increased by about 350 percent between the mid-1970s and the mid-2000s.[20] Given the explosion of the Internet and devices since 2009, we can safely assume that, whatever the number is now, it's probably higher than it was when the study was published. The estimate from that study was that we are exposed to about 100,000 words per day, whether heard or read. As a point of reference, the lengthy book *The Brothers Karamazov* comes in at slightly under 400,000 words. In short, we come across a lot of information in our daily lives.

The negative effects of this increase are likely compounded by our general resistance to effortful thinking, as other studies suggest. While there's natural variation at the individual level in the extent to which we avoid it, the tendency appears to be unrelated to things like intelligence. One of the ways this resistance to deep thinking is manifested is in how we simplify and filter information.

Many readers will likely be familiar with what psychologist Daniel Kahneman refers to as system 1 and system 2 thinking, where system 1 is quick and easy and system 2 is more effortful. Similar to Kahneman's framework, but perhaps less well-known, is something called the Heuristic Systematic Model (HSM).[21] This model breaks our thinking into two modes: heuristic and systematic. Heuristic thinking is our default. It's characterized by a readiness to form opinions and judgments by following basic cues. Systematic thinking, by contrast, is what we do when we take a careful look at evidence and make connections between ideas. Unsurprisingly, we tend to prefer the former over the latter.

While academic psychologists have different terms for this preference, one is "cognitive miser." As "cognitive misers," we often seek simple ways to solve problems, rather than sophisticated and demanding ones.

So, how might cognitive miserliness relate to certainty? When we simplify concepts and problems, we cast aside nuance and ignore complexity. And when we shut out nuance, we lose our ability to question the thinking that drove us to our position on a particular topic in the first place. What if, in part, we're more certain because we're filtering out more and more of the available information? Here's one way to think about it.

In some ways, there's considerable overlap between system 1 and heuristic thinking and between system 2 and systematic thinking. After all, they both spotlight this desire to simplify. That said, an interesting component of the HSM is the idea of a *sufficiency principle*. It suggests that the transition between the two modes of thought—heuristic and systematic—is triggered by our subjective assessment of how much information we need to have before we make a judgment. The idea is that we assess what we *think* we need to know in order to make a judgment and compare it to what we *actually* know. When the gap between those two is sufficiently small, heuristic thinking is more likely. When we sense that we need more information, systematic thinking is triggered.

The HSM model suggests that one way to think about the role of the Internet, particularly when it comes to heated issues, is that it's led us to misread the size of that gap. There are three main ways this could happen. We could think we know more than we actually know, we could think we need to know less than we actually need to know, or some combination of the two. There's reason to believe that a combination of the two is happening. This conclusion is broadly consistent with the thesis of Nicholas Carr's now-famous *Atlantic* article titled "Is Google Making Us Stupid?"[22] In that piece, Carr argued that our time on the Internet has diminished our capacity for both concentration and contemplation.

I offer this not as a definitive answer to the question of why the problem of certainty is so salient now but as something to consider as we try to figure out that puzzle. While we continue to ponder this, I can comfortably say that notwithstanding how we got here, the costs of remaining are too high to bear.

Reversing the trend we're seeing won't happen without intentionality. Because it's one thing to point out that we're treating different aspects of heated issues as settled and that leads us to demonize and dismiss one another. It's another to break free of it. It requires putting words to our assumptions, as well as being willing to examine them.

As a reminder of how this works, let's return to the example of witnessing a car theft. We talked about how, when I look down on the person stealing the car, it's because the act violates my principle that stealing is wrong. Now let's imagine that, instead of observing someone stealing a car, I see a pro-choice (pro-life) sign in someone's yard. And let's say I then conclude the person is a murderer (misogynist). As with the car stealing example, that judgment comes from a belief, value, or principle that I'm treating as both given and inviolable. If I'm judging the person with the pro-choice sign, it might be because I think there's no reason anyone could have such a sign in their yard and not be a murderer. And if I'm judging the person with the pro-life sign, it's probably because I am assuming that it's not possible to respect or value women and also oppose abortion rights. In the next chapter, we'll look more closely at what happens when we fail to challenge these kinds of assumptions.

Chapter Summary

- By not asking questions, we fail to explore "unknown unknowns"— things we don't even realize we are ignorant of or treating as certain. This failure limits our understanding of one another and of potential discoveries.
- Assuming certainty can prevent acknowledgment of the possibility of doubt, leading to rigid thinking and the inability to recognize that some questions lack definitive answers.
- Harsh judgment and demonization are signs that we may not be questioning or clarifying our thinking sufficiently.
- The Internet and social media may contribute to polarization not

just by what we're exposed to, but also by the overwhelming volume of information, leading to more certainty due to the simplification of complex topics.

• Certainty can drive people towards extremism by leading them to associate only with like-minded individuals who may hold more extreme views.

Practice Uncertainty

Create a mind map that starts with a belief you hold strongly about a social or political issue. Draw branches to represent why you hold this belief and potential biases you might have. This can help you visualize, question, and clarify the structure of your own beliefs.

4

The World When We Fail to Challenge Our Thinking

"The quest for certainty blocks the search for meaning. Uncertainty is the very condition to impel man to unfold his powers."

Erich Fromm, *Man for Himself*

When we aren't committed to interrogating our thinking, when we're convinced that we know everything there is to know and that the right path forward is clear, it becomes difficult, if not impossible, to understand why someone would disagree. So, we do what comes naturally and we draw our own conclusions. Racist, libtard, bigot, snowflake. The conclusions we draw rarely paint a flattering picture.

The Fallacy of Equal Knowledge

When we're sure we're right and we're closed to criticism, we tend to see two reasons why someone might hold an opinion that's different from ours: ignorance or hate.[1] Ignorance is the more charitable of the two. The term "ignorance" is sometimes used to refer to a lack of knowledge rooted in a lack of intelligence. But knowledge and intelligence can actually be decoupled. The Fallacy of Equal Knowledge assumes a lack of the former that is not necessarily tied to an absence of the latter.

When we assume that someone disagrees because they don't have the right information, we're saying something very specific, perhaps without even realizing it. We're saying that if this person had the information that I have, if they knew what I know, they'd agree with me.

One of the questions I often get when I talk about this fallacy with groups is, "Well, are you talking about the kind of knowledge you learn in a classroom, or are you talking about experience, as in what happens to a person in their life?" I believe the thinking behind the question is that while classroom knowledge alone might not be enough to get everyone to agree, life experience might be. I tend to answer this question in the same manner whenever it's asked. "Make it the strongest case you can. Assume two people have the same knowledge *and* the same life experience. Now, can you assume they'll agree on abortion, gun control, affirmative action, immigration, etc.?"

I've never had the person asking the question come back with an answer other than "no." Then it's time for the next question. That is, "Why is this the case? Why does having the same information and the same experiences *not* get everyone on the same page?" While the answer is complicated, part of it can be found in the simple fact that people interpret and respond to experiences differently.

Imagine two children—same age, sex, economic background, etc.— who experience similarly traumatic upbringings. Perhaps it's having an alcoholic parent. One child might draw energy and drive from that experience, growing up to be resilient and high achieving—perhaps even never drinking alcohol. The other might, as a result, drop out of school, struggle with her own addiction, and ultimately have a hard time finding her place in the world.

We don't fully understand why these hypothetical children might have such divergent responses to what appear to be similar experiences, but we know they can. This is one way to think about the idea that even if everyone had the same experiences, they still wouldn't necessarily agree.

I stumbled into this fallacy in class one day. At the height of the pandemic, when learning was happening remotely, I often used the polling tool on Zoom in an attempt to coax students to participate. And in the fall of 2020, one of the polls I did was about George Floyd. It was in a "Social Problems" class, where we had been having continuous conversations about race, racism, and policing. One day, I asked the class a version of the following question: Is it possible that a reasonable person could view the killing of George Floyd through the lens of bad policing rather than through the lens of race? I was surprised when the poll returned a result of about 60 percent saying yes. Slightly less than two-thirds of the class thought this was possible. I had underestimated their openness.

As the discussion continued, however, it became clear that there was something deeper going on. I heard from several students some version of the following point: "It's possible someone wouldn't see it through the lens of race if they just didn't know any better." There it was. The assumption that, if the person just knew more, they'd have a different opinion.

Let me pause for a moment. I want to be clear that pointing to the limits of knowledge's ability to get everyone to agree on contentious issues is not a declaration that knowledge and education aren't valuable or that it isn't important to be well-informed. Nor is it a statement that new information can't change people's opinions. I'm making the narrower observation that, on heated issues with a strong moral component, there's no reason to believe that having the same information will lead to agreement. The underlying assumption that an asymmetry in information is what separates one side from the other is flawed.

So, I re-ran the poll with the students. This time, I changed the wording a little. I wrote: "Is it possible that a reasonable person could view the killing of George Floyd through the lens of bad policing rather than through the lens of race, if they had the same information that you have?" The responses came in. This time, the percentage saying "yes" dropped to 30 percent. It was much harder for them to understand how someone would disagree in this revised case. The Fallacy of Equal

Knowledge was born.

The assumption that the other person is simply ignorant is easy. And it's a way to avoid a disagreement. What's more, dismissing someone's opinion as being the result of not having enough or the right information gives me permission to move on, not really engaging with what they're saying. We can take this even a step further. If I think my position is the one *anyone* would come to with the right information, I am free from having to interrogate or challenge my own thinking. The Certainty Trap is a reminder that we *always* have to interrogate our own thinking when it comes to heated issues.

Follow the Science

In some ways, the appeal of the Fallacy of Equal Knowledge comes from an oversimplified way of thinking about what we know about the world in the first place. After all, insisting that we're seeing the world through a window—treating our knowledge as definitive—has the advantage of helping us make sense of what can often otherwise be complicated issues. One of the most common ways we arrive at pseudo-definitive claims is through science.

Confusion over how science works and what it can and can't tell us became clear during the most intense periods of the Covid lockdowns in 2020. Understanding this confusion can help us understand why "follow the science" became a slogan trotted out by anyone and everyone looking to appear informed. And why it was used as a mic drop moment by people on opposite sides of vaccines, shutdowns, and other Covid-related policies.

What got lost was the notion that science doesn't give us definitive answers. This means that our knowledge is always subject to change. A failure to recognize this turned "follow the science" into a tug of words between two sides, each of which claimed that the scientific scales were clearly tipped in their favor. Covid vaccines were either for mindless sheep or concerns about Covid vaccines revealed you as a tinfoil hat-wearing crank.

Science does not provide definite answers. Forgetting this sets us up for the Fallacy of Equal Knowledge. After all, if science removes any shadow of doubt, then disagreement on "science-dependent" issues must be the result of one or another party refusing to accept the right answer.

When it comes to the ways we judge one another, the idea that science provides definitive answers implies that anyone who doesn't agree with the "follow the science" person's opinion is an anti-science moron. The simplicity of "follow the science" makes me think of a giant conference room into which people walk to discuss a particular issue—say Covid vaccine efficacy. Then, everyone sits down at a giant oak conference table, and together, they read the latest peer-reviewed studies. A discussion follows. Afterward, they walk out smiling and laughing, all in full agreement now. And yet, of course this can't happen because *science doesn't provide definitive answers.*[2]

At its core, science is a process. It's a way of trying to understand the world that's both iterative and grounded in probabilistic thinking. In many cases, it looks something like this.

Let's start with a question. Maybe we want to understand whether women and men drive at approximately equal speeds on the highway. Perhaps our question is driven by a concern that people are, in general, driving too fast but we have limited funds to target both groups with a slow-down message. So, we want to know: Should we market our message more toward women or more toward men (let's assume for the moment that there's a meaningful difference in what marketing toward one group versus another would look like in this case)?

Maybe our hypothesis is that men drive faster than women. We might think this is the case because men exhibit, on average, a higher tolerance for risk than women do. Assume we've drawn this conclusion from previous studies. There are a couple of ways we could test our hypothesis.

We could stand on the side of the highway with a radar gun, measuring the speed of passing cars while trying to observe whether the drivers are men or women. This approach has clear challenges. For starters, it might be difficult to figure out the sex of the driver of a car that's passing at 70 mph. And, of course, there's bound to be some measurement error in the radar guns. In other words, they probably don't always get the speed exactly right.

There are other ways to try to gather this information if we don't want to stand on the side of the road with a speed gun. For instance, we could do a survey. We could ask people their sex and questions about how fast they drive. We might ask: *What was the fastest you drove in the last week?* Of course, we'd have to assume that most people both remember accurately and that they answer honestly.

Regardless of how we decide to collect the data, once we have it, we can analyze it. When we have our results—when we have calculated the average speed for men in our sample and the average speed for women in our sample—we could compare them. And we would see whether the average speed for men is higher or lower than the average speed for women. If it's higher, this is evidence in support of our hypothesis that men drive faster. If it's equal to or lower than the average speed for women, it's not.

While this is the general gist of the scientific method, it doesn't end here. It continues with the reporting of findings and, sometimes, the conducting of additional research. Going back to our example, however, regardless of what our findings ultimately show—whether men in our sample drive faster, whether women do, or whether the average speeds are the same—we cannot conclude anything definitive. Why? Because there's always the chance that, even if we did everything in our analysis right, whatever conclusion we draw is wrong. One way to think about this is that we're trying to draw conclusions about a large number of people (a population) from a small number of people (a sample). And it's always possible that, in this case, we ended up with especially fast or

THINKING IN PROBABILISTIC TERMS MEANS UNDERSTANDING THERE'S ALWAYS A CHANCE OUR CONCLUSION NEEDS REVISING.

slow drivers. This variation is one of the reasons why, when it comes to our conclusions, repetition is so important.

Here's another way to think about it. One of the questions I'll often ask students when I teach statistics goes something like this: Let's say you're interested in the average temperature that people leave their thermostats on at night in January in the state of Illinois. So, you draw a random sample of one hundred households and ask them what they set their thermostat to at night during that month. And let's assume, for the sake of this argument, that you somehow know that the *actual* average winter thermostat setting in Illinois is 68 degrees. Is there a chance that the average setting for your hundred households might be 66.5 degrees? Or 70 degrees? The answer, which students usually get right, is yes. You might do everything right and happen to get a sample of households who like it really cold. Or really hot.

We don't need to dive into the underlying concept of sampling distributions to say that what we're illuminating here can help us understand why answers that come from science, or the scientific process, aren't definitive. But the variation we're describing isn't the *only* reason for this limitation. Another reason our answers aren't definitive is the fact that when it comes to heated and contentious issues, we're usually talking about human beings and human behavior.

Studying people brings challenges that, for instance, running a chemistry experiment does not. Many of those challenges come from the fact that we can neither observe nor measure everything we'd like to when it comes to why people do what they do. This means that there are going to be multiple possible explanations for what we find.

Here's a simple claim. Taking more tub baths is associated with a lower risk of coronary heart disease and stroke.[3] This might be because baths are relaxing and good for you. However, it might also be the case that people who are more stressed just have less time to take baths. In other words, there might be something fundamentally different about people who choose to take regular baths and those who do not. And whatever it is that makes one group different from the other might also be linked to rates of coronary heart disease and stroke.

The previous example blurs together personal choices (taking a bath) and health outcomes (having a stroke). But we can imagine a non-medical social science example that focuses solely on behavioral choices. For instance, let's say I want to understand the relationship between alcohol use and grade point average among college students. My hypothesis might be that higher levels of alcohol use lead to lower GPAs.

Perhaps the easiest thing to do would be to run a survey where I ask students to tell me how much alcohol they consume and what their GPA is. To narrow the scope of the question, maybe I could specify that I'm asking about alcohol consumption in the preceding week.

Let's say I gather a random sample and I collect the data as described. And let's assume the data shows that students who report consuming more alcohol also have lower GPAs. Is this evidence in support of my hypothesis? Maybe. The problem is that I can't tell, from the data I've collected, whether heavy alcohol consumption is making the students struggle in their classes or whether students who are struggling with their classes are drinking heavily. Perhaps they're drinking precisely *because* they're struggling academically. In short, there's more than one possible explanation. A failure to challenge our thinking often leads precisely to a corresponding failure to consider multiple possible explanations.

One of the ways researchers sometimes try to tackle this problem is with longitudinal data. Longitudinal data is generally the result of a study where information on respondents is gathered at multiple points in time. The idea behind collecting this kind of data is that it allows the analyst to establish time order—to identify which factor came first, which is important for trying to demonstrate causality. If the increase in drinking came before the drop in GPA, I'll have a stronger case for saying that one caused the other. Although even then, it wouldn't be definitive. After all, it's entirely possible that some other event—perhaps a death in the family—led to both the increased drinking and the drop in GPA.

To be sure, there are complicated statistical techniques that try to get at these types of analytic challenges in an attempt to rule out alternative possible explanations. My point is that, when it comes to human behavior in particular, our answers, explanations, and theories are always probabilistic in nature. This means there's always a chance we're wrong. After all, this is why Haldane said that the presence of rabbits in the Precambrian would destabilize how he thinks about the theory of evolution.

Hopefully, the fuzziness of the phrase "follow the science" is coming into focus.

To make matters even more complicated, sometimes the scientific method is described as but one way of acquiring knowledge. What people often mean by that is that science stands next to things like reason/rationality, authority, and intuition. For instance, if I tell my child that he shouldn't kick his teacher in the shins, he's not learning that through the scientific method.

The scientific method rests on observation. It's based in the powerful idea that we can both test and criticize our knowledge. It also hinges on the idea that our tests can be repeated, where repetition that leads to the same or a similar conclusion strengthens credibility. However, because it's based on observation, one disadvantage of the scientific method is that it has little to say about things we care about in the world that we *can't* see. For instance, most parents would be enormously grateful for a surefire way to teach their kids to be resilient. And while there are different theories on how to foster this, resilience, for many reasons, is an extremely difficult thing to measure or test for. In some ways, we can observe it after someone has experienced something traumatic, but it's difficult to predict ahead of time. Another disadvantage of the scientific method is that it emphasizes and prioritizes objectivity. Objectivity in science is the idea that we've removed all relevant biases. And yet, it is itself open to criticism: As in, can we ever remove every trace of bias? Moreover, how would we know if we did?

That brings us to rationality, another way people think about knowledge. While it's related in many ways to reason and logic, it does not require direct observation in the way the scientific method does. For instance, the conclusion that the changing tides in the ocean are due to the gravitational pull of the moon is the result of reason and logic. Like science, however, rationality is not without its challenges. For one thing, reasoned arguments might mask logical fallacies (like the Settled Question Fallacy). That means that, for instance, what may first seem logical might turn out to be merely cultural convention. Consider how I might argue that it's only *logical* that I get angry when you show up an hour late for dinner. But, in fact, there's a question about whether my expectation that you show up on time is simply a cultural norm and not a matter of logic.

Authority—another way of knowing things—at its best uses the accumulated wisdom of notable people and traditions. It's why, I hope, my child listens to my warning and doesn't kick his teacher in the shins when he's mad. In many cases, people who are recognized as authorities on a particular topic earn that title over time, suggesting that trust in them has been tested and is therefore less likely to be misplaced. But, of course, even the most experienced and well-credentialed authorities can be wrong. Not to mention that the mechanisms that make someone an authority might be dysfunctional. Consider, for instance, professions that have institutional gatekeepers, like the fields of medicine or law. If the bar exam or medical licensing exam dramatically dropped the standards required to pass, the authority conferred to doctors and lawyers would likely—and largely understandably—lose credibility as well.

Then there's intuition. Intuition often allows us to know things that

are unavailable through any of the other methods of knowledge acquisi-
tion. As such, the knowledge that comes from intuition is deeply personal and can be powerful. Intuition might be the thing that keeps you from
going on a second date with someone who seems a little strange, or it
might be what leads you to trust (or not trust) a new babysitter. However,
intuition tends to yield knowledge that is largely inaccessible to people
outside of ourselves. And what we feel we know from intuition can be
difficult to put into words. Of all ways of knowing, intuition might be
the most susceptible to our own self-delusions and misconceptions.

What I've described here is in no way meant to be an exhaustive
study of different types of knowledge or of how we know things. On the
contrary, we've barely scratched the surface. After all, these are questions
that philosophers have pondered for centuries and will probably continue to ponder for centuries to come. My point is far narrower. While I
make no claim of equivalence, it seems clear that each of these methods
of accumulating knowledge has value. And each has shortcomings.

When I teach "Social Problems," I often have students read the book
Factfulness, by the late Swedish physician and educator Hans Rosling.
Part of what Rosling is most remembered for is the way he promoted
and advocated for the use of data in decision-making in international
development specifically, but for all policies more generally.

When I teach Rosling's book in class, students' first reaction to it is
almost always favorable. They tend to be pleasantly surprised by many of
the positive trends—like declining infant mortality rates and increasing
literacy rates—he reports in the book. They appear to take comfort in the
possibility that the world isn't as horrible as it seemed before they read
it. Then I tell them that some people take issue with Rosling's argument.
Some people disagree with how he interpreted the data or argue that he
cherry-picked his findings. Others think he's too cheery and failed to
bear in mind how bad things could get again in the blink of an eye. But,
I say to the class, still others take issue for a different reason.

When the students look puzzled, I ask them the following question:

What happens when two forms of knowledge lead to conflicting conclusions? Which one should triumph and why? Or what happens when data tell two different stories? As they nod, I'll often bring up a tangible example, like policing in minority communities.

One way to understand the threat that members of the black community face by the police is by looking at the rates at which they're killed by officers relative to members of other communities. This yields headlines like "Report: Black People Are Still Killed by Police at a Higher Rate Than Other Groups."[4] Another way is to look at the work of researchers like Harvard economist Roland Fryer. In his paper titled, "An Empirical Analysis of Racial Differences in Police Use of Force," Fryer finds no evidence of racial differences on the most extreme use of force by police.[5] A commitment to interrogating our thinking means thinking both openly and critically.

The lack of agreement about something like policing can lead to even bigger questions. Like, how important is it that, in a society, we have a shared sense of what's true and real? How do we reconcile competing views (some choose one conclusion and others choose another)? *Can* we reconcile competing views? What does it mean if we can't?

One of the most important aspects of any kind of knowledge is the willingness to be wrong. Acknowledging the provisional nature of what we know fosters both trust and credibility. In many ways, it serves as a form of inoculation against certainty.

While the scientific approach to knowledge has its flaws, some of which we've talked about, when it's done well, it has the recognition of fallibility built-in in a way that intuition, authority, and logic often don't. For starters, most people don't respond well to having their gut feelings questioned, and many authority figures don't appreciate being challenged.

We brought up these different types of knowledge in the context of the Fallacy of Equal Knowledge—the idea that if only the other person had the same information I have, they'd agree with me. But now we know this isn't necessarily true. Not for scientifically generated knowledge and not for rational knowledge, intuitive knowledge, or authoritative knowledge. In short, scientific knowledge is probabilistic (meaning there's always a chance it's wrong and often there's more than one possible explanation), rational knowledge can be lost behind logical fallacies, intuitive knowledge can be riddled with self-delusion and misperceptions, and authorities can be just plain wrong.

As we'll talk see when we talk about certainty and confidence, the fallibility of our knowledge doesn't mean that everything we understand to be true about the world is simply a toss-up or a roll of the dice. What it *does* mean is that knowledge alone, especially when it comes to the kinds of contentious issues we're talking about in this book, won't get people to agree.

We started this section with the slogan "follow the science." Here's another problem with the idea that science, in particular, will get people on the same page. Science, at its best, tells us something about the way the world is. Or at least, something about the way it's likely to be, in a probabilistic sense. But, as philosopher David Hume famously pointed out, it doesn't tell us anything about how it *ought* to be. In the context of the Fallacy of Equal Knowledge, even if we all were to agree on what *is*, we wouldn't agree on the *ought*, because the *ought* is based in values that vary. Consider: *We put fluoride in our water.* That's a statement about what is. *We should continue to put fluoride in our water.* That's an ought and it's based on other values. We conclude the *should* because we've decided, for instance, that the benefits of having healthy teeth outweigh any of the possible side effects of fluoride.

Some scholars have argued that Hume was wrong and that you *can*, in fact, get ought from is. I'll leave that to the philosophers to debate. I'm relieved to say that, for our purposes, it doesn't really matter. Even if someone wanted to argue that there is a single way human beings think about how the world ought to be (let's say, a world where all human beings can flourish), we're still going to be faced with thorny questions. For starters, what does it mean to flourish, who defines it, and how will we know if we're doing it? But there's an even more difficult question. That is, what happens when the flourishing of two different groups comes into conflict? In other words, what do we do if or when the flourishing of one group comes at the price of the flourishing of another group?

In short, in the face of disagreement, ignorance is put forth as a first, sometimes charitable, explanation for why the other person doesn't see things the same way. However, that charitable interpretation doesn't often last. It becomes difficult to sustain when that other person either demonstrates adequate knowledge and still doesn't agree or when they don't change their mind after hearing the opposing information-filled argument. Once the difference of opinion can no longer be blamed on ignorance, the Fallacy of Known Intent often takes over. And, sometimes, of course, the Fallacy of Equal Knowledge is skipped altogether.

THE FALLACY OF KNOWN INTENT

There's something satisfying about drawing conclusions about someone else's intent—to draw a line between good and bad, us and them. It's so tempting it can be hard to resist. The Fallacy of Known Intent is the name I've given to this tendency to act as though we know another person's motives. When we do this, the motives we ascribe are rarely charitable. It's worth pausing to point out here that if we're going to say that assuming bad intent is a problem, we're making at least one big assumption: Intent matters. Yet, this is an assertion some people will dispute. Those inclined to dispute the role of intent often do so because they see impact as the only factor we should focus on or care about.

This kind of thinking is often rooted in a desire to neither dismiss nor minimize a person's sense of feeling hurt or offended. If intent doesn't matter, a declaration like, "Well, that's not what I meant or how I meant it," is no longer a defense or excuse.

However, the assertion that intent doesn't matter is fraught with problems. It's easy to see this in a legal context. There's a reason why me accidentally backing my car into yours in the supermarket parking lot is treated differently than me deliberately flooring it in reverse and slamming into your car in that same parking lot. The police will view the two instances differently, as will the insurance company.

But parking lot accidents aside, there are other reasons intent has to matter. A society where it doesn't matter is one where the norms of what's acceptable will be set by the most sensitive person in every room. To get a handle on the implications of this, ask yourself whether you've ever known anyone who you view as too sensitive. Or ask yourself a more general hypothetical question—is it *possible* that a person could exist who's too sensitive? It doesn't matter who's defining "too sensitive"—it works with a strict or a relaxed version. The point is that if you think the answer to either of those questions is yes, it becomes hard to imagine how someone's sense of being offended can be the way we determine what's in and what's out when it comes to social acceptability.

There's more. A society where intent doesn't matter is one that creates persistent confusion for its citizens when it comes to how to move through the world. Let's say I'm offended by people who don't say "good morning" to me at the start of the workday. In my mind, not greeting me is unfriendly and rude. But let's say you're offended by people who *do* say "good morning" to you. Perhaps to you, it feels intrusive, and it minimizes the stress you're feeling. Under conditions where intent doesn't matter, someone passing by both of us in the corridor would, in theory, be expected to either know this about each of us or to apologize to whichever of us she offends. Suddenly we're all expected to navigate a minefield of potential emotional responses.

Earlier in this book, I referenced how the failure to challenge our thinking has downstream effects that include concerns over things like free speech and self-censorship. We can tie this directly to this point about intent. One of the reasons intent and free speech (or self-censorship) are linked is this: There are multiple examples of language use where intent is the only thing that differentiates a simple question or comment from something odious or hateful. When intent is treated as irrelevant, however, all versions of a statement get lumped together.

Let's suppose someone says, "I think the most qualified person should get the job." One way to see this comment is as code for something like: *We should not give members of minority groups a leg up because, if people don't succeed in life, it's their own fault. A person's lack of success stems from their own stupidity, laziness, and bad choices.*

There are several things someone might object to in this statement. Perhaps the most obvious are the character insults of stupidity, laziness, and bad choices. Another might be the callousness of unilaterally blaming people for their lot in life. A third is the broader assumption about obstacles to success. The sentiment suggests certainty that real barriers don't exist, and that success is wholly determined by an individual's grit, tenacity, and work ethic. But is that correct in some broader sense? Might there be some factors at play that are outside an individual's control? Again, the answers to these questions matter less for our purposes than the questions themselves.

Here's another way to see the original statement—"I think the most qualified person should get the job." *We shouldn't treat identity categories (race, gender, etc.) as job qualifications. Doing so is unfair, creates resentment, and leads people to question the capability of the people who benefit from the policy.*

This second version has a fundamentally different feel to it from the first. It appears to be grounded in principles—a sense of fairness and the importance of personal dignity—that many people would identify with.

To get a sense of how much the distinction between the two statements matters, imagine if, instead of the actual statement, "I think the most qualified person should get the job," a person used the direct words of the italicized interpretations. It's hard to believe that anyone in earshot would be indifferent between the two. And yet, if intent doesn't matter when we hear "I think the most qualified person should get the job," this would mean treating the following two motivations the same:

We should not give members of minority groups a leg up because if people don't succeed in life, it's their own fault. A person's lack of success stems from their own stupidity, laziness, and bad choices.

We shouldn't treat identity categories (race, gender, etc.) as job qualifications. Doing so is unfair, creates resentment, and leads people to question the capability of the people who benefit from the policy.

SOCIAL PENALTIES

Intent also comes into play because it leads us to determine the costs, social or otherwise, we might insist on when someone violates a norm. Let's look at a somewhat inflammatory example. In late fall 2022, the Chancellor of Purdue University, who is white, stepped up to speak at a commencement ceremony. The speaker immediately before him had told an anecdote about how he sometimes used a made-up language with his family. In an apparent attempt to play off of this comment, the Chancellor stood at the podium and began his remarks with what sounded like an effort to mimic the sounds of Mandarin Chinese. He then laughed a little before saying, "That's sort of my Asian version of his."

Few people stepped forward to argue that what the Chancellor said was okay. That said, there are substantial differences in what we might think should happen next. Here's why this gets tricky. I'll pose two questions: one that will probably seem easy and one that doesn't.

Here's the deceptively easy question: *Is what the Chancellor said racist?* Many people would find this an obvious yes (and might even think I'm crazy for posing the question). But here's where even a statement such as this can be confusing. There are multiple ways to understand his cringy words.

One goes something like this: *All Asian languages sound like the same mishmash of syllables stuck together, and it's not worth my time to learn them or even how to distinguish between them.* This sure sounds diminishing of other languages and cultures. But another possible way to hear it is something like: *It's really hard for me to understand or differentiate between the sounds of several different Asian languages. And my attempt at a joke is really about making fun of myself.*

If I try, I can even imagine a world in which, in this latter interpretation, the Chancellor's comment might be seen as awkwardly self-effacing. To be sure, that doesn't make it okay in some broader sense. It's simply a recognition that there is more than one way to interpret it. And, again, if the difference seems meaningless, imagine that the italicized versions have been swapped for the actual statement.

Does the Chancellor's statement warrant this much analysis? Maybe not. But given the calls for his resignation that followed his blunder, it seems worth reflecting on. He might well be a racist who thinks little of other cultures, and his language here reflects his sense of superiority. Or he might be someone who generally means well, tried to say something funny, and overstepped. Now, here's the harder question: Should the consequences be qualitatively different for one version (deliberately demeaning other languages) than for the other (trying to be funny and using poor judgment)?

The Fallacy of Known Intent would tell us that the answer to that question is no. It brings us to a no either by ruling out the possibility of an alternative benign explanation or by asserting that the difference between the two—that the Chancellor's *intent*—doesn't matter. In both cases, it's doing its work through certainty.

Here, the Fallacy of Known Intent has echoes of something referred to as the Principle of Charity. In the fields of philosophy and rhetoric, the Principle of Charity calls on people to interpret the statements of others in the most rational way possible.

The Principle of Charity, however, papers over a couple of distinct points. One is that, for it to take root, it requires people to first recognize

that there are ways of seeing the motives behind an objectionable statement or action that *aren't* hateful. In other words, in order for me choose
the Principle of Charity, I have to be able to see at least two possible
interpretations in the first place. Option A might involve odious intent
and option B might involve a justification that would make sense to me.
In that case, the principle tells me to allow space for B. But seeing B is
precisely what becomes difficult when we're not questioning our thinking.

The Principle of Charity is also silent on the question of *why* the
benefit of the doubt is so important to give. In other words, someone
might reasonably ask: Who cares if we get our assessment of someone's
intent wrong? The answer to that question brings us full circle to the
costs of certainty itself—resentment, polarization, extremism, the erosion of trust, and simple inaccuracy in our assessment of others. To see
how this can play out, let's consider a specific example of racism.

RACISM: WHEN INTENT DOESN'T MATTER

At this point, many people recognize that the meaning of racism has
changed over time. The shift has been away from one where intent (the
belief in the superiority of one race over another) was once the defining characteristic toward something broader. The first *Merriam-Webster*
definition of racism reflects the original way of seeing it. It reads "a belief
that race is a fundamental determinant of human traits and capacities
and that racial differences produce an inherent superiority of a particular
race."

But the second reveals this shift. As of 2020, another option was
added. That is, "the systemic oppression of a racial group to the social,
economic, and political advantage of another." The third reads, "a political or social system founded on racism and designed to execute its
principles." Intent plays no role in definitions two or three. In order to
understand the significance of this shift, it helps to have some under-

standing of how we got to this point.

The second half of the twentieth century and the early part of the twenty-first saw unprecedented declines in many measures of attitudinal racism. For instance, the percentage of white respondents saying they support school integration went from about 30 to 95 percent. The percentage opposing laws against interracial marriage went from just under 40 percent to about 90 percent. The percentage approving of interracial marriage went from just 5 percent to almost 90 percent.

At the same time, the percentage of white respondents holding negative stereotypes about other groups declined. The percentage saying that whites are more intelligent went from just under 60 percent to about 20 percent. The percentage saying that whites work harder went from slightly under 70 percent to just over 30 percent.[6] In other words, while there was clearly still work to be done, things were trending in the right direction.

At the same time we saw signs of remarkable—and long overdue—attitudinal improvements, many people—social scientists and others—observed that racism did not appear to be a thing of the past. It persisted as something people experienced in their lives, in both overt and subtle ways. This raised a question: Did the measured improvement in attitudes reflect actual change or was there another possible explanation?

This question is not as straightforward as it may seem at first. If we take the trend at face value, the answer seems to be a clear yes—attitudes improved. This interpretation would be consistent with the massive cultural and social shift toward greater equality that occurred in and around the 1960s and 1970s. However, this interpretation only really makes sense if we think that many or most people were being honest in their survey responses throughout the survey period. If that assumption *doesn't* hold, if people were denying racist attitudes they still held, the data becomes extremely difficult to read.

This leads us to another possible explanation: Racism either didn't decline or it declined only minimally. In this version, the social norms around what was considered an acceptable response to the survey questions changed. In other words, a respondent might think something like: "I don't support school integration. That used to be something I could say out loud, but now I can't. I'm still opposed to it, but I know I am supposed to give a response that is socially acceptable." In this light, the answers to the questions on racist attitudes are next to meaningless because the data, especially after the norms changed, is unreliable. This, in turn, would be consistent with the observation that racism hadn't vanished.

The possibility that some respondents were only telling interviewers what they thought they wanted to hear meant that the old questions were no longer useful. That meant we needed new ones. Since asking people directly about whether they had openly racist attitudes was no longer an option, the only other choice was to ask people *in*direct questions.

Indirect questions can be used in all kinds of ways. Let's say I want to know how tall someone is in a survey, but I can't ask them to tell me their height. Maybe I could instead ask them if they can reach, without a stool, a plate on the top shelf of their kitchen. It is probably going to be the case that the people who say yes are taller, on average, than the people who say no. But my measure could be noisy for any number of reasons—people misjudge how high their arms reach, there are different shelf heights, a tall person has shoulder pain, etc.

In the case of something like racism, where there's a perceived "good" answer, assessment becomes even more challenging. The best solution would be to find some trait that's correlated with or that predicts racist attitudes but that doesn't trigger people to hide their true responses.

The old direct questions included things like, "Do you oppose interracial marriage?," where responses of yes were interpreted as indicators of racism. The new questions attempt to sidestep this. They include, "How responsible, in general, do you hold blacks in this country for their outcomes in life?" Responses indicating "very" are generally seen as indicators of racism.[7]

As with the example of asking people if they can reach something on a tall shelf, using indirect questions isn't inherently a nonsensical idea—if you can tolerate the messiness in the results. The problem in the racism example, relative to the height example, though, is more severe because how we understand the level of racism in a population is, arguably, of more consequence than how we think about a few inches of difference in average height. What's more, with the word "racist," we're talking about a label that we need to function as a social deterrent. In other words, we want the term to pack a metaphorical punch that keeps people in line with social norms. A watered-down, disputed, or controversial version will work against that goal. Particularly one that's disputed across political lines.

The core problem with this indirect question to get at racism is its assumption of symmetry. It assumes that because people who are racist (under the old measure) are more likely to say they hold blacks responsible for their outcomes, people who hold blacks responsible for their outcomes are, therefore, racist.

If you think intent matters—and as we've argued, if we care about the problems associated with certainty, it has to—this erasing of intent should worry you, even though it emerged in response to a real problem. And yet, this is how confused measurement has become on this important topic. For instance, the Modern Racism Scale includes the following additional questions (this is not a complete list of prompts used):

- How much discrimination against blacks do you feel there is in the United States today, limiting their chances to get ahead?
- Has there been a lot of real change in the position of black people in the past few years, only some, not much at all?[8]

Each of these points raises issues upon which there is little agreement, including within the black community. The questions tap into a common theme: our understanding of the causes of inequality and our sense of what the right solutions to it are. More specifically, they're asking for respondents' perceptions of barriers to opportunity and success for members of the black community. Answers that suggest that the barriers are more internal (for instance, motivation, work ethic, and preferences) than external (for instance, discrimination) are viewed as indicators of racism.

But for this to make sense, we have to treat the causes of inequality as settled—and that they're all external. Because if we're willing to see uncertainty in this claim, it's difficult to justify labeling as racist anyone who questions this.

Categorical Thinking

Much of what drives the Fallacies of Equal Knowledge and Known Intent comes from a very human need to categorize the world around us. Plato, recognizing this need, famously said that categories should "carve nature at its joints." Perhaps a simpler way to think about the idea put forth by Plato is that categories should make sense. There should be breakpoints where sufficient differentiation warrants a new grouping. Cats and dogs are both mammals, but they're clearly different animals. So, when I encounter one or the other, I can be highly confident of what it is and call it what we collectively understand it to be. Part of the reason I know to call a cat a cat is that we broadly agree on what the defining characteristics of a cat are. When I visit a friend and she has a pet that looks like a cat, there really aren't any other plausible explanations of what it could be. Of course, it helps that, for most people, labeling an animal as a cat or a dog isn't a high-stakes matter.

I came across an especially interesting example of our need to categorize in a *Harvard Business Review* article.[9] The article starts out by telling the English-speaking reader to say, out loud, "ta" and then "da." I remembered from an undergraduate linguistics class that these are called voiceless and voiced alveolar stops. The author reminds us that there's actually no difference between what's happening in your mouth when you make these two sounds. The difference lies in something called the "voice onset time"—the elapsed time between when you begin to move your tongue and when you begin to vibrate your vocal cords. Here's where it gets interesting.

It turns out that if that time is more than about 40 milliseconds, English speakers will hear "ta," and if it's less than that, we'll hear "da." This dividing line is so robust that 50 and 80 milliseconds will both sound like "ta." But 35 milliseconds will sound like "da," and 45 milliseconds will sound like "ta." Such a hard line has obvious value in communication. After all, it's what lets us tell the difference between "town" and "down" and "tech" and "deck."

The instinct for these kinds of clear dividing lines persists when it comes to many aspects of life, including heated issues. We like to know who's with us and who's against us. But in this case, the categories are either you see things the way I do, or you're ignorant/hateful.

While Plato tells us our categories should make sense, they should also be useful. The "t" and "d" distinction clearly meets this criterion. The obvious utility, for English speakers, is its ability to help us differentiate between words. By asking whether categories make sense, we're asking whether the difference maps onto an actual distinction we can observe in the world. Let's go back to our two categories: ignorant/hateful or agreement with my position. Does this distinction consistently map onto a real-world difference? Certainty tricks us into thinking it does.

But that's not the only relevant question. Another is: Is such a categorization useful? From what we've seen so far, not only is it not useful to think of our ideological and political opponents this way, but it's actually counterproductive.

Categories are coherent when the thing on one side of a line is reliably and clearly different from the thing on the other side of a line. To go back to our earlier example, we can easily imagine a line where dogs are on one side and cats are on another. Now imagine a line where good people are on one side and bad people are on the other. This is essentially what we're drawing when we are stuck in our thinking. Let's run a thought experiment. Let's say we've come to an agreement that there's one and only one thing that gets a person on the "bad" list: taking the life of another person. If you take the life of another person, you're automatically on the "bad" person side. Otherwise, you're on the "good" side.

This line seems fairly straightforward, but our commitment to interrogating our thinking still leaves questions. As in, is there any way for a person, once they've taken a life, to move back to the other side of the line? Or is taking a life *always* irredeemable? What if the murder was committed in self-defense? What if the killer was insane or high on drugs at the time? What if the victim was also a murderer? Do any of these questions matter? Who decides? If we're going to put people on one side of the line or another, don't we have an obligation to engage with them?

The complexity I'm describing is familiar to many authors and thinkers. It's visible in Aleksandr Solzhenitsyn's *The Gulag Archipelago.* He wrote, "If only there were evil people somewhere insidiously committing evil deeds, and it were necessary only to separate them from the rest of us and destroy them. But the line dividing good and evil cuts through the heart of every human being. And who is willing to destroy a piece of his own heart?"

Let's say that, instead of a stark line, we decide to come up with a different approach. Maybe we could create a list of questions to determine how bad an action is. If we were to do so, what would go on that list? Perhaps some indication of the severity of the offense? Would the severity have to do with the number of people harmed? But what counts as harm and who decides? Why? And what about an act that harms few people but is more morally abhorrent than one that harms many people? Say someone in a bakery inadvertently taints a batch of cookie dough so that several hundred people get sick. And say a person in a different bakery spits into a single cookie (apologies for the gross mental image), and no one gets hurt at all. Which is worse, according to our evaluation system?

The reality is we will always disagree not only on what moves someone from the good side of the line to the bad, but also about when and if someone can move back in the other direction. Going back to the Chancellor's blunder for a moment, this maps onto the two questions we posed. One was: Is he racist? The other was: What, if anything, should the consequences be?

Most of us judge others all the time. This tendency is so pervasive that I imagine it's part of being human. But when we judge without paying attention to the underlying process of how we got there, we treat that process as though it doesn't matter. Consider the example of four white undergraduates at Colorado State in 2019.[10] After picking up some samples of a facial mud mask from the student union, the students went back to their dorm, smeared it on, and took a photo of themselves. The mud mask made it look like they were in blackface. Presumably this is why, in the photo, each student's arms were crossed, making an "X" in front of them. The photo was captioned "Wakanda forevaa," an apparent reference to the Marvel film *Black Panther*. They posted it on social media.

The backlash was significant, with the students receiving death threats and calls being made for their expulsion. The father of the girl in the picture (the other three students were boys) released a statement she'd written in which she apologized for her actions.

I described this situation to my students one day, and I asked them what they thought about it. Most of them thought that there should be consequences for the students' actions. I asked them to think about whether a couple of different factors might change their minds. One was: Would it matter if the students turned out to be huge Marvel movie fans? Or if they had a history of posting photos in various Marvel poses? Would it matter if it turned out that the students volunteered every weekend at a homeless shelter or if they supported Black Lives Matter? What should be done if one person thinks the Colorado State students' action is racist, and another person thinks it was just an off-color joke? Or thinks they did nothing wrong at all? Again, the answers aren't the point; it is to understand that reasonable people could think about them differently.

I also specifically asked what they thought about the girl's apology. Their main concern seemed to be that they felt it wasn't genuine. The comment that came up repeatedly was, "She was only apologizing because she got caught." I pointed out that, while that was most likely true, did it necessarily mean that the apology couldn't be sincere? I asked the class whether there was anything she could do that would redeem her in their eyes—whether there was any form of an apology that would be sufficient. They weren't sure.

A recognition of the Settled Question Fallacy, the Fallacy of Equal Knowledge, and the Fallacy of Known Intent brings us into a new space. It's not a space where the answers are known, but it is one where our thinking is clearer, we judge less, and we see the world and one another in full complexity. In other words, it's one where we start to understand we're not seeing the world through a window.

Chapter Summary

- The Fallacy of Equal Knowledge asserts that if someone had the same information we do, they would share our opinion.
- People process and respond to similar experiences in vastly different ways due to individual differences, leading to diverse perspectives even with shared knowledge.
- Scientific knowledge is always subject to change and to interpretation, explaining why "follow the science" doesn't uniformly lead to consensus on issues like COVID-19 policies.
- The Fallacy of Known Intent involves assuming we understand the motives behind someone's actions, leading to oversimplification and potential misjudgment of others' actions.

Practice Uncertainty

Go to the social media or regular media site of your choosing. Look through the posts or headlines and select an article or two to read on a heated issue. Look for instance of each of the Fallacy of Equal Knowledge and the Fallacy of Known Intent.

5

The World When We Question Our Thinking

"The novelist teachers the reader to comprehend the world as a question. There is wisdom and tolerance in that attitude. In a world built on sacrosanct certainties the novel is dead."

MILAN KUNDERA, *THE BOOK OF LAUGHTER AND FORGETTING*

I was reading the *New York Times* one day when I came across the Ethicist's column. The title grabbed my attention: "Is It OK That My Co-Worker Keeps Her Anti-Abortion Views on the Down Low?"[1] The author of the query wrote of her co-worker, "She actively restricts who she tells about her pro-life views, because she fears it will hurt her advancement prospects and could end friendships. She hopes people will see her as a good person and not judge her first on her anti-abortion views. I cannot decide if this is lying. And while I disagree with her views, it is the potential lying that is most questionable to me."

The column then proceeded to address the question of whether the co-worker was ethically in the wrong for concealing her views. As I was reading, my left eyebrow went up almost involuntarily. I leaned back in my chair to think about why I reacted this way and I realized that the column failed to address what I saw as a far more fundamental question.

That was: What kind of climate was it where the co-worker felt she had to hide her views in the first place? The most would seem to be: the kind of climate where, at least on the question of abortion, good people are pro-choice and bad people aren't.

As I said in the previous chapter, when we fail to question our thinking, we often see just two possible reasons for disagreement: hatefulness or ignorance. In the case of the co-worker described above, potentially being seen as either would be reason enough for her to want to conceal her position on abortion. When we allow for uncertainty, however, the world becomes more complicated. Many people find that stressful. After all, nuance takes work. Ambiguity as a threat takes more effort to think through, and it makes it harder to put people into the categories we like to use to organize the world. In this sense, the absence of clarity tends to be something we feel forced to tolerate while we're on our way to some place where the lines are clear and we can relax once again.

But thinking this way reflects a fundamental confusion when it comes to what we know about the world and how we know it. Doubt isn't a rainstorm we push our way through on our way to the clear skies of conviction that lie just on the other side. Doubt is around us all the time—it's the ambient noise in the background.

Questioning our thinking means recognizing doubt's persistence. This can help slow down our thinking and make it easier to understand why someone might think in a particular way. This can, in turn, help reduce many of the social ills we've talked about.

Avoiding the Settled Question Fallacy means trying to understand how a person who holds an opinion you find objectionable got there. This makes their values, experiences, and worldview not just relevant but central. One way to do this to read widely, listen to a variety of podcasts, or, in other ways, expose yourself to thoughtful expressions of that position. These kinds of activities can lay the foundation for productive conversations that seem impossible when we're stuck in our thinking.

Another way to do this is to simply talk to people and ask them questions. However, one challenge with relying on asking another person to explain their thinking is that it requires their willingness to engage with you. It also assumes that the person is clear with themselves about motivates their own thinking and why. Unfortunately, sometimes the person simply won't be able to answer you in the way you're looking for.

One spring, I was asked to lead a teacher training at a high school in Tennessee. The school had been facing some challenges, with both parents and students, when it came to communicating across ideological differences. One of the situations that emerged was that some of the conservative students had formed a club because they felt uncomfortable expressing their views among their peers and in their classes. However, not long after the conservative club began meeting and finding its voice, some of the more politically progressive students said that they felt disturbed by some of what the conservative group was promoting.

What I said to the director of the school was something along these lines. "Without knowing exactly what the students in the conservative club were saying, I'm willing to bet that they have little experience expressing themselves in a way that communicates their thinking effectively and clearly." Often, when it comes to contentious social and political topics, our thoughts and justifications aren't even clear enough for us to put words to. So, for the school director, this meant choosing: Did they want to try to convince the conservative students to change their minds about their group or tell the progressive students to tough it out? Or, alternatively, do they want to show the conservative group how to clarify their own thinking and the progressive group to challenge theirs?

Here's the thing: Most of us are not in the habit of asking ourselves why we think what we think or how we got there. This doesn't just apply to high school students; it is the case for people of all ages. After all, it's not high school students who are driving political polarization in this country. Put simply, sometimes we often hold our opinions without exactly knowing why. The Certainty Trap is the commitment to trying to figure this out.

Fortunately, this commitment doesn't require a conversation partner. There is just as much, and sometimes even more, value in thinking through how a *hypothetical* person might justify getting to the position you're trying to understand. Plus, this option has the benefit of being something you can work on either alone or in a room full of people who entirely agree with you. It also has the advantage of being a way to really challenge yourself—you might come up with questions that get to core assumptions in a way that an actual opponent might not. In some ways, practicing this in the absence of actual disagreement lets you proceed at your own pace. We'll say more on this shortly.

There's nothing about understanding someone's justification for their position that requires you to accept it, agree with it, or like it. And there's nothing about doing this that requires the claim that all opinions are created equal. It *does* mean you can't simply brush off the person's justification as irrelevant. It *also* means that your justification for your opinion is subject to parallel scrutiny. And it requires that you, in general, start with the belief the other person is being sincere and honest in what they're telling you. After all, avoiding the Fallacy of Known Intent means that, unless you have reason not to, you are committed to giving the other person the benefit of the doubt.

What Do We Mean By "Justified" Anyway?

If being willing to challenge our thinking opens the door to a third possible explanation—beyond assumptions of ignorance or hatefulness—for a position we find objectionable, it's worth being clear about what that implies. Here, I've used the word "justified," as in the person might be "justified" in their thinking. In earlier versions of this work, I used the words "legitimate" and "principled." Neither of those were quite right. I was searching for a word that conveyed neither approval nor condemnation—a word that simply describes how the other person sees things, without judging them.

What this looks like in practice is openness. But still another way to think about it is as a reminder that everyone believes their position is warranted. That means that every position is consistent with the holder's values and understanding of the world. Avoiding certainty isn't about determining whose reasons are valid and whose aren't. It's, at least in part, about making that thinking explicit.

As I mentioned earlier, there are a couple of ways to do this, and one is easier than the other. The first is to simply ask someone with an objectionable opinion why they think what they think or how they got to their position. This approach is straightforward and has the advantage of making the other person feel heard. What's more, if it's a person who can clearly articulate their thinking, the conversation can be eye-opening.

The second approach is to do this by thinking through justifications with other like-minded folks or without even asking anyone for help. In other words, you can actually think through what the justification might be for the position you find objectionable. Challenging your own thinking is important to be able to do, even in the absence of conflict and even if you're alone with your thoughts.

But let's pause for a moment on the word "justified." We said that the other person's position is consistent with their values and understanding of the world. In other words, the opinion comes from *somewhere*—the person didn't pull it out of thin air. Thinking about justification in this manner can be used to describe any position, no matter how abhorrent it may be. Let's take a grim example, just to try to make a point.

Let's say I meet someone who thinks kicking puppies is fine. Maybe that person is a straight-up sadist. At the same time, is there a version of their position where they're not? What if the puppy is attacking them or their child? There is nothing in this line of thinking that suggests that I have to sit back and watch while they continue to kick puppies or that I have to accept their reasoning. But there is, I submit, a difference in how we'd think about the sadist and the person who's defending herself.

In other words, the fact that someone thinks their actions and opinions are justified doesn't necessarily mean the rest of the world has to see them that way. Our commitment is to being clear about what the principle or value is that's being violated when we object—even when it comes to kicking puppies.

If there's no version of this position that makes sense to me, it's my job to figure out why. In this example, maybe that principle is simply that intentionally inflicting harm on another living creature is wrong. However, that too requires clarification, given we do things like test products and drugs on animals. So, maybe the principle is that intentionally inflicting harm on a living creature when there's no resulting benefit to humanity is wrong. But now we'd need to be clear about what we mean by benefit, when the benefit is considered sufficient, and who decides.

A judgment, if we choose to make one, can come later. But, as with the puppy example, we have to be clear about what we're condemning and why we're condemning it. And we have to understand that the principles that lead us to condemn it are also subject to questioning.

You might be reading this and feel sure that I'm mistaken. To take it back to the kinds of heated issues that define our current polarization— maybe you're convinced that everyone who is opposed to immigration is, in fact, racist. And say you think that asking them to justify their position will only lead to lies as they hide their true racial resentment. If this is where you are, then I refer you back to the Fallacy of Known Intent. There likely are people opposed to immigration who are racist, using a definition of racism that everyone would get behind. Avoiding the Fallacy of Known Intent just means you're willing to set aside the assumption that you know who's who and what's what.

The lion-sized question of which justifications are valid from a moral standpoint and which aren't is one that rightly occupies the thoughts of many of us. We desperately want to know that there are clear lines between right and wrong. And we want to know where those lines are. After all, if we don't know this, how do we identify people as being on one side or the other?

Think of it this way: In some fraction of situations where we put people on the "bad" side of the line, if we had stopped to do the kind of examination I'm suggesting, we'd realize we were assigning them that position based on assumptions that aren't always supported. These are people we judged unfavorably because we didn't have full information.

It is, of course, conceivable that someone would have a justification for a position that many people—from across the political spectrum—would find truly morally abhorrent. Let's say someone is of the opinion that people with an IQ under 70 should not be allowed to reproduce. And say they got to this idea by concluding that people in that IQ range are more likely to be a drain on society than a benefit.

If someone objects to this (as many of us would), my commitment, as the person objecting, is to be clear about what principle this is violating for me. In this case, it might be the belief that *all people should be treated equally*. Or the belief that *all human beings have equal moral worth*. It might be an objection to what can be seen as a narrow way of thinking about what it means to be a loss or a benefit to society. And so on and so forth.

Ultimately, the person who thinks people with an IQ under 70 should be prevented from having children may indeed be ignorant or hateful. But, when you're willing to let go of certainty, you can disagree with that person's justification for any of the reasons I've listed (or more) without condemning their character for an assumption you've made about their motives.

Disagreement with a position on a contentious issue requires at least three things: clarity on what the other person's thinking is (a net loss to society), clarity on what principle of yours it violates (all people have equal moral worth), and the recognition that this is not the same thing as demonizing someone for their opinion, position, or question (I can reject this justification without demonizing the person offering it). The reasons to avoid the character demonization go back to the core motivation for this book.

Putting this into practice can be even more difficult than it sounds for a simple, practical reason. Figuring out the possible justification for another's position and putting words to a principle that you hold require the use of language in a way that both people recognize and agree with. For instance, "I disagree because I oppose evil in the world" is not a clear statement. In fact, in the earlier example, the puppy kicker might also think he's eliminating evil in the world.

In the last chapter, we talked through the specific example of racism and how the meaning of the word has changed. So, if your justifying principle is that you oppose racism and you're using that term to mean something different from the person you're trying to engage with, that conversation will likely remain at an impasse until or unless you get on the same page with regard to what you're talking about. And even if you can't come to an agreement on what defines—in this case—racism, you have still named the source of the disagreement. That alone can provide a layer of clarity that you didn't have before.

Ultimately, there's a world of difference between condemning someone's character for an opinion they hold and disagreeing with the justification on which that opinion is based. Here's what that might look like: A person who doesn't support the use of race in college admissions might have arrived at his position because he resents the members of minority groups who stand to benefit from the policy. It's possible that he knows little about college admissions, and if he did, he'd think differently. But he also might have a justification for his position that has nothing to do with either resentment or ignorance. For instance, the use of race in admissions decisions might violate his sense of fairness and equality.

In fact, fairness is another word that people on opposite sides of hot-button issues tend to use differently. I can be opposed to the use of race in college admissions and claim fairness as my justification (I want all applicants to be considered equally, regardless of their race). Or I can support the use of race in college admissions and claim fairness as my justification (given the historical treatment of members of minority groups, they should be afforded an advantage). In this case, both perspectives use the word "fair" to justify their positions, even though they're clearly not using it the same way.

To take a different example, a person who stridently criticizes this country might, in fact, hate it. They might be anti-patriotic in the strictest sense of the world. Or they might simply be unaware of the good that has come out of the United States, and if they knew, they'd feel differently. But the person who criticizes this country may have a justification for how and why they arrived at their critical position that has nothing to do with either of those things.

Understanding what another person's justification might be is one of the hardest yet most important things to get used to in the commitment to challenging our thinking. I see students struggle with this every semester when I ask them to write a paper analyzing a heated issue in a way that doesn't communicate their personal opinion. Fortunately, this is something we can all get better at. We can notice when we demonize someone's character for the opinion they hold and try to put words to what it is that leads us to the judgment we're making.

Figuring out where the certainty is can be a real challenge. Although knowing that it's there actually makes this search easier than it would otherwise be.

It's a little like losing your car keys in your house when you live alone. You know you had them when you last got home (because you drove home), and you haven't left the house since. It's easier to find them when you know they have to be there *somewhere*. Similarly, if you're feeling righteously indignant, certainty is there somewhere.

With this in mind, let's dive more deeply into an example. One topic I end up in frequent conversations about with students is cultural appropriation. It's an issue about which many students have a strong intuitive sense of right and wrong. They often have an equally strong sense that they can tell the difference between cultural appropriation (which they see as exploitative) and cultural appreciation (which they see as rooted in admiration). The topic often brings out both a strong sense of conviction and a tendency to demonize, which makes it ripe for using as a test case.

There's a second reason cultural appropriation is a useful example to think through. People objecting to what they see as cultural appropriation tend to be fairly clear about why they're objecting—they see exploitation. But people who aren't entirely convinced by those arguments don't always have a clear sense of how to put words to their concerns. As we'll see, it can be a pretty slippery topic to pin down.

EXAMPLE: CULTURAL APPROPRIATION AND CULTURAL APPRECIATION

Loosely speaking, cultural appropriation is the idea that someone, usually of European descent, borrows from another culture (often that of a non-European group) in a way that fails to give credit or mocks. It's seen as exploitative, disrespectful, and diminishing. In its extreme formulations, it's seen as theft.

The people most concerned about cultural appropriation generally recognize that the distinction between appropriation and appreciation is largely one of intent. When the person's intent appears to be to treat the culture with deference, admiration, and respect, they are less likely to object. When the intent appears to be to use it to advance their own agenda or as a target of derision, they are more likely to object. One of the main challenges with this, of course, is that this core distinction depends on something we can't observe.

When I teach classes like "Social Problems" and "Bigots and Snowflakes," I usually take a few minutes at the start of each period and invite students to talk freely about what's going on in the world. I ask them to share things they've come across that make them think of our class. It could be something they saw on the news, something they saw on social media, something that came up in another class, or even a conversation they had with a roommate. At the start of class one day, a hand went up from the back of the room. Based on previous comments made by that student, I knew she was of Mexican descent.

She said that she'd gone into Target over the weekend and saw a display that bothered her. The display had tchotchkes and knickknacks for el Día de los Muertos (the Day of the Dead). El Día de los Muertos, in Mexican culture, is a holiday where families welcome back the souls of deceased loved ones for a gathering that involves food, drink, and festivities. The day is often associated with various symbols of skeletons and skulls.

According to the student, the Target display contained an assortment of various plastic versions of traditional symbols and items associated with the holiday. I asked her what about the display bothered her. She said she felt that the cheap knock-off items weren't sufficiently respectful of an important cultural holiday. I told the class, "That concern makes sense to me," before asking if I could push a little further.

I thought for a minute and then posed the following question. "Let's assume that someone who's never heard of el Día de los Muertos walks by this tchotchke-filled display in Target and wonders what it's for. And let's say that, with minimal effort—perhaps a single question to a salesperson—the person learns that it's for a Mexican holiday. Now, this person who walked into the store unfamiliar with el Día de los Muertos walks out knowing something she didn't know before. Does that mean the display is now a good thing? Or is it still objectionable? What if instead of one person learning about the holiday from the display, ten people do. Or fifty? Is there a point where the scale would tip?"

As you probably know by now, the goal isn't to answer these kinds of questions; it's to generate them. My point isn't to convince the student (or the class) that her concerns are or aren't valid. It is to get them to uncover the complexity that is there anyway but usually goes unnoticed.

Here's another example: In 2016, during a trip to Puerto Nuevo, Mexico, two non-Hispanic white women from Portland, Oregon, came to love the local tortillas. In their broken Spanish, they inquired about the basics of how to make them and, combined with a little reconnaissance (which apparently involved peeking through some windows), they gathered enough information to try on their own.[2] When they returned to the States, one of the women committed her mornings and evenings to perfecting the tortillas. When she felt she had it down, the two women opened a food truck, where they sold breakfast burritos.

On May 19, 2017, an article in a local outlet was written about them. It was titled "These White Cooks Bragged about Bringing Back Recipes from Mexico to Start a Business."[3] One of the main concerns raised by the author was whether the Mexican women who shared their recipes ever received anything in return. The article generated a strong response, including anger directed toward the Oregonian women for their act of cultural appropriation. By May 25, they had shut down their food truck.

Failing to press beyond the outrage and the closing of the food truck leaves interesting questions on the table. Among other things, the reaction to the article conflated two kinds of objections that are better considered separately. One is objections to *how* the knowledge of the tortilla-making was acquired. The other is objections to *who* was acquiring it.

Let's assume, and I believe this would be correct, that the women in Puerto Nuevo who helped the Oregonian women with the tortillas were never given anything in return. Given that, we might imagine a couple of different scenarios.

What if the tortilla recipe was proprietary? Imagine a scenario where, of all the people making tortillas in Puerto Nuevo, one family had modified the recipe in a way that made it distinct from all the rest. And the only way the women from Portland could get the recipe was to sneak into that family's house at night and steal it (assuming it was written down somewhere). This would seem ethically wrong to most of us. After all, it fits a classic definition of stealing.

Now let's imagine a different scenario. What if, while in Mexico, the two Oregonian women overheard a local woman sharing with a friend the details about opening a breakfast burrito truck business in Portland, Oregon. Imagine they then scooped the business opportunity, sprinted back to Portland, and opened the exact same thing, but did it first. This, too, would seem wrong to many people.

Now imagine the recipe is *not* proprietary. Imagine that it's something all the women who grow up in that part of Mexico learn how to do. In this version, no one owns it, and no one can claim credit for coming up with it. Is it still a secret? Or imagine that the overheard conversation wasn't about opening such a truck in Portland, Oregon, but rather in Omaha, Nebraska. Do these differences matter? Should they?

Or what about this scenario? The two white women went to Mexico, loved the tortillas so much that, through trial and error, they figured out how to make them. Then, they opened a breakfast burrito truck. Let's say they had asked a Mexican woman in Puerto Nuevo for help, and she was happy to oblige at no charge. Would that matter? Or what if the women figured out 90 percent of the recipe through trial and error on their own and got 10 percent of the method from the women in Puerto Nuevo? What about 99 percent and 1 percent? 80 percent and 20 percent? What if the women simply used the tortillas as the inspiration for something they then created on their own? At what point, if any, would their product be differentiated enough to call it their own creation?

While those are questions mainly about how the information was acquired, we might dig into a similar set about who's acquiring it. If the breakfast burrito truck had been started by two Latina women who had been born in the United States, would that have been different? What if they were Latina women of Mexican origin who'd been raised in non-Hispanic white households with no connection to their heritage? For that matter, what if the non-Hispanic white women had lived in Mexico for an extended period of time and hadn't simply taken a short trip there? Is there a duration of time they could have lived there that would make it okay for them to open a breakfast burrito food truck? Five years? Ten years? Twenty? And for all of these questions, who should decide and why?

To be clear, I don't have answers to these questions. The students don't usually either. Fortunately, that doesn't matter because the answers aren't the point. The reason to do these thought exercises is to understand that there's more to the issue than we originally thought. That's the case, regardless of whether we change our position.

It's entirely possible that the points I just raised are not the kinds of points that would be voiced by someone who said they don't like the outrage associated with cultural appropriation, unless they happened to be someone who's given it a lot of thought. But they don't have to be the points the person voiced out loud to be worthy of engagement. Because by making this thinking explicit, we come to a clearer understanding of possible justifications driving the position. More importantly, however, remember that the challenge in this book isn't just to navigate disagreement with the person standing in front of you. It's to challenge and clarify how we think about the world and one another, even when we're on our own.

EXAMPLE: CANCEL CULTURE

Cancel culture might be tied with cultural appropriation when it comes to the frequency of being brought up in class. It's another topic where, once it comes up, people nod and appear to have a shared understanding of what it is but struggle to define it clearly. When I ask students for examples, they'll often talk about the latest YouTube star or social media influencer who's been defenestrated for stepping over a line—usually socially, but sometimes criminally.

"Cancel Culture Is Toxic" was even the title of a 2021 event held by Open to Debate. As is typical of much of the conversation on this topic, it centered on the question of whether its consequences are truly harmful. While this is reasonable to ask, it also misses the broader point.

Often, heated debates over cancel culture unfold with some people wanting to dismiss it with a wave of the hand. They offer up examples like Matt Damon and Scarlett Johansson. Damon was "canceled" after comments he made at the height of #MeToo suggesting that there was a spectrum of inappropriate sexual behavior and that actions at one end of that spectrum should be treated differently from actions at the other end. The objection to Damon's words was largely based on the idea that, as a man, he was speaking at a time when he should be listening. However, despite any backlash to his comments, not long afterward, Damon could be found on *Saturday Night Live* playing the character of Supreme Court Justice Brett Kavanaugh. In other words, Damon's career in entertainment appeared to be no worse for the wear.

Johansson found herself being "canceled" after expressing her opinion that she, as an actor, should be allowed to play any character or role and shouldn't be constrained by her identity. Her comment was in response to backlash she received after being cast as a transgender man in a film. Although Johansson subsequently stepped down from the role, her career, like Damon's, appears to be no worse for the wear.

If the only worthwhile examples of cancel culture were situations like these, and the question was whether the consequences were harmful, there would be little cause for concern.

That said, other cases are harder to dismiss. Like the San Diego Gas and Electric employee who was fired after he was spotted with his hand out a window making what the person who captured the image interpreted as a white power sign. The former employee, however, says he was fired for cracking his knuckles.[4] In this case, we're not talking about a movie star but a blue-collar worker who's lost his job.

Let's go back to Damon and Johansson for a minute. What if, as with the co-worker who was hiding her views on abortion, the question of whether cancel culture's consequences are actually harmful isn't the right one to ask? There's a version of Damon's comment where it's little more than an observation that more severe behaviors should be viewed differently from less severe behaviors. And the fact that he is a man gives him no less standing to make that point than anyone else. Similarly, Johansson's statement might simply be the expression of her opinion about what the role of an actor should be.

But the real question isn't whether the consequences of the "cancelations" were powerful enough to cause harm. It's whether the behaviors or the words warrant any condemnation at all. Here's one more example before we tie some of these together. Meg Smaker is a documentary filmmaker who made a film that was initially called *Jihad Rehab* before the name was changed to *The UnRedacted*. The film has been described as an in-depth and careful examination of a facility in Saudi Arabia devoted to rehabilitating Islamist jihadis. The fact that Smaker is a white woman and an outsider to Islam drew complaints that ultimately led to the film's cancelation from numerous film festivals, including the prestigious Sundance.[5]

Damon, Johansson, and Smaker (and, to some extent, the Oregonian food truck women) have something in common. They all were perceived to have stepped outside of their identity boxes in unacceptable ways. But it only makes sense to talk about whether the consequences they faced were too severe or not severe enough if we agree that what they did was over some line. This raises the question: Is there agreement on who can say what depending on their identity markers? Do we have a clear sense of who is allowed to speak and under what conditions? If so, on what are those norms based?

Damon was speaking on the topic of sexual assault of women when he is a man. Johansson was going to be speaking (acting) as a transgender man when she's a biological woman. Smaker was telling the story of Muslim men from her position as a non-Muslim white woman. To be sure, there are real questions here to contend with. Like: Who has the right to tell whose stories? When it comes to heated issues, should all opinions be given equal weight? How much does our identity (referring here to race, ethnicity, gender, gender expression, sexuality, etc.) shape our experience in the world? Does it define us so completely that no one outside of our group can relate? Does this then mean that people inside an identity group share the same or similar experiences? Do all members of an identity group make sense of their experiences in the same way?

These are the kinds of questions that we should be thinking about. And to be sure, some people are doing just that. One notable example is the site Free Black Thought, which has the apt tagline "Black thought varies as widely as black individuals."[6]

Ultimately, the questions we ask have the power to shift the conversation. And when it comes to cancel culture, the question isn't so much whether the punishment fit the crime as it is: Was a crime committed at all?

The Challenges of Life in a Sea of Uncertainty

The willingness to interrogate your thinking brings challenges. One is learning how to find the kinds of questions that can reveal uncertainty. We've talked through a few examples, but it's worth pointing out that this gets easier with practice. In part, that's the case because you'll start to see some questions—such as who decides and why?—that come up repeatedly.

Another challenge, however, is that once you commit to questioning your thinking, you're probably in uncharted territory. It's where you're sidestepping assumptions about bad intent unless you have reason to believe otherwise. And this a space that can be challenging to navigate.

It's worth pushing a little at the edges of this idea of "unless you have reason to believe otherwise." Let's say I learn that you support kneeling in protest during the national anthem and let's assume this is something I am opposed to. It is possible that you support kneeling because of your contempt and disdain for this country. But, if I'm committed to avoiding assumptions about your motives, I won't assume that's correct. After all, you also might think that kneeling during the national anthem is an important, necessary, and powerful form of political expression. It's even possible that your position comes from a love of this country and a desire to see it live up to ideals you feel have been lost. Questioning my thinking means I'm looking to understand how you might justify your position, not how I justify it for you.

It also means that, if I want to argue that your motives are hateful, I should have a clear reason for coming to this conclusion. And as a matter of clarity and coherence, that justification can't be that you knelt for the national anthem last year, too. Nor, for that matter, can my reason be that, for instance, you advocate for defunding the police. In other words, defending my conclusion that your motives are bad on one issue by arguing that your motives are bad on some other issue is no defense at all.

Think of it this way: The only way support for defunding the police (or kneeling during the national anthem) is evidence of hating this country is if there's no other possible reason for holding that position. When we've left certainty behind, support for defunding the police is evidence of little more than . . . support for reducing police department funding. In this context, it makes no sense to use assumptions about the intent of one opinion to justify assumptions about the intent of a different one. What's more, even if you tell me in your own words that you, in fact, hate this country, avoiding certainty means I'm committed to trying to understand why.

Here's a perhaps less complicated example of life with uncertainty: Let's say Theo and Michelle work at a marketing firm, and they have to do a joint sales presentation before a client. To maximize the likelihood that the client wants to hire them, they need to make their presentation as professional as possible. Theo thinks they should use a design that has a lot of moving images and animation. Michelle thinks they should choose a design that's simple and classic. Theo thinks Michelle's design idea is boring and forgettable, and Michelle thinks that Theo's design looks busy and unserious.

This makes for a pretty ho-hum example of an interaction so far. But what happens when we add a layer of certainty? Maybe Michelle thinks Theo doesn't like her design because he's sexist and doesn't value the contributions of his female colleagues. Or maybe Theo is a member of a minority group that is underrepresented at the firm, and he feels Michelle isn't valuing his contributions because of her internalized racism. Suddenly, what was, at first, a yawn of an exchange takes on new meaning. Avoiding certainty—specifically, in this case, the Fallacy of Known Intent—means questioning precisely these kinds of assumptions.

Nothing in what I'm saying means that Theo can't be sexist or that Michelle can't be racist. The point is that certainty in those assessments changes the dynamic. How might Theo feel if he's accused of sexism if that's not really what's driving him? How might Michelle feel if she's accused of racism if that's not what's driving her? Theo feels that he's calling out racism. Michelle feels that she's calling out sexism. But are they?

Some people will make the point that Theo and Michelle might not be honest about their motivations, not just with one another but also with themselves. In this line of thinking, they could be motivated by internalized sexism and racism and not realize it. While that's possible, treating that explanation as correct requires treating a whole other series of questions as settled—including the definitions of racism and sexism themselves. Further, if I'm going to say that Michelle is acting on unacknowledged internalized racism, is there anything Michelle can do or say to convince me that's not true? If the answer is no, then I'm not willing to be wrong. And if I'm not willing to be wrong, then I am not questioning my own thinking.

I once had a student ask me why I thought it was so important to, as she saw it, bend over backward trying to defend someone from a charge of racism. If it's a possible explanation, why not go with it? What's the problem with using a broad definition, casting a wide net, and calling a few people racist who might not be? If we catch in our net people who are simply hiding their motives, it's not such a big deal. Or so goes the thinking. I responded that seeing this problem that way makes two assumptions. One is it denies any obligation we have to one another to give each other the benefit of the doubt—bringing us back to our earlier discussion of the Principle of Charity. The other is that it's a profound underestimate of the costs discussed in chapter 4.

In the eyes of some people, Ursula Franklin took the commitment to understanding others' perspectives about as far as it could go. Franklin was a German-Canadian educator at the University of Toronto for more than forty years. She was a deeply committed pacifist and Quaker who won the Pearson Medal of Peace for her contributions to the cause of human rights. Not long after the 2001 terrorist attacks on the United States, Franklin was on a panel where the topic turned to the hypothetical question of the value of talking with the people who committed the atrocities. Franklin suggested that she would still find some benefits to talking with them.[7]

The response to her comment by her fellow panelists was unequivocal condemnation. The consensus among those who objected seemed to be: What could the people who committed those acts have to say that would be worth hearing? The answer, and these are my words, not Franklin's, is that even the people who flew planes into buildings had some thinking behind what they did. Hearing what that was doesn't mean condoning it. The reason to hear it is because you care about how they justify their actions, not how you do. The example of Ursula Franklin is a dramatic one where we're talking about an act that directly resulted in the loss of thousands of lives. But the commitment to understanding others' justifications knows only the limits we place on it. In chapter 9, we'll talk about what to do when this just feels too hard.

Perhaps the way to think about questioning our thinking is as a series of commitments. One is the understanding that harsh judgment and demonization always come from certainty. A second is that nothing, in the physical world anyway (as we'll talk about in chapter 6), is certain. A third is that no idea, value, principle, or belief is exempt from questioning, examination, or criticism. A fourth is the recognition that to question something, we have to name it. It's hard to examine something we can't put words to. A fifth is that people always behave in ways they see as justified. And understanding what those justifications are requires neither condoning nor condemning them. A sixth is that any movement toward condoning or condemning is going to be based on a set of principles that are themselves subject to questioning and examination (see the third commitment).

None of these commitments requires us to change our mind about any particular issue. But they do mean we have to be clear when it comes to our thinking. And, perhaps most importantly, we have to be open to challenges and to the possibility that we're wrong.

Let's think this through with what I found to be an especially challenging example. There's a quote, usually attributed to James Baldwin, that I sometimes come across. It goes like this, "We can disagree and still love each other unless your disagreement is rooted in my oppression and denial of my humanity and right to exist." The quote is usually brought up when someone's explaining the limits of viewpoint diversity and of talking with people who disagree. As in, we can disagree as long as this—what's described in the quote—isn't the case. And to be sure, it's a powerful statement. It's a way of standing firm in who we are and refusing to diminish our self-respect for anyone or anything. In other words, there's good reason the quote resonates with so many people.

It wasn't until someone brought up this quote during a workshop I was leading on talking across political divides that I decided to dig in. I figured if I was serious about there always being questions when heated issues are presented definitively, that must be the case here too. Ultimately, while there might be other threads of uncertainty to pull on in Baldwin's powerful words, I found two.

The first is that the statement sets up a binary. It implies that our choices are either to disagree and love each other or to not engage at all. But are these really the only two options available to us when we're figuring out how to interact? The second has to do with intent and may be even more significant. In this case, what does it mean for someone to have an opinion that's *rooted in my oppression and denial of my humanity and right to exist?* How can we know if someone's opinion is rooted in those things?

One possible rebuttal to what I'm saying is that you can know by the position itself. For instance, here's an opinion: *Unauthorized migrants should be deported.* If I'm an unauthorized migrant, I might feel that this position is itself rooted in a denial of my right to exist. But is that necessarily the case? Could this opinion be rooted in one of the concerns mentioned earlier, like maintaining a proper queue for lawful immigration or a desire to protect domestic workers?

I can imagine a version of Baldwin's quote that would lead us into even more complicated territory. What if it instead read, "We can disagree and still love each other unless your disagreement leads to policies and laws that oppress me, deny my humanity, or deny my right to exist." In this modified version, we've moved away from speculations about intent. However, such a move would likely just lead to different questions. For instance, what is meant by rules or laws that oppress? And, more challenging still, what if the rules that would oppress one person or group would provide freedom for another? This is certainly the case when it comes to some of the tensions we see unfold over religious freedom and anti-discrimination law.

Again, the point is to recognize the importance of the questions themselves. And to see that the justification for different answers may not be what we initially think.

The Limits of Time

There's an important limitation that has, thus far, gone unaddressed. It's the question of time. In other words, there's one way to think about the questions we might ask and the conversations we might have—if time were unlimited. As in, what might we do in a world where we had nothing else to do and limitless patience? We could, if we wanted to, spend hours each day conversing with people we disagree with to better understand their perspectives.

Of course, this isn't the world in which most of us find ourselves. We have demands that pull us in different directions. But even in the face of those demands and in the context of finite time, when it comes to the kinds of topics at issue in this book, we can make significant changes in how we think and communicate. We can slow down our thinking, be more intentional about it, demand clarity of ourselves, and ask it of others.

The good news when it comes to taking on this challenge is that, while the ideal setting might be one where we have unlimited hours and patience to explore different topics, it's not necessary. What is necessary is to recognize certainty's effects and to be aware of the commitments outlined earlier, even when you don't have time to generate all the questions. There's a world of difference between saying *there is no justification I can imagine wanting to hear for that position I don't like* and *I believe that person has a justification, even if I don't know what it is.*

The practical limitation of time points us to one more question worth considering. That is, whose responsibility is it to push for clarity? Take the example of *I think that unauthorized migrants should be deported.* Is it the responsibility of the person holding the opinion or of the person listening to move toward clarity on what the justification is or might be?

The answer is it's the responsibility of anyone who cares about minimizing the costs we've talked about and of anyone who cares about understanding the world. This means it's on all of us. Ultimately, no one can force anyone else to change what they think or believe—we saw this tried in George Orwell's *1984*, everyone's favorite dystopian reference—but you also can't force someone to lean away from certainty and engage with you if they prefer to remain closed to questions.

That said, what I've found is that when you approach topics with an obviously genuine interest in thinking through and understanding the possible justification of different conclusions, more people are on board than you might think.

Chapter Summary

- When we assume our knowledge is complete, we fail to understand the nuances in others' opinions, often ascribing ignorance or malice to those who disagree with us.
- Cultural appropriation versus appreciation shows us an example of the importance of understanding intent and context.
- Cancel culture raises questions about identity and who has the right to speak or tell stories, suggesting the need for a more open understanding of these issues.
- We face practical time limitations when it comes to engaging with complex issues. But the responsibility for seeking clarity and understanding rests with everyone interested in reducing conflict and increasing comprehension.

Practice Uncertainty

Pick a controversial topic that you have strong feelings about. Come up with a version of the opposing argument that you can't dismiss as rooted in hate or ignorance. Notice whether this is easy or difficult and reflect on why.

6

Freedom from Certainty Isn't Really Free

"Between certainty and chaos, there's a huge space, that's where
humans need to conduct their business."

CARLO ROVELLI

One day, late in the semester of a "Social Problems" class, we were discussing what is known and how when it comes to biological differences between men and women. We'd been talking as a class for thirteen weeks about uncertainty and assumptions and, in this particular case, we were discussing the potential limitations of that knowledge for how we think about gender inequality.

A student in the front row who had been an active and attentive participant throughout the semester raised her hand. She was engaged with the material so her quiet voice surprised me when she asked, "When does it end? Is there anything we can't question?" I said, "It either ends when you want to stop thinking about it or it doesn't end." She then dramatically slumped her head on her desk in exasperated frustration. I responded by telling her this.

In a scene early on in the movie *Men in Black*, the older, wiser, alien-fighting agent played by Tommy Lee Jones and the new, young recruit played by Will Smith are sitting on a bench talking. The older agent says to the younger one, "Fifteen hundred years ago everybody knew the earth was the center of the universe. Five hundred years ago, everybody knew the earth was flat, and fifteen minutes ago, you knew that humans were alone on this planet. Imagine what you'll know to-morrow."

A commitment to questioning our thinking—avoiding the Settled Question Fallacy, the Fallacy of Equal Knowledge, and the Fallacy of Known Intent—puts us on that bench every day. While we probably won't be asked to fight aliens, it does require a degree of commitment and vigilance. Especially in the beginning, as you begin to notice how you think. Because most people find it easier to treat what we know about the world as definitive rather than provisional, the pull to return to thinking that way can be strong. Given that, a few points are import-ant—and hopefully helpful—to bear in mind.

What Does It Mean to Be Certain?

As a rule, words like always, never, every, and none make me bristle. So, it is with great care and intentionality that I write that *certainty always leads us to think we're looking out a window.* That "physical world" refer-ence I made in the previous chapter? It comes back here. We'll get to it shortly.

If we're going to attempt to understand how the world is funda-mentally uncertain, a reasonable place to start is with the definition of certainty itself. According to the *Oxford English Dictionary*, its various meanings include "The quality or fact of being (objectively) certain" and "The quality or state of being subjectively certain; assurance, confidence; absence of doubt or hesitation." The meaning of "certain," meanwhile, includes "Sure to come or follow; inevitable" and "Definite, fixed, sure." However, the most relevant definition might be: "Established as a truth or fact to be absolutely received, depended, or relied upon; not to be doubted, disputed, or called in question; indubitable, sure."

I have a quibble with some of the dictionary's definitions of certainty and certain that is worth pointing out. While almost all of the definitions listed resonate with how I think about the term and how I use it in this book, there's one that doesn't: the one that uses the word *confidence*. While we haven't gone into the importance of confidence yet, it is not to be confused with *certainty*. Sometimes, these two words are used in the same context and yet have differences in meaning that matter enormously. Confusing? You bet.

When I was a graduate student in demography, we talked a lot about fertility. Together with mortality and migration, it is one of the three subfields that make up the discipline. One of the first things you learn as a demographer is that fertility has a different meaning to demographers than it does to people outside of demography. Even though, in both cases, it has to do with having children. Outside of demography, fertility generally refers to the ease or difficulty with which a woman or a couple can conceive. Meanwhile, to demographers, fertility strictly refers to the number of children born. Further complicating things, to demographers, *fecundity* is the word that refers to how easy or difficult conception is. Same word, same context, two meanings, and the difference matters.

In a similar manner, *certainty* is sometimes used in a way that suggests it can exist in degrees, such as at a high or a low level. I'm using the word in a much stricter sense.

Picture a number line bounded by zero on the left and one on the right. Because it's a continuous function, there are an infinite number of possible points on that line. If you think you've exhausted them all, you can always add one more decimal place. But the fact that it's bound means you can't go lower than zero or higher than one.

In this model, the two endpoint values represent the only positions on the number line that indicate certainty. The value of zero means I'm certain something will *never* happen or isn't true, and the value of one means I'm certain something *will* happen or is true. Everything in between zero and one represents possibility, ranging from remote to strong. This is the space that refers to confidence, which we'll talk about in more detail in the next chapter.

But how do we know we should chop zero and one off the number line? In other words, how do we know nothing is certain? This question is something philosophers have pondered and debated for centuries. When Descartes famously wrote, in the seventeenth century, *Cogito, ergo sum* (I think, therefore I am), he did so in search of a truth that cannot be doubted. What's more, the entire field of epistemology is devoted to questions of how we know things and how we distinguish fact from opinion. In other words, the topics of certainty and knowledge are fertile ground for a wide variety of thinkers.

Sometimes recognizing uncertainty is easy. Am I certain that if I pick up the eraser on my desk and apply it to what I've written in pencil on this piece of paper, it will do its job of erasing what I wrote? Many of us have had the experience of old, hard erasers that just smear the graphite across the paper. I know that's a possibility when I use it. Or, if someone says to me, it's going to snow tomorrow, I don't need to remind them that they can't be sure. They know and I know that the prediction could be wrong.

And sometimes, uncertainty can be harder to think through. For instance, am I certain that, if I drop my glass on the floor, it will shatter? Perhaps it lands in such a manner that it absorbs the impact without somehow breaking. Of course, because I also know that the chance that happens is incredibly remote, I try to avoid dropping glasses on the floor.

The other day I was driving home from an appointment. I noticed my certainty that if I continued on the road I was on, made a right, then a left, then a right, I would arrive at my house. Of course, I wasn't judging anyone or feeling righteously indignant, but I decided to challenge my thinking anyway. So, I wondered, how could I be wrong? Then I thought, perhaps road construction had begun in the brief time I was gone, forcing me to alter my route. Or, more dramatically, perhaps an accident had happened that would change how I got home that day. Or, even more improbably, could something have fallen from the sky, landed in the middle of the road, and now there was no more road there? My point isn't that I believed any of these things (I didn't). It's the recognition that the probability associated with them wasn't zero, which meant that I couldn't be *certain* that continuing to drive on my usual path would, in fact, get me home. In case it needs to be said, I ignored these small probabilities, kept driving my usual route, and made it home just fine.

I was on the phone with my brother one day, talking about the uncertainty of everything, when he took this idea as far as I'd heard anyone take it. I was throwing out various things to think through, such as "I'm certain that's a tree" and "If I fall in an active volcano, can I be certain I will die?" And, without directly engaging with my questions, he responded, "At a high enough level of abstraction, can we be certain we were here yesterday?" I was rather stunned to realize that there was nothing I could say that would answer his question in a way that would eliminate every speck of doubt.

At the beginning of this book, I referenced writer David Foster Wallace's 2005 commencement address at Kenyon College. I retold the story he told about a barstool conversation between a man of faith and an atheist. In that same address, however, he told another parable:

> There are these two young fish swimming along and they happen to meet an older fish swimming the other way who nods at them and says, "Morning, boys. How's the water?" And the two young fish swim on for a bit, and then eventually one of them looks over at the other and goes, "What the hell is water?"[1]

There is more than one lesson we could take from this story. It could be a reminder to pay attention to things we take for granted. It could also be a reminder of the wisdom of elders and the naivete of youth. But it can also be a reminder that, much like the earlier example of water freezing at 32 degrees Fahrenheit even before we knew that to be the case, the young fish are no more or less in water if they don't realize it. In what we're describing in this chapter, the "water" is uncertainty and doubt.

But Doesn't 2+2=4?

The idea that nothing is certain comes with a noteworthy exception. The world of physical reality, often what we think of as the real world, stands in contrast to abstract worlds. And when we're talking about the physical world where entities are interacting with one another and where we're relying on our senses and on measurement, indeed, nothing is certain. However, when we're talking about an abstract world, this is no longer the case. It's a distinction that is subtle, but it can help clarify the example of 2+2=4.

To be sure, someone could point out that my statement isn't sufficiently specific. After all, it doesn't state base 10 math. And 2+2 in base 2 or base 4 doesn't equal 4. So, let's say we specify base 10. Is there uncertainty now in the statement that 2+2=4? The answer is no—and this is why the difference between the physical and the abstract matters. Let's say there are two apples on the table. I tell you that I'm going to reach into my bag and put two more apples on the table. Does 2+2=4 here? Are you sure? What if I don't put two more apples on the table (even though I said I would)? I said I was going to, but I don't. What if I pull out one apple and one kiwi? What if I pull out an apple and a red ball that looks kind of like an apple? What if I pull out four pieces of fuzz? Or what if I pull out nothing?

The difference between the two scenarios—2+2=4 and what I pull out of my bag—is one way of thinking about the distinction between the physical world and an abstract one. When we're saying 2+2=4, it's certain because mathematics is inherently abstract. In a sense, it's a little bit like a game of Monopoly. If we're playing and you land on Park Place while I own it and have a hotel on it, I can be certain that, if you're following the rules and you have the money (or property to mortgage), you'll pay me the price on the Park Place card, 1500 Monopoly dollars. That certainty comes from having rules that are precise, well-defined, and exhaustive.

This distinction between physical and abstract worlds is reflected in a famous quote by Albert Einstein when he said, "As far as laws of mathematics refer to reality, they are not certain; and as far as they are certain, they do not refer to reality." While there's some haggling over the precision of the translation from the original German, the idea is persistent.

There's one more complication to point out when we think about physical and abstract worlds. While abstract worlds *can* contain certainty, they don't *have* to. They are simply places where certainty is possible, as with the Monopoly game. But I could also imagine a game where the rules are determined by rolling the dice. In other words, one where the rules aren't known ahead of time. In this sense, such a world would be both abstract and, until the rules are established, at least, uncertain.

The uncertainty in the physical world doesn't mean any choice is as good as any other. Let's think back to the earlier example of *I'm certain I'll die if I jump into an active volcano*. This is one of the questions I was tossing out during the conversation with my brother. In this case, we're talking about the physical world, so we're back where nothing is certain. There's some chance I'll land on a rock ledge and avoid the pit of lava entirely. Or that a large bird will swoop in and carry me to safety. Even if I tried to anticipate a million different conditionalities, a clever person could always find one more. Does this mean I want to jump into an active volcano? Of course not. Even though the probability of surviving is not zero, I have no desire to see if I get lucky.

Abraham Lincoln Is Dead

We've talked about how nothing in the physical world is certain. Even if it's in the context of scenarios that have infinitesimally small probabilities—like the chance that something fell from the sky, forcing me to alter my route home. But recall, the tiny nature of any particular probability isn't the point—the point is that it isn't zero. Imagine a situation where we would almost never have occasion for doubt, like walking on the sidewalk with a friend. You're casually putting one foot in front of the other, certain that your next step will land on firm ground just as the last one did and the one before that. Now, imagine the friend says to you, "You know, I read in the news that someone has been drawing strange optical illusions on city sidewalks so that it looks like there's a hard surface you're going to step on, but it's actually a giant hole. People have been spraining their ankles left and right. I know a guy who even broke his leg last week." Could that friend create the smallest bit of doubt so that you hesitate ever-so-slightly before you take your next step? You do this because you know that, as unlikely as it is that what your friend is saying presents a real risk to you, you also know the chances aren't zero.

In thinking some of this through, I tried to come up with a statement that people, myself included, would normally not question. And I challenged myself to come up with where the uncertainty lay in it. That, combined with a few fascinating and thoughtful email exchanges with theoretical physicist Carlo Rovelli (quoted at the beginning of this chapter), led to some interesting ways to think about how agreement on and precision in language, as well as a belief in reality itself, also relate to how we think about certainty.

Abraham Lincoln is dead.

This seems like a straightforward, unobjectionable claim. Something we should be able to claim certainty about. So, what is there to pull at?

Let's start with, who is Abraham Lincoln? There are, I assume, multiple people alive today with this name, so we probably need to clarify who we're talking about. But that seems doable. We're talking about the sixteenth president, who was shot in 1865. Now, what does it mean to be dead? If Lincoln believed in resurrection, might he, in some sense, be alive today? For that matter, might we say today, "Abraham Lincoln is alive"? After all, we could be referring to the fact that his legacy is still with us. Many people would consider that to be a true statement, in how we usually think of what it means for something to be true. But then, how can "Abraham Lincoln is dead" and "Abraham Lincoln is alive" both be true?

We find out fairly quickly that we end up in a space where precision and the meaning of words matter enormously. The statement feels certain largely because we have a shared understanding of everything that goes into the sentence: *Abraham Lincoln is dead*. When we get to the point where we've eliminated all ambiguity in the name and the words, we arrive at something like certainty because we've defined all the rules of the game. Kind of like Monopoly.

Of course, we're pulling apart an example—the statement that Abraham Lincoln is dead—that few people would feel compelled to analyze. But, in doing so, we find that a simple phrase lives in a cloud of conditional statements. We move through the world as though there are sentences and declarations that have a unique and unquestionable meaning that everyone hearing them immediately agrees upon. But, especially when it comes to contentious topics, this simply isn't the case. What *is* the case is that there are many statements that come from a shared bucket of knowledge, and when they come from that bucket, agreement tends to be taken for granted. It is also the case that much of the time, this works just fine. Until it doesn't.

Uncertainty, Bias, and Seeing People as Individuals

Certainty leads us to generalize in part because of the way we discard information. We're certain about a conclusion we draw about someone because we ignore anything possibly disconfirming. And we discard disconfirming information because we're certain about our conclusion.

On the one hand, generalizing allows us to navigate the world efficiently. It's what makes it possible to not stop and analyze whether every object with four legs and a seat that looks like a chair is, in fact, a chair. On the other hand, when it's applied to groups of people, it can lead to well-known types of bias. If I treat all members of a particular group as having a particular characteristic, I'm generalizing or stereotyping. But it's worth noting that generalizing and stereotyping are often seen as distinct insofar as the former allows for people to change their views with new information and the latter doesn't. However, because the two tendencies stem from a similar instinct, they have a similar solution.

Some scholars see our tendency to generalize as one of the most basic instincts there is. But it can stunt our thinking, nonetheless. Countering this instinct often involves seeking out new information—like looking for differences within groups and similarities across groups.[2]

A willingness to continually challenge and question our thinking has implications for how we think about bias itself. Let's say two people are talking in the break room at work. James's background is East Asian. Felicity's is not. Both work in marketing. Felicity has found herself faced with a problem that requires a level of mathematics higher than what she's familiar with. She turns to James one day as they're getting their coffee and says, "Hey, James, can you help me with this math problem?" Let's assume Felicity has no specific reason to think this is something that would be of interest to James. In other words, assume James never said to her, "You know, Felicity, I really love math."

In this context, many people would cringe at what Felicity said to James. But *why*? Here's one version: Felicity said what she said to James because she's making assumptions about James based on his East Asian background—specifically that he's good at math. Her assumptions about East Asians reflect, at best, Felicity's ignorance and, at worst, her deep-seated racism. Here's another version: what Felicity said was in poor taste because she's generalizing. We don't know what's in her heart or whether she's truly and deeply racist, but we do know that she's not seeing James as an individual with his own strengths, weaknesses, and interests.

The difference between the two ways of thinking about Felicity's comment is that condemning it/her as racist makes assumptions about her motives (this goes back to the tangled definition of racism we talked about earlier). But, absent other information—for instance, let's assume this isn't the third time in a week that Felicity has been told to stop asking her East Asian colleagues for math help—there's no need to jump to this assumption. Not only is there no need to do so, but doing so may actually make the desired change in Felicity harder to come by. This could easily be the case if Felicity resents the implication about her intent.

Let me be clear. This is *not* a statement that we shouldn't call out racism or other hateful language when it rears its head. It's an argument to avoid the Fallacy of Known Intent. There's a way to address the content of what Felicity said that doesn't require making unnecessary assumptions that cause a series of other problems.

This kind of example suggests that the way to navigate interactions is by doing everything possible to cease seeing people as members of the identity groups they inhabit or appear to inhabit. And that means viewing people as individuals, evaluated on their own personal traits.

At face value, this might appear to be a broadly unobjectionable goal. In fact, the idea of *not* evaluating people based on the perception of group identity has led to some interesting efforts. For instance, orchestras used to hold auditions in such a way that the people determining who got an offer could see the person playing. In other words, the judges could see what race they were and whether they were male or female. And at the time, the leading orchestras were heavily dominated by men. As people began to pay more attention to the representation of different identity groups, a decision was made to move to blind auditions. In this new model, to remove bias, musicians tried out from behind a screen, hidden from those who were evaluating them.

The fact that this blind audition approach has come under criticism in recent years suggests a desire on the part of some to move back toward seeing people as representatives of their identity groups. However, this is a move that, especially in the absence of clear and open conversations, we make at our peril.[3]

CERTAINTY IN THE PAST, PRESENT, AND FUTURE

The only thing as uncertain as guessing about what hasn't yet happened might be trying to reconstruct a series of events that happened when no one currently alive was there to witness them. History is a constant process of triangulation where, if A corroborates B and B corroborates C, and there isn't D or E that contradicts everything else, we draw conclusions. It's a process of reading the residue past events have left behind.

In some ways, we accept more easily the uncertainty involved in looking into the future than in the past. After all, when the United Nations makes its population growth predictions, they don't just do one. They'll often have three different models, conservative, moderate, and aggressive. However, our willingness to speculate about the future becomes complicated when it's accompanied by fear.

In 2017, columnist Bret Stephens published his first column at his new job at the *New York Times*. The piece was titled "Climate of Complete Certainty."[4] Stephens opens the column talking about Hillary Clinton's 2016 presidential campaign and the ultimately devastating consequences of her campaign's overconfidence in its own victory. He then transitions to a Pew Research Center poll indicating that only 36 percent of Americans care a "great deal" about climate change. He uses this as a starting point to argue that he thinks this low percentage is in part due to hyperbole associated with the forecasted consequences of climate change combined with the certainty with which they are presented.

In the piece, Stephens carefully acknowledges the overwhelming evidence in support of man-made climate change. He says, "Anyone who has read the 2014 report of the Intergovernmental Panel on Climate Change knows that, while the modest (0.85 degrees Celsius, or about 1.5

degrees Fahrenheit) warming of the earth since 1880 is indisputable, as is the human influence on that warming." The rest of that sentence says, "much else that passes as accepted fact is really a matter of probabilities." Stephens writes, "Claiming total certainty about the science traduces the spirit of science and creates openings for doubt whenever a climate claim proves wrong."

My read of Stephens's piece is that he was trying to make a narrow warning against making claims that are inherently probabilistic sound definitive. Specifically, he's pointing to those that are based on models and simulations, as climate forecasts are.

The backlash to Stephen's column was swift. While people who write in the comments section on the *New York Times* website are likely angrier than a random sample of readers, the tone is telling. The top comment (among "Reader Picks") includes the following admonishment, "Mr. Stephenson (sic) agrees that human-caused climate change exists, but says we shouldn't be certain about it, and that science is good and climate scientists are honest, but people who push for environmental laws and regulations are bad because they strongly believe the scientists are correct?"

If I were to talk about this article and comment in a classroom setting, several questions would come to mind. Did Stephens say we shouldn't be certain about whether climate change is occurring, or did he say that we shouldn't be certain about the predictions? I read the latter and not the former. But let's set this question aside for the moment.

Stephens's piece raises another question that relates to the commitment to questioning our thinking. Is there a "right" way to express skepticism, even or especially of something with the potentially profound impacts of climate change? If we're taking seriously the idea that no value, belief, or principle is exempt from questioning and examination, then the answer has to be yes. This then forces us to grapple with the question of, well, what is that acceptable way, and who decides?

Uncertainty about the future is scary in part because of what it can mean for our lives and the lives of our children. Uncertainty about the past, however, brings with it its own set of problems. Perhaps one of the clearest examples of this is the *New York Times'* 1619 Project. The tagline of the project is "to reframe the country's history by placing the consequences of slavery and the contributions of black Americans at the very center of our national narrative." The project has been the source of controversy on at least two levels. One seems to be the historical accuracy of the project's claims.[5] In a letter to the *New York Times*, four academic historians wrote:

> [W]e are dismayed at some of the factual errors in the project and the closed process behind it. These errors, which concern major events, cannot be described as interpretation or "framing." They are matters of verifiable fact, which are the foundation of both honest scholarship and honest journalism. They suggest a displacement of historical understanding by ideology.

Referring to the letter, the editor responded:

> [W]e disagree with their claim that our project contains significant factual errors and is driven by ideology rather than historical understanding. While we welcome criticism, we don't believe that the request for corrections to The 1619 Project is warranted.

How do you reconcile disagreements about historical facts? You can start by not claiming to have a definitive answer.

A second controversy is tied to the assumptions the project makes about intent. The 1619 Project seeks to make the following assertion: "One critical reason that the colonists declared their independence from Britain was because they wanted to protect the institution of slavery in the colonies, which had produced tremendous wealth. At the time there were growing calls to abolish slavery throughout the British Empire, which would have badly damaged the economies of colonies in both North and South."[6]

Is this right? Is it wrong? Knowing the answer to those questions would require being able to peer into the hearts and souls of the long-since-dead men and women who were alive at that time. The problem isn't in proposing a new way to think about history—the problem is in presenting it as the answer. Making a thoroughly convincing argument about the intent of anyone in any time period is a challenge. This book is based partly on the understanding that we can't even do this reliably for people we encounter in our daily lives who are alive, well, and can speak for themselves. Ultimately, assertions based on assumptions of intent—past, present, or future—are made on the shakiest of shaky ground.

At the same time, there's something powerful about the 1619 Project. When its creator says on NPR, "Black people are largely treated as an asterisk in the American story," she's tapping into something compelling.[7] Similar in some ways to the James Baldwin quote we talked about earlier, her words are empowering and demand attention. But acknowledging them raises more questions than answers.

First of all, if we're saying a group is being treated as an asterisk, I take that to mean that their role is being diminished in a way that is incompatible with reality and is not being taken sufficiently seriously. For the sake of carefully thinking this through, let's simply grant that it's right—that the story of black Americans has been sidelined in the broader American story in a way that is both historically inaccurate and degrading. It seems plausible, after all. What, then, is the best way to correct for it?

In the world of the 1619 Project, the corrective appears to be to center slavery and the treatment of slaves and their descendants in American history, focusing on the persistent impact into the present.

Let's further assume that the central claim of the 1619 Project is right. Assume we have good reason to believe that the American Revolution was primarily fought to defend slavery in the New World. That only raises other questions. How much of today's inequality can be traced to slavery? All of it? 50 percent? More? Less? Let's say all of it. If we knew that to be true, too, does it answer the question of what to do now to correct this? And, more complex still, if we knew the claim surrounding the motives of the Revolutionaries to be true, what *should* it mean for the way we think about the founding of this country?

In other words, how should we evaluate or judge their intent, even if the 1619 Project is right? To our ears today, any attempt to defend slavery is abhorrent. And to be sure, it was abhorrent to the ears of the abolitionists of the day as well. But, as with many things, it's more complicated than it initially appears.

In this case, the complexity shows up in the question of whether historical figures should be viewed with the norms of today or with those of the time and context within which they lived. Princeton Professor Robert George has attempted to get at this complexity by posing the following scenario to his students:

> I sometimes ask students what their position on slavery would have been had they been white and living in the South before abolition. Guess what? They all would have been abolitionists! They all would have bravely spoken out against slavery, and worked tirelessly against it.
>
> Of course, this is nonsense. Only the tiniest fraction of them, or of any of us, would have spoken up against slavery or lifted a finger to free the slaves. Most of them—and us—would have gone along. Many would have supported the slave system and happily benefited from it.
>
> So I respond by saying that I will credit their claims if they can show evidence of the following: that in leading their lives today they have stood up for the rights of unpopular victims of injustice whose very humanity is denied, and where they have done so knowing:
>
> (1) that it would make them unpopular with their peers; (2) that they would be loathed and ridiculed by powerful, influential individuals and institutions in our society; (3) that they would be abandoned by many of their friends; (4) that they would be called nasty names; and

(5) that they would risk being denied valuable professional opportunities as a result of their moral witness. In short, my challenge is to show where they have at risk to themselves and their futures stood up for a cause that is unpopular in elite sectors of our culture today.[8]

I read Professor George's point not as excusing or condoning slavery but as challenging the impulse to evaluate the past with today's sensibilities.

So, what is the "right" way to talk and think about history? Failing to recognize the complexity—and uncertainty—that sits underneath these questions leads to various other problems. One example came in the shape of a response to the 1619 Project rolled out by then-President Trump in 2020. He established the 1776 Commission as an attempt to reverse the damage he saw as being done by the 1619 Project. The motivation for the commission, as taken from Executive Order 13958, is described as follows:

> Throughout its national life, our Republic's exploration of the full meaning of these principles has led it through the ratification of a Constitution, civil war, the abolition of slavery, Reconstruction, and a series of domestic crises and world conflicts. Those events establish a clear historical record of an exceptional Nation dedicated to the ideas and ideals of its founding.
>
> Against this history, in recent years, a series of polemics grounded in poor scholarship has vilified our Founders and our founding. Despite the virtues and accomplishments of this Nation, many students are now taught in school to hate their own country, and to believe that the men and women who built it were not heroes, but rather villains. This radicalized view of American history lacks perspective, obscures virtues, twists motives, ignores or distorts facts, and magnifies flaws, resulting in the truth being concealed and history disfigured. Failing to identify, challenge, and correct this distorted perspective could fray and ultimately erase the bonds that knit our country and culture together.[9]

Trump responded to the conviction of the 1619 Project with more certainty. Ultimately, rather than broadening a conversation about what we can know, the implications of our assumptions, and the different ways we might think about the history of this country, both the 1619 Project and the 1776 Commission make untestable claims that can't be proven right or wrong—and they demonize people who aren't on board.

I am not coming at the study of history from the position of a historian. I'm not looking to make a universal claim about the nature of historical knowledge, nor am I looking to redefine tried and true terms. I'm taking something intellectual luminaries like Einstein and Rovelli have known intuitively to be the case—that the world is uncertain—and trying to pull back as many layers of it as I can.

Knowledge and Certainty

One of the questions that philosophers have long pondered is whether knowledge itself requires certainty. In other words, is it possible to know something without being certain of that thing? If you're not certain, does that mean you do not know it? Cogito aside, most philosophers have come to believe that one does not require the other. So, what, then, does it mean to know something? We can look at one of the ways of thinking about knowledge that persisted for many years: *justified true beliefs*. In this context, "knowing" something meant that each one of those terms was satisfied.

Let's start with "justified." While we talked earlier about what it means for an opinion to be justified, here we're coming at it from a slightly different angle—what the idea of justified means for knowledge.

The need for justification comes, at least in part, from an effort to separate actual knowledge of something from the sheer coincidence of being right. Say, for instance, I'm holding a fair, unweighted, six-sided die. And I declare that the next roll will be a five. Then I roll the die and it is, in fact, a five. Did I "know" it was going to be a five? After all, I believed it would be a five, so I satisfied that part. It turned out to actually be a five, so it was also true. But before rolling the die, I had no justification for thinking that it would be a five. I just got lucky. According to the definition of knowledge as a justified true belief, I could not say that I "knew" it when I just happened to be right.

To say that something is true is usually understood to mean that it maps on to some aspect of reality. Truth, in this sense, doesn't necessarily have to be proven or known to others. What's more, as we know, what's true and what we observe aren't always the same. Let's say you're dressed as Taylor Swift for Halloween and your costume is really, really good. It's so good that someone actually takes you to be Taylor Swift. We can safely say that what that person observes isn't what's true.

That brings us to belief. In the context of justified true beliefs, the word belief refers to a *full* belief or something akin to conviction. In other words, something we lightly hold wouldn't qualify.

Thinking about knowledge in this manner lasted, among philosophers, until about the middle of the twentieth century. That is when Edmund Gettier published a short paper that upended how they had previously understood it.[10] Gettier's original challenge to the idea of the justified true belief version of knowledge was the following: He described the case of Smith and Jones. They both apply for the same job. The company president tells Smith that Jones will get the job. Smith also notices that Jones has ten coins in his pocket. Smith is not guessing about the coins in Jones's pocket because he (as strange as it may sound) had occasion to count Jones's coins himself. Smith then infers, based on this inventory, that whichever person gets the job will have ten coins in his pocket. This also isn't a guess, given what he was told by the company president and, again, what he knows about the number of coins in Jones's pocket.

In the scenario, Smith both gets the job (contrary to what the president said) and has ten coins in his pocket. So, what Smith believed—that the person who would get the job would have ten coins in his pocket—was true, but not in the way that Smith thought it was true. Does it count as knowledge? What Gettier did was present a case where a belief was both true and justified but would not generally be considered knowledge.

There have been other subsequent examples of this. For instance, there is the fake barns example by Goldman.[11] Goldman describes Henry, who's driving in the countryside. As Henry is driving, he's looking at different objects in the fields he passes by. He sees something that looks like a barn. As a result, he believes he is seeing a barn *and* he has good justification for this belief. What Henry doesn't know is that this neighborhood has a lot of fake barns—buildings that are made to look like barns on the front when they're spotted from the road. It turns out the one Henry was looking at was, in fact, a real barn. As is, his belief was both justified and true. But given the prevalence of barn facades in that neighborhood, was it knowledge?

Gettier successfully poked a giant hole in the idea of justified true beliefs. But the question of what it really means to know something is one that philosophers disagree about to this day. For our purposes, we just need to know that, when it comes to the physical world (when we're not playing a Monopoly game), our knowledge is provisional.

MORALITY AND COMPLEXITY

Perhaps one of the most difficult things to really internalize is that moral questions are usually complex. I have two ways I try to make this point stick with students. Sometimes I use one, sometimes I use the other, and sometimes, over the course of the semester, I use both.

The first is a story called "The Ones Who Walk Away from Omelas," by Ursula K. Le Guin.[12] In the beginning of the story, Le Guin describes the idyllic community of Omelas. It's a place of unbound joy, happiness, and well-being. It's a land of frolicking children and summer festivals, one where music plays, no one goes hungry, and no one knows sadness.

Le Guin encourages the reader to make the utopia her own. Whatever you think would make society perfect, imagine that's Omelas.

But, Le Guin then tells the reader, there's a price for this unbounded joy. The price comes in the form of a child. The child is locked away in a space the size of a closet, with no daylight. The child is given gruel to eat and left to sit in its filth. Omelas will remain, we are told, a utopia only as long as the child remains in this state. If someone so much as offers the child a kind word or a gentle touch, the idyllic setting of Omelas will fall to ruin. What's more, past a certain point in adolescence, all the inhabitants of Omelas are aware of the child and its suffering. The "ones who walk away" refer to the people in Omelas who can no longer bear the burden of the child's suffering, nor can they live with the guilt of destroying the utopia of Omelas. So, they do the only thing they feel they can, and they leave. After playing an audio version of the story in class, I ask the students to think about what they would do if they lived in Omelas. In talking it through, they tend to see how there isn't always a single choice that's obviously right or wrong. There are only tradeoffs.

The second tool I use to make this point is a website called moralmachine.net.[13] The site cleverly sets up a series of scenarios, each of which contains two self-driving cars. In each scenario, the car is going to crash because its brakes fail (no crashes or violence of any kind is shown—it's just implied). The user—in this case, the student—has to decide whether the car should swerve or go straight. Going straight invariably leads to running over some people or animals on the crosswalk but saving whoever is in the car. Swerving invariably leads to crashing into a barrier and killing every person or animal in the car but saving whoever is on the crosswalk. The program varies the characteristics of the people on the crosswalk and in the car.

When I pull up the site, the first scenario I'm presented with is as follows: If the car goes straight, it'll hit an adult man crossing the street on a crosswalk. If it swerves, it'll avoid the man on the crosswalk and kill the elderly man in the self-driving car.

The website presents a series of choices like this, where the details vary. Sometimes, there are other passengers in the car or on the crosswalk. They might be young or old. Sometimes there's a pregnant woman or a homeless person. Occasionally there's a dog or multiple dogs either in the car or on the street. And sometimes the person (or people) on the street has a green light to cross, and sometimes they don't.

In thinking through these scenarios, users are forced to make their thinking explicit about the decisions they make. Do we sacrifice the people in the car because they made the choice to get in a self-driving vehicle in the first place? What if the car contains a pregnant woman and there's one dog on the crosswalk? Does it matter if the people on the crosswalk had the right of way? Do they value the life of the homeless person differently than the life of the businessperson? And, to all of these questions, why or why not?

Depending on the class, sometimes I'll add another wrinkle. Getting autonomous cars to do what you want them to do isn't always straightforward. Autonomous cars are programmed to respond based on how they read their surroundings. If a particular set of circumstances occur or are present, then they are to behave in a particular way, in a series of "if X, then Y"s. And, of course, for everyone's safety, we want them to be right as much as possible. This system can work as long as the assumption that X (say, a 40 mph sign) is, in fact, X (a 40 mph sign) holds. If this isn't the case, there's a problem.[14]

The point is to get the students to see that any answer is based on a set of principles, values, and tradeoffs. As we've said throughout the book, observing that is not the same thing as saying all principles and values are or aren't equally valid. It's a way to recognize that they can all be named, questioned, and criticized. As in, *why* is the life of the pregnant woman more important than that of the homeless man? *Should* you avoid killing the dog on the sidewalk, even if it means killing the driver? How does a human life compare to a dog's? Does the number of dogs on the sidewalk matter? And so on and so forth.

Now that we have a handle on what it means to say nothing is, in fact, certain, it's time to turn our attention to the question of how, given this lack of certainty, we can make sense of anything about the world.

Chapter Summary

- Certainty is possible in abstract worlds like the world of mathematics but not in the physical world, where everything is within the realm of probability.
- Historical facts and interpretations are subject to the uncertainty of evidence and perspective, making the past challenging to reconstruct with complete confidence.
- Morality is generally complex and often involves difficult trade-offs.
- Leaving certainty behind leads to a focus on people as individuals.

Practice Uncertainty

Go to moralmachine.net and work through the simulations. Think about how you justify your responses and how someone might come to a different conclusion.

7

Down with Certainty, Long Live Confidence

"The minute one utters a certainty, the opposite comes to mind."

MAY SARTON, MRS. STEVENS HEARS THE MERMAIDS SING

There's nothing about questioning everything that suggests that all explanations have an equal probability of being correct or that all outcomes are suddenly left to nothing more than a coin flip. A lack of clarity on this point could lead to the conclusion that, since we can't actually be certain of anything, we might as well just take a wild guess. When, in fact, it's *because* outcomes aren't all just a coin flip that I am not going to, for instance, take a drinking glass out of my cabinet and drop it on the floor to see if it breaks. For that matter, I'm also not going to jump into an active volcano to see if I survive. To be fair, I probably wouldn't jump into an active volcano even if my survival *were* determined by a coin flip. In the previous chapter, we described a continuous number line that ranged from zero to one. We said that the zero and the one were positions of certainty, and everything in between indicated confidence. This chapter is about how to think about that space in between. It turns out that going from a position of one on that number line to a position of 0.99 is qualitatively different from going from 0.99 to 0.98, even though they both reflect a reduction of 0.01. When faced with someone who disagrees on a heated issue, a person who's at a one is simply more likely to have a reaction that involves harsh judgment than a person who's at a 0.99.

When we're at a one on the number line—when we're certain—we've decided, either consciously or unconsciously, that we don't need any more information. After all, there's no point in listening to other ideas or thoughts when we know all we need to know already. Sometimes, when I describe being at a one in these terms—implying that complete knowledge of *anything* is a possibility—people realize how unrealistic it sounds. They're able to quickly recognize the absurdity of thinking there's nothing left to learn. And yet, especially when it comes to heated issues where the stakes feel high, this can be all too easy to forget.

Untangling Cause and Effect

Avoiding certainty means not occupying the zero or the one on the number line. However, that leaves the infinity of numbers between those two book ends. So, under what conditions should I have confidence that the right position is closer to one, and under what conditions should I have confidence that it's closer to zero? In other words, what counts as evidence? Or what *should* count as evidence? When it comes to social problems and challenges, we often want clear answers. We want to know which factors cause what so that we can tackle the problem efficiently and successfully. However, this turns out to be elusive.

We draw conclusions all the time about how different parts of society fit together and interact. And in some cases, we're aware that we don't have full information. When a friend tells me she had an argument with her husband, I know I'm hearing the story filtered through her. After all, I haven't heard the husband's side of the story. But this information asymmetry arguably matters little in the sense that my role is primarily to provide a sympathetic ear to my friend. I'm not, for instance, sitting in judgment in a court of law or even in the court of public opinion about her husband's guilt or innocence.

Let's say instead that I'm talking with someone about US immigration. Whatever I believe—that immigration hurts US workers or that it's good for US workers—how confident should I be that I am right? One way to think about this is to ask what the ideal case would look like for drawing conclusions on these kinds of questions, whether we're talking about the impact of immigration or anything else.

In general, the most persuasive evidence comes from experiments. Experiments get their explanatory power from their ability to isolate how a change in a single factor results in a change in another factor (or set of factors). When it comes to certain fields, this is relatively easy to do. For instance, if I'm working in a chemistry lab, I can probably control a wide range of aspects of the environment that might affect the way two solutions interact. I can set the temperature, control the humidity, and change the lighting. Importantly, as far as I am aware, there are no ethical challenges when it comes to manipulating these things (provided you're not, for instance, asking someone to withstand a subzero room in a T-shirt and shorts). But what if instead of running a chemistry experiment, we're trying to understand a social problem?

Maybe we're wondering whether people who have been incarcerated have shorter life expectancies than people who have never been incarcerated. We may even have reason to believe this is true. It's easy to imagine that the experiences—both physical and psychological—that one has in prison could either directly or indirectly reduce life expectancy. Now, imagine that to answer this question, we gather data such that we're able to follow people until they die. And let's say the data is consistent with what we expected: people who were in prison have shorter life expectancies than those who weren't. Does that mean we were right? Does being in prison make people die younger?

In this example, many people would recognize that such a conclusion isn't warranted. But it's important to understand *why*. The why is that, to attribute their shorter life expectancies to the time in prison, we'd have to be able to assume that, without spending time in prison, their life expectancies would be similar to those of people who never spent time in prison. This assumption might be fine. But it won't hold if the two groups—those who spent time in prison and those who never did—are different in some other way that could affect their life expectancy. For instance, if the people who spent time in prison have fundamentally different levels of tolerance of risk than those who didn't, the assumption falls apart. After all, it could be their preference for risky behavior, and not the incarceration, that led to the lower life expectancy.

A way around this would be to remove the element of choice when it comes to who gets put in prison. Removing choice would mean randomly assigning one group to be incarcerated and another group to remain free. If the randomization were done right, it would make reasonable the assumption that those in one group don't significantly differ from those in the other group in any way that matters for life expectancy. However, for obvious reasons, arbitrarily incarcerating people violates all kinds of moral and ethical principles.

We can apply this thinking about causality to a wide range of social issues we might be interested in studying. Let's say we want to understand whether having a baby during high school leads to lower earnings at age 40. We may have intuitive reasons to believe that this would be the case. After all, having a baby in high school probably makes it harder to graduate, harder to pursue a college degree, and, in many cases, harder to work full-time hours. In fact, given all this, we might wonder how it's possible that having a baby during high school *wouldn't* cause lower earnings. To be clear, having a baby during high school might do all of the things I just described—I have no secret knowledge that it doesn't. But it's not the only possible explanation.

What if, on average, young women who have a baby during high school are different from young women who don't have a baby during high school in some other way that affects their earnings at age 40? For instance, what if the two groups are fundamentally different in the extent to which they're focused on school and learning? Recall that a strong claim that having the baby *causes* lower earnings later on requires this not to be true. In other words, we need to be able to assume that the earnings of women who had a baby during high school wouldn't have been different from those of women who didn't have a baby during high school, but for the fact that they had the baby.

Here again, one way we could know with greater confidence how one affects the other would be to randomize which young women have a baby during high school and which don't. And once again, we're not running a chemistry experiment—we're talking about people's lives.

None of this should be read as a lamentation of the fact that we can't run unethical experiments on human subjects. The point is simply to observe the inherent limitations in the claims we can make when it comes to many issues we care deeply about.

Here's one way of thinking about it. If we compare two groups—one who has experience A and the other who doesn't—on an outcome and they differ in some way that we're not measuring, we have no reason to assume they'd be the same in the absence of experience A. They could differ in ways we can't see but that matter, nonetheless.

In general, when it comes to the issues we care most about, it's nearly impossible to know conclusively what is causing what or even what the best solutions are. Because of this, the "right" level of confidence is itself an open question. We can't be sure if we're right in our conclusion because we're talking about people who make choices about what to do and how to behave. And ultimately, there's no definitive way to know whether the people who make one set of choices are different in an important and relevant way from those who make another set of choices.

This is all important to bear in mind when we think about evidence and what moves us along the slide rule between zero and one (excluding those two endpoints). So far, we've talked about data in the form of experiments. Of course, that's not the only way to study a subject or to look at relationships between factors. Surveys and polls, which we'll talk about more in a moment, are often used to inform our thinking, especially on polarizing questions.

Another approach involves qualitative, in-depth interviews. The challenges that accompany this approach are often fairly straightforward. For instance, with qualitative interviews, researchers gather detailed data on a relatively small sample of people. However, it's not just the smaller sample size that matters—it's how the study participants are identified. Often, with qualitative data, interviewees are found through word of mouth or through other informal means. To be sure, this is often a necessary strategy to study populations that can be hard to identify or find. For instance, if I want to study unauthorized migrants, I'm trying to locate a group that has a powerful incentive to stay under the radar. So, I will need to be creative in how I gain access to that population. However, because of its nonrandom approach to sampling, qualitative data rarely generates conclusions that can be generalized to a broader population.

Anecdotes, another source of information, are similar in some ways to what people call lived experience and have some overlap with qualitative data. They can provide deep insight into how people understand their place in the world. Our personal experiences can be an important force when it comes to how we form opinions, including or especially on heated issues.

We can recognize the power of all these types of data and information and also ask how much they should move us one way or another along our slide rule of confidence. We can disagree about the answers, too. After all, that's part of being willing to have our own thinking questioned.

It's worth noting that nothing about avoiding certainty means that I can't take a stand that, for instance, survey or census data should inform policymaking more than people's lived experiences—as Hans Rosling argued in *Factfulness*. The intellectual commitment I'm describing is simply a willingness to explain why I stand by that position, to be clear about what assumptions I'm making, and to recognize the possibility that I'm wrong. Maybe I think that our personal experiences are too misleading or too driven by various biases. As long as I'm willing to have my position examined, to have its weaknesses exposed, there's nothing preventing me from arguing that one approach is superior to the other.

The point isn't to say with finality that a well-run study moves you to a 0.72 on our number line and a powerful personal experience moves you to a 0.34, while a randomized experiment puts you at 0.96. It's to realize that those numbers—whatever you think they should be—can be questioned, examined, and criticized, just like everything else. If someone wants to make the argument that lived experience should be treated as though it's as compelling as any other type of evidence, they can make that argument. And it can be challenged on its merits just as the counterargument can be.

As we try to make our thinking about evidence and the conclusions we draw more explicit, many of us will notice that this is easier to do for some kinds of issues than for others. And, as you might have guessed, it's often harder for issues that are polarizing.

What This Means for Polarizing Questions

Let's dive in with what might be one of the most contentious yet important questions that comes up: What percentage of US adults are racist? The question asks about percentage, which means that possible answers could range from 0 to 100. It's probably the case that few people would place the number at 0, but that doesn't do much to narrow down our answer. Where *should* it fall? It matters because how we think about the answer shapes how we interpret a wide range of circumstances where racism is one of multiple possible explanations.

So, what *is* the right number? Earlier, we talked about the changing definition of racism and the challenges associated with measuring it. Going back to that discussion for a moment, let's say I think racism is best measured by asking people if they hold specific racist attitudes—this would be one of the older measures we discussed and would bring with it the question of whether people answer honestly.

I could look to a survey or a poll to ask people whether they think it's okay to use certain kinds of racially charged language or how they'd feel if their child married someone of another race. But, if such a questionnaire returned relatively low numbers, I'd face the problem we outlined before. That is, I can't tell if the number is low because people are actually not racist or because they're racist but have changed their answers to conform with what's considered socially acceptable.

Given this challenge, we could try to measure the level of racism using one of the recent, more adaptive indicators we talked about—like asking people if they think discrimination is mostly a thing of the past. Such a question casts a much wider net, but it's also likely to ensnare people who wouldn't fit a description of a racist that requires actual racist attitudes or behavior.

It is, of course, possible to make the argument that the mere position that discrimination is no longer a real problem is in itself racist. But it's hard to imagine that argument without additional and simultaneous assumptions. One is that intent doesn't matter—something we've talked about in detail. After all, if intent matters, it becomes possible to think discrimination isn't a problem *without* that opinion coming from a place of racial resentment or hostility. In other words, if intent matters, the question arguably becomes an unreliable indicator.

Treating the belief that discrimination is no longer a significant barrier as an indicator of racism requires at least one other significant assumption. This time, it has to do with how we think about what counts as evidence of discrimination in the first place. Here, things can get even more complicated. The most convincing test for something like labor market discrimination based on a given characteristic, like race, would require circumstances that simply aren't possible in the real world.

Let's make this concrete. Say I'm interested in identifying labor market discrimination based on age. How might I test for it? A pure test might be to compare two people, A and B, who are applying for a job. In this case, A and B would need to be alike in every way except for their age, as this is the factor that I think is leading to discrimination. They would need to have the same skills, the same personality, the same background, the same work ethic, the same grit and resilience, and the same everything else that might possibly affect their job performance. The reason for this requirement is straightforward. If anything differs between A and B that might relate to how well they do their jobs, I would have no way to know if the person was hired due to their age or because of this other trait that differed between the two. The problem in practice, of course, is that no two real people are identical in every way.

In the real world, when doing research, we often try to find people who are alike in a list of ways that we can observe, and we compare their outcomes. But our conclusions are going to be susceptible to the criticism that the people ultimately differed in other ways that we didn't account for.

The problem we're describing here is why, especially when it comes to understanding something like labor market discrimination, approaches like correspondence studies can be so powerful. In correspondence studies, researchers apply for jobs using applications made up of fake people. To test for labor market discrimination based on race, for instance, they might make up what are essentially identical resumes that differ only in the racial sound of the name. In one of the most well-known of these studies, one set of resumes was sent out with typically white-sounding names and the other was sent out with typically black-sounding names.[1] The other qualifications were the same. When the white names were called for interviews more often than black names, the researchers had powerful evidence of labor market discrimination. The study's results were compelling because, with two imaginary applicants that exist only on paper, it's possible to make the candidates identical in all other ways.

In other words, because the applicants were otherwise indistinguishable, we can be confident that any difference in who got interviews was due to the one thing that differed: the racial sound of the names. However, it's worth noting that, as compelling as correspondence studies are, there is at least one relevant question they can't answer, which makes them somewhat less than definitive.

In the world of scholars who do this kind of work, there are (at least) two kinds of discrimination. There's taste-based or preference discrimination, and there's statistical discrimination. Taste-based discrimination largely refers to prejudice in the sense of dislike or a sense of superiority over specific groups of people, usually minorities. Statistical discrimination, while still discrimination, does not require prejudice or the dislike of members of other groups. It is thought to stem from the fact that, in this case, employers have imperfect information about applicants. In the study described above, employers might be using what they infer from the names to fill in gaps about characteristics that they believe will shape work performance. While most people would still find it unacceptable, it differs in an important way from preference discrimination.

The distinction of note is that statistical discrimination, in theory, could lead to differential interviewing patterns even if all the people reviewing applications and making recruitment decisions were themselves without prejudice or racial animosity. It could even, from an employer's perspective, be the rational choice. While it makes sense to view either type of discrimination as a problem, the question of what to do about the unfair outcome would likely vary depending on which type is thought to be driving it.

INDIRECT EVIDENCE

Earlier we posed the question: What percentage of adults in the United States are racist? And we're exploring how people come to their intuitions about how they answer that question. We've talked about surveys that ask attitudinal questions and correspondence studies that provide a test for discrimination even though they, perhaps, can't determine which kind of discrimination is driving it. Still, another possible way to think about the answer to the question we posed is in terms of inequality.

As we saw earlier in our discussion of racism, racial disparities in a wide range of outcomes—wealth and education, for instance—have persisted or, in some cases, even increased over time. Some people will argue that those disparities themselves are evidence of racism—whether at the level of individuals behaving in a discriminatory manner or with what people have come to call institutional racism. Institutional (or systemic or structural) racism is a reference to systems that are understood to create and sustain inequality.

However, using inequality as evidence of racism requires another assumption. That is, that the disparities we observe between groups have no other relevant cause. In other words, as with our age discrimination example, it requires the assumption that the groups in question differ, on average, in no relevant way other than race.

But what if the inequalities *aren't* caused by or aren't *entirely* caused by discrimination or other racist forces? In other words, what if this underlying assumption is wrong and the inequality is actually something that itself needs to be explained? We might think through a couple of different scenarios.

In the first one, all of the persistent disparities we see across outcomes are, in fact, due entirely to racism and discrimination. In this case, one way to reduce those disparities is through tackling the prejudice that lives in the hearts and minds of people making hiring and promotion decisions.

In another scenario, *none* of the persistent disparities are due to discrimination or racism. They are due entirely to differences in preferences and behaviors across groups. (To be clear, I'm not arguing this necessarily is the case.)

To continue with the thought experiment, however, the latter would suggest that the work to be done in reducing racial inequality is to encourage the modification of preferences and behaviors to ones that will lead to more favorable outcomes. And yet, this explanation is fraught. Because of the historical context of slavery and unequal treatment, it can be seen as blaming the victims of decades of mistreatment and dehumanization for their position in life. And that, understandably, sits poorly with many people. Too often, we fail to realize that, while the fact that this explanation sits poorly with people is rooted in concerns that many would see as legitimate, this discomfort is separate from the question of whether the explanation is accurate.

Let's think through two more scenarios before we bring this together. One is probably fairly obvious. It's the idea that neither of the extremes I've presented is correct. In this case, understanding why disparities persist requires looking at both external (racism, discrimination) and internal (preferences, behaviors) causes. But here's our last scenario. Let's say that all of today's disparities are, in fact, due to differences, on average, in preferences and behaviors that lead to unequal outcomes across racial groups. I could imagine an argument that says that all of those preferences and behaviors are themselves due to racism and discrimination. In this version, what I've delineated here into two separate causes—external and internal—are, in fact, traceable to the same root cause of racism. This is indeed worth thinking about. However, it still leaves open the challenge of how to remedy the current situation. When we think about blaming today's circumstances on past conditions, even those not in the distant past, we are quickly confronted with uncomfortable questions. Like, is there a line to walk between thinking people's disadvantage has nothing to do with choices they've made and treating anyone who struggles as though they deserve what they got? Fundamentally, there are questions here about the importance of human dignity, what fosters it, and how to promote it.

When we think about indirect answers to the question about the prevalence of racism in the United States, there's at least one more piece to consider. In recent years, many conversations have centered around the role of unconscious bias. The idea is that racism we're not aware of permeates how we act toward and treat people of different racial and ethnic backgrounds. One of the main ways people measure or assess unconscious bias is through something called the Implicit Association Test (IAT). It attempts to measure how people unconsciously relate mental images to positive or negative words or concepts. Ultimately, it captures how and whether people link words with negative or positive connotations to different racial or ethnic groups (it's also been done with genders, political orientations, and other groups). In particular, researchers look at the user's reaction time. A user who takes longer to associate a positive word with, for instance, the side of the computer screen indicating a word tied to "black" is seen as having unconscious bias.

Results of the IAT suggest that the vast majority of people, including members of minority groups themselves, are at least a little bit racist. (So maybe, if we rely solely on this assessment, the answer to our question—what percentage of US adults are racist?—is close to 100 percent.)

This measure, however, has come under considerable criticism because, as some scholars argue, it's simply not clear what it's tapping into. In other words, while a latent or ambient level of unconscious bias clearly isn't a good thing, what does it actually tell us? Specifically, unconscious bias turns out to be a weak predictor of both racist attitudes and racist behavior, raising the question of whether the IAT is, in fact, measuring something meaningful. Here's one way to think about it: If I know that everyone everywhere is at least a little racist, according to this measure, do I or should I worry about people who don't appear to have racist attitudes or behave in racist ways? It's not immediately clear to me that the answer to that question is yes.

Intuitions and Experience as Evidence

When it comes to polarizing questions, we sometimes justify our positions not based on surveys and polls but on personal life experience and, perhaps more importantly, our interpretations of those experiences. Let's think about one more race-related question before we apply our thinking to other issues.

Here's a question related to the one we just posed: Are members of minority groups better off than they were fifty years ago? A few years back, in my "Social Problems" class, after several weeks during which we'd been talking on and off about race and policing, the students had specific questions about policing that I felt unequipped to answer. So, I decided to bring in a guest speaker. I reached out to the University of Illinois Police Department and asked if there was someone who would be willing to come to my class and talk with us. The Lieutenant who came on the appointed day was friendly, knowledgeable, and patient. She was with the University of Illinois Police Department, but she'd also spent years working with the FBI. Because of this, her experience was broader than just the college community of Champaign-Urbana.

The students were respectful yet pointed with their questions. And toward the end of the fifty-minute conversation-filled class period, we had time for one more. A student raised her hand and asked: Why should we (where "we" referred to members of minority communities) trust you (where "you" was the police)? The Lieutenant thought for a moment before saying, "We've put a lot of systems in place that didn't use to be there. For instance, there's a formal system for complaints now and that's taken very seriously." She concluded by saying, "Really, I think things are a lot better than they used to be."

When the Lieutenant made that final comment, the student's jaw dropped, and she shook her head. The conversation remained respectful, but the student said, "I just don't see how things are better." Clearly, they had deeply divergent views of the world. The student saw a world where members of her community were afraid of the police, feeling that they could be abused or killed at any time by officers who would never be held accountable. The Lieutenant saw a world of officers doing the best they could in what was often a difficult and high-stress job. To her, it was one where, while more training was needed in some cases, the vast majority of officers were not motivated by racism or racial hostility. And it was a world where, over the course of her decades-long career, much had changed for the better. Based on their experiences, however, the student and the Lieutenant would have quite different answers to the question of whether members of minority groups are better off than they were fifty years ago. And which would be right?

While haggling over the answer to this question might be an interesting exercise, it's not the point. After all, this book is largely about recognizing that reasonable people could come to different conclusions based on what we believe we know for certain. Think back to the earlier question: What percentage of US adults are racist? Whatever number you had in your head when I first posed that question doesn't need to have changed. But now, regardless of whether your number is low or high, hopefully you can recognize that it's not *certain*.

When we forget this, it can shade how we see the world. Consider, for instance, one of the scenarios described earlier in the book. Theo and Michelle were preparing a marketing presentation. Theo thought Michelle's design idea was boring and forgettable, and Michelle thought that Theo's design idea was busy and didn't look serious. Whether Theo thinks Michelle's criticism is driven by a racist devaluation of his work will, in many ways, trace back to how he thinks about the answer to the question about the percentage of adults who are racist. In other words, if he puts that percentage high and if he feels certain about it, he's likely to conclude that Michelle is racist. Not only that, but he might also view anyone who doesn't see Michelle as he does as willfully denying racism. If he's certain it's low or even zero, that too will shape how he sees Michelle's comments. And all of this will probably happen without Theo realizing or questioning it.

Our tendency to treat answers to questions on heated issues as certain or definitive isn't unique to asking about the percentage of racists in the United States. Consider this question: What percentage of men would commit sexual assault if they knew they could get away with it? Here again, most of us, if we pause to reflect on it, recognize that we don't have a clear answer. At the same time, our intuitions about the answer do their work in the background, shaping how we think about a wide range of situations. Imagine a scenario where, after a sexual encounter, the woman says it wasn't consensual and the man says it was. It's not hard to see how this figure that lurks in the back of our minds could affect our reaction.

How we think about the answer to the question about men and sexual assault will shape both our response and how we view people who disagree. It's easy to imagine someone saying, "You're a misogynist for believing the man" or "You're a naïve idealist for believing the woman." What's more, we do not have to consciously be thinking about the question "What percentage of men would commit sexual assault if they knew they could get away with it?" in order for this to be the case. Its effects operate in the background regardless of whether we're aware of them.

Consider another example: Is gender-affirming care good for children? Do we have a clear and known answer to this question? Gender-affirming care generally refers to "a range of social, psychological, behavioral, and medical interventions 'designed to support and affirm an individual's gender identity' when it conflicts with the gender they were assigned at birth."[2] It's a way of working with children who identify as transgender that treats as a given—in other words, affirms—the disconnect between their physical bodies and the gender they identify with. This approach stands in contrast with one that might involve probing at other psychosocial issues among gender dysphoric children, including other mental health challenges, that might correlate with or otherwise explain the child's challenges. Such an alternative approach wouldn't assume that a child who presents as gender dysphoric actually needs to transition socially or medically.

Some people view gender-affirming care as nothing less than lifesaving. They see it as the only way to help children exhibiting signs of gender dysphoria, some of whom otherwise might suffer from depression or even attempt suicide. Others see this approach as neglectful or even abusive. They see an automatic decision to affirm whatever a child claims their gender to be, without exploring alternative possible explanations for the problem, as leading the child down an unnecessarily painful path. In this view, for instance, a child who is gay and doesn't yet understand their sexuality or who is experiencing some other kind of crisis might have his or her problems manifest as gender dysphoria. And the root cause could remain unexplored. One concern, then, is that gender-affirming care can put the child on a particular trajectory without addressing the underlying problem the child is facing. This certainty can lead to demonization and judgment is if I take as given, for instance, that gender-affirming care is a net positive. I might then see anyone who disagrees as wrong-headed (through the Fallacy of Equal Knowledge) or even transphobic (through the Fallacy of Known Intent).

Let's talk about one more example before we move on. Was the 2020 presidential election stolen? We could also pose the question using more neutral language. Was there sufficient fraud in the 2020 presidential election to warrant disputation of the results?

Most people can probably agree that there's some level of election malfeasance that, if witnessed, each of us would see as justification for questioning the results of an election. For instance, if I went to a polling place on election day, stood there for a few hours, and watched the same people cycle through the line over and over again, I might grow wary of the results.

Of course, most of us are not hanging around outside polling places, but even if we were, presumably that's not what we'd see. So outside of what we can personally observe, how do we make this determination? It's not the kind of question surveys and polls can help us with. It's actually the kind of question that points to the importance of how public trust can shape our intuition. After all, when a court (or multiple courts) determines that there is no evidence of fraud—as happened with the

2020 election—trust in the legal system is largely what will shape our sense of whether that decision was arrived at fairly. As we think this through, we might consider a different but related question: Would you feel comfortable claiming with *certainty*, for this or any election, that there was no fraud whatsoever?

Here's one way to think about our intuitions in the face of this kind of ambiguity: What's the difference between the following statements?

The election was stolen.

There was no fraud in the election.

I have some concerns there was fraud in the election.

Based on what we currently know, there is not sufficient evidence of fraud to suggest that it could have had a significant impact on the outcome of the election.

Aside from the fact that the statements increase in word count, the first two come across as definitive. In fact, they're expressions that probably would sit at the one on our number line. And if a person holds one of those first two, they have all the justification they need to judge as stupid or demonize someone who doesn't agree. The second two, on the other hand, sit somewhere in the space of confidence, leaving the door open for the tiniest bit of doubt.

In differentiating between the statements and in pointing to the definitive nature of the first two, I am not suggesting that what we currently know doesn't point us in one direction, although it's a direction that assumes trust in the legal system. And as I've said with other examples, I am also not saying that the answer to the question of whether the 2020 election was stolen simply becomes a toss-up.

I'm saying that the certainty behind the claims is unwarranted and it changes how we view and interact with other people. If you're reading that sentence and thinking that what I'm suggesting is, for instance, too risky and that election deniers need to be stridently and unambiguously condemned, I invite you to read again what I wrote. There is nothing in what I'm saying that says the conviction that the election was stolen is necessarily justified. What I'm saying is that responding to this claim of certainty with a counterclaim of certainty leads nowhere useful.

MAKING SENSE OF AN UNCERTAIN WORLD WITH CONFIDENCE

As we try to remain within the bounds of confidence and avoid certainty, it's worth thinking about how we find ourselves certain in the first place. There are (at least) two ways of thinking about this. In one version, people come to heated and contentious issues—like those that touch identity, fairness, and inequality—with an open mind and an unformed opinion. Then, over time, some people become increasingly sure they're right, up until the point when all doubt is gone. The erasure of doubt is helped along through a continuous feedback loop provided by things like social media siloes, echo chambers, and confirmation bias. Countering this requires early exposure to the importance of and prevalence of finding uncertainty.

But there's another version too. One that's, in some ways, more alarming than the first. In this version, from the beginning of a person's educational experience, specific types of information are presented as given, creating certainty from the start. For instance, in some schools these days, information about gender is presented in a manner that suggests the state of our knowledge is definitive. Specifically, the message is that we know that gender isn't binary, exists on a spectrum, and is unrelated to biological sex.

To be clear, challenging long-standing assumptions about gender has value in the same way that challenging any assumption has value. The assertion that gender *is* binary, as with any other assertion, should not be considered infallible or definitive. It, too, exists on a spectrum of confidence and requires clarity when it comes to how we got there. In other words, the problem isn't with the suggestion that what we think we know about gender might be flawed or incomplete. It's with the suggestion that we now know the answer and the way that, with an issue like this, it leads to precisely the kind of demonization we're trying to avoid. To make this concrete, here are a few questions that might guide an approach that doesn't swap one set of definitive claims for another.

What *do* we know about the relationship between gender and biology? For what percent of people are these two things aligned? Has the percentage for whom they're aligned changed over time? Why? For all of these questions, how do we know? Surveys are one possible source of data but, as we saw with the earlier racism example, they can be fraught. Especially if there is social pressure to answer in one way or another.

Here's an alternative, even deeper, discussion we could have: Let's say there are two ways to think about gender. In one version, there are primarily two genders, and there's a range of how those are expressed. There can be masculine girls and feminine boys, but most people largely fall within these two conventional categories. In another version, many of the variations within the categories of boys and girls are ill-fitting. Now, what were, in the first version, simply considered variations within conventional categories are treated and understood as being their own self-defined groups. This leads us to a long list of different possible genders.

This second, newer version raises interesting questions, not only about sex and gender, but also about social identity. For instance, is our identity entirely self-determined? If it is, it seems reasonable for me to expect that my identity, whatever it is, will be reflected back to me by the people around me. In other words, whatever I say I am, or whatever I feel I am, is how you should refer to me. In this sense, if I look like a woman in every clearly visible way, but I identify as a man, the people I encounter have a moral and social obligation to refer to me as "he."

Or we might ask whether our identity is, at least in part, socially negotiated? Is how you respond to me, to some extent, determined by how I appear to you, regardless of how I identify myself? In this case, you referring to me as "she" makes perfect sense. Which is the more apt description of how we think about who we are? Which is better? And what do we mean by "better"?

I'm not suggesting that all of these questions should be tackled in middle school sex education classes. But having them in the back of our minds could reshape the conversation on sex and gender in a way that brings it more in line with what we know. It could pave the way for an age-appropriate presentation of information that recognizes not only the uncertainty but also some of the fundamentally moral questions that underpin how we think about these topics.

The goal of walking through these two versions is to say that a failure to challenge our thinking can have multiple sources. One is information siloes and echo chambers, where we consistently hear only opinions similar to our own. But another in is when an institution we trust to be authoritative presents disputed information as definitive. This is something we'll go into in more detail in the next chapter.

We've talked about the fallacies we're prone to—Equal Knowledge and Known Intent—when we don't question our assumptions. It's worth pointing out as well that certainty often has what we might think of as a cascading effect. Let's go back for a moment to the question: What percentage of US adults are racist? Wherever I place that number, if I feel certain about it, will shape how I view other interactions. Consider any interaction that goes sideways between people of different racial backgrounds. The determination of whether it goes sideways *because* of racism, in contrast to some other reason, both shapes and reflects the way someone thinks about the answer to the initial question.

One of the reasons leaning into confidence and away from certainty can be challenging is that certainty serves a valuable function. It lets us arrive at what psychologists call "cognitive closure," which is the elimination of ambiguity and the identification of conclusions that are definitive. Cognitive closure is something most people tend to seek out, often in response to something psychologists call "cognitive dissonance." This is to say that when we hold on tightly to beliefs as we do when we feel the stakes are high, letting them go doesn't often come easily.

In the field of psychology, cognitive dissonance is the idea that holding contradictory information is mentally taxing and people will go to great lengths to avoid it. According to the theory, when there are two actions or ideas that are psychologically incompatible with one another, we'll do just about anything, psychologically, to make them consistent.

Cognitive dissonance, one of the most well-known findings in the field of psychology, was initially inspired by the results of a 1935 study.[3] In that study, the author found that, following a severe earthquake in India, people who had not been directly affected by the earthquake developed and spread rumors about an even worse disaster that was going to hit at any time. Reflecting upon this study, psychologist Leon Festinger suggested that this was their way of making sense of the deep fear that they felt. The rumors served the purpose of closing the gap between the fear they felt and the fact that they had not actually suffered any damage from the earthquake.[4]

In another example of how cognitive dissonance might play out at the individual level, consider a smoker who knows smoking is bad for his health, and who also cares about his health. In order to reduce the dissonance that comes from doing something he knows will hurt him, he might either tell himself that the reports of smoking's harm are overblown, or he might convince himself that the benefits—for instance, smoking can help prevent weight gain—outweigh the costs.

Ultimately, leaning into uncertainty—thinking in terms of confidence—requires us to think differently about cognitive dissonance. We've been saying throughout this book that ambiguity is ever-present and that our conclusions, in the physical world anyway, are not definitive. This means that the very things we lean on for cognitive closure—like certainty and simplicity—further our distorted sense of the world (tricking us into thinking we're looking out a window). But what if the recognition of uncertainty can, by coming at the problem of cognitive dissonance from a different direction, be an alternative solution to the search for cognitive closure?

Let's make this concrete. When it comes to heated issues, one of the areas where many of us come face to face with cognitive dissonance is around the topic of inequality. How we think about this issue ties into deeper beliefs about whether people generally "get what they deserve" and whether meritocracy—the idea that hard work and talent are generally rewarded—works.

If my cognitive framework is that meritocracy largely works, I have reason to view people who don't succeed as lacking in some trait that would have led them to a better outcome. In this case, seeing people who don't succeed as hard-working and competent can create cognitive dissonance. Conversely, if my cognitive framework is that the world is fundamentally unjust and unfair, then I will likely view people who succeed as not having earned it and being the beneficiaries of unearned advantage. In this case, seeing people who succeed either despite having faced adversity or who appear to be exceptionally competent and hard-working can create cognitive dissonance.

The point here isn't that we can't arrive at better and worse answers to the question of whether or how well the meritocracy works. Any answer we might arrive at would require us to define *and* agree on what success looks like and, perhaps more importantly, what the *barriers* to success look like. And, of course, these are precisely the kinds of questions for which answers can be the most challenging.

To be sure, there have been significant efforts to demonstrate that, particularly when it comes to ideas around merit, one worldview or the other is correct. Along those lines, in the middle of the twentieth century, psychologist Melvin Lerner developed something called the "just world hypothesis."[5] Lerner's theory was that the mistaken belief that the world is ultimately a fair place—that people largely get what they deserve—leads people to view others as being deserving of their suffering.

Through his work, Lerner showed that when participants observed study confederates being electrically shocked for making mistakes during a task where they were supposed to be learning (or so the participants believed), they tended to derogate the victim. More suffering led to more derogation. Lerner said that the two ideas that were dissonant and being reconciled were (1) a sense that the world is fair and (2) the observation that people were being shocked for missing an answer, something many people would view as *un*fair. Lerner's work was particularly influential when it comes to something we now often think of as victim-blaming. Although, of course, the work raises questions, too.

Does recognizing unfairness in the world mean agreeing that any suffering is due to factors out of one's control? The link to ideas around merit is clear. Do people "get what they deserve"?

There's another question, too. When it comes to inequality, how should we think about cognitive dissonance that runs in the other direction? In other words, is there an analogous tendency to assume *un*fairness when reconciling inconsistent ideas? If I think the world is fundamentally unfair, and I see someone who works hard and succeeds, am I then thinking about subtle ways this person benefited from the world's unfairness in order to reconcile the two ideas? To be sure, the temptation to claim that one comprehensive view—justness or unjustness in the world—represents reality and the other is built on bias is powerful.

Here's an exercise I've done with students to try to think about this a little more deeply. Standing at the front of the room teaching class, I'll use myself as an example. I'll say, "I'm a tenured professor at the University of Illinois. While I realize that some academics might see the U of I as insufficiently elite, others would see my position as one of success. So, let's ignore the naysayers for the moment and say I've had some degree of success."

I'll continue with, "How should I think about my trajectory? Did I get where I am because of my own grit, hard work, competence, and tenacity? Did I get here because of advantages I was born into, like because

I'm white? Is there a way to know how much of my success is because of what? Is it 2 percent because I'm white? 0.2 percent? 97 percent?" As with so much of what we're talking about in this book, the point isn't to answer these questions—although it might be interesting to try—it's to recognize the questions themselves.

A blanket denial of unfairness in the world can be difficult to justify. Look no further than the random lottery of birth—something none of us controls. But there are other examples, too. Most people would probably agree that the way particular diseases strike is the height of unfairness. After all, would it make sense to hold someone responsible for developing breast cancer if they carry a mutated BRCA gene? Doing so would be absurd, because they would have been born with the mutation, and it would be difficult to attribute the cancer to the person's lifestyle choices. But what about lung cancer? We probably see it as unfair when a non-smoker gets it. Is it also unfair if the person smoked two packs a day for thirty years? What if they smoked half a pack a day for five years?

In general, it can be hard to separate our psychology from our thoughts about fairness. On the one hand, explanations that center responsibility on the individual often sit poorly with people as it sounds like we're—back to Lerner for a moment—blaming victims. On the other hand, sometimes the only way we can make sense of people's suffering is to tell ourselves that they brought it on themselves. That allows us to believe that if we don't make the same mistake they made, we're safe from that particular circumstance.

In fact, one of the main reasons biological explanations can be so powerful is because they cut to the heart of questions of personal responsibility and blame. In some cases, they're seen as exculpatory. For instance, in the case of health problems, biological explanations take the onus off of individual behaviors. It's not Jim's fault he has type 2 diabetes; it's biological. This can work for mental health issues as well. As in, it's not Bob's fault he has a gambling addiction. It's how his brain is wired. On the flip side, as we noted earlier in the case of women and nurturing tendencies, biological explanations—because they represent things we can't change—can be, and have been, used to justify and perpetuate inequality and even atrocities.

I want to be clear—I am not making a declaration about whether type 2 diabetes or gambling has a genetic component. Nor, for that matter, am I declaring that women aren't still discriminated against in the labor market. I'm pointing to the way a desire to minimize or eliminate cognitive dissonance can show up in the form of certainty.

Let's go back to the question of fairness and who deserves what. A couple of extreme cases might be helpful in thinking this through. If someone is deprived of an education and barely given what they need to survive, the vast majority of people would concede that if they don't succeed in life, it's not really their fault. After all, how could someone possibly flourish under those conditions? In other words, there is almost always some set of sufficiently dire circumstances where we can all imagine a lack of success isn't the fault of the person themselves.

Similarly, imagine someone who is born into the kind of wealth and privilege that provides every advantage and who can pass with ease through barriers that other people have to earn their way past. If they don't succeed, we often tend to assume that it's because they did something wrong or were lazy. Either scenario provides, relatively speaking, a clear way of thinking about the presence or absence of barriers to opportunity and fairness. And many of us are more sympathetic toward people we feel have barriers in their way than people who don't. The question then returns to what extent do external barriers keep people from succeeding? And, more importantly, how do we know?

The importance of the ability to consider questions—the kinds we can only ask when we're committed to avoiding certainty—is difficult to overstate. It has allowed for enormous medical advances we've seen across history. It's why we no longer treat depression with cocaine, coughs with heroin, or ulcers with a nasal tube of milk.[6] And we can probably all agree that we're better off because of those who came before us and were willing to ask the questions that led to these better treatments.

But, as we've shown here, not all questions are created equal, which means not all uncertainty is created equal. In some areas, uncertainty raises far more tension than others. If we go back to the question about racism for a moment, for many people, asking whether Officer Derek Chauvin killed George Floyd *because* Floyd was black or *because* Chauvin lacked adequate police training would be seen as fundamentally intolerable. This feeling, as understandable as it may be, comes from certainty.

Taken to an extreme, thinking in terms of confidence rather than certainty can be paralyzing. If we can't know anything for sure, how can we make any decisions at all? This could bump up against the very practical issue that, as a society, policies need to be put into place in order for us to live together. Fortunately, a commitment to asking questions and engaging with doubt doesn't mean we do nothing. But thinking in terms of confidence does have other important implications. It means that we remain open to the possibility that our policies or decisions might be flawed and, therefore, may need to be changed in the future. And, at least as importantly, it has crucial implications for how we respond to people who disagree with those policies, decisions, and positions. Ultimately, when we're confident, rather than certain, that the path we're on is right, it's possible to understand how someone could arrive at a different conclusion.

CHAPTER SUMMARY

- Think of a number line from zero to one. Zero and one represent absolute certainty, and the in-between reflects levels of confidence.
- Determining causality in social issues, especially given the necessary ethical constraints that prevent certain types of experimentation, is difficult and means there is usually more than one possible explanation for an outcome.
- Clear answers are often elusive in social problems due to the multi-

faceted nature of evidence, including experimental, qualitative, and anecdotal data.

- The concepts of cognitive dissonance and closure illustrate how people seek to resolve contradictions in their beliefs to achieve a state of mental comfort.

Practice Uncertainty

Think through the question of What percent of American adults are racist? How did you arrive at the number you got to? What assumptions did you make? Try to think through how someone could come up with an entirely different number.

8

Certainty in Our Institutions

"You have to test your hypothesis against other theories. Certainty in the face of complex situations is very dangerous."

Richard Holbrooke

In his 2020 book titled *Trust: America's Best Chance*, former US presidential candidate Pete Buttigieg wrote, "Our ability to trust in institutions and in one another—the ability to trust that we are subject to the same facts, even living in the same reality—is now endangered. A combination of causes has brought us to this point, a crisis of trust that has the potential to be paralyzing."[1]

Buttigieg is right about the loss of trust reaching a crisis point and the potential for paralysis as a result. At the institutional level, trust is necessary for legitimacy. We pay taxes because we trust the government not to use our tax dollars to buy yachts for everyone who works at the Department of the Treasury or Exchequer. We abide by legal decisions because we trust judges to be impartial. We send our kids to school because we trust teachers to educate them. And we lean on the media to inform us about the world because we trust they'll get the story right.

Or at least it seems like this is how it's supposed to work. Trust in institutions usually requires things like transparency, a sense that the

179

employees and leadership are competent, and a feeling that people from a wide variety of backgrounds are valued. Unsurprisingly, institutional certainty makes all of these difficult to sustain. After all, what does transparency mean when an organization is not clear—even, or especially, with itself—about its values, assumptions, or priorities? What happens to the public perception of competency and credibility when information presented as definitive or final turns out to be, well, not quite right? Or what is the right way to interpret institutions that take a public stand on political issues while simultaneously insisting that they welcome and value different perspectives?

The loss of trust in institutions is both cause and effect of the problems Buttigieg described in his quote. We live in different realities in part because we don't trust what's coming out of our institutions. And we don't trust what's coming out of institutions because we live in different realities.

People lose trust in institutions for all kinds of reasons. And sometimes those reasons have little direct connection how we think about heated issues. For instance, if I find out that the director of the local library has been embezzling money, that will probably affect the extent to which I place my trust in that institution. In other cases, the link is more direct. For instance, many of us look to some institutions to advise us on how to live, like the Centers for Disease Control and Prevention (CDC) or the American Academy of Pediatrics. When these organizations have to walk back definitive-sounding claims, we begin to question other assertions they make. In this case, one of the main ways they get things wrong is by communicating *certainty* about what they know.

Certainty also leads to the erosion of trust in institutions by, as with individuals, weaving its way into contentious social and political issues. It leads institutions to take positions on heated issues, without even necessarily realizing that's what they're doing. And when this is done by an institution that the public expects to either be unbiased or to welcome and be open to a wide range of perspectives, trust is eroded. This is the inevitable result of the public seeing that the institution is not living up to the values it claims to hold.

Because this latter piece relates specifically to individual's expectations of institutions, it's worth diving into a bit more. As individuals, when we meet others for the first time, or even for the thirty-first time, we don't necessarily expect them to set aside their opinions on heated political issues. In fact, we often assume the opposite. Unless, of course, we're meeting the person *because* they've been brought into a situation based on their expertise as a neutral conflict resolution expert or mediator. In that case, we expect them to be deliberately and carefully as unbiased as humanly possible. That narrow set of circumstances aside, many of us assume that part of getting to know someone means learning what they think about different things.

When it comes to institutions, however, our expectations are often different.[2] For instance, how would you feel if you walked into your child's public school one morning to find they'd hung a giant, *school-sanctioned*, pro-life (or pro-choice) banner in the entryway? Many parents would probably not be happy about such a display. We have an expectation that a school, especially a public one, won't take political sides. After all, the thinking goes, they're responsible for educating young people in a way that teaches them to live harmoniously with disagreement.

Would we feel differently if the school in question was private? What if it was Catholic? In that case, we might think it strange—perhaps we'd even be disappointed—if they *didn't* take a stand on abortion. What if the school is private but not religious? Maybe our expectations in that case would be closer to the public-school scenario than the Catholic school one.

We can apply similar thinking to higher education. Let's say I'm a high school senior looking at colleges and I pick Hillsdale College—a four-year liberal arts institution known for its politically conservative and Christian ethos and approach. Would it be reasonable for me to be indignant when I get there and find that the vibe on campus is more sympathetic to Republican Party concerns than Democratic Party ones? Or would that be on me for having unrealistic expectations? Similarly, what are the expectations about the many colleges and universities that deliberately don't have a clear political orientation? In this case, many of the institutions themselves play an active role in the perception that they welcome a wide range of political and ideological viewpoints.

And what about non-educational institutions, like stores and businesses? How would I feel if I walked into Target and they had a pro-life banner in the front of the store? I would be surprised, to say the least. At the same time, would I be surprised if I saw a similar banner hanging in the entrance to Hobby Lobby? Should I be? To the best of my knowledge, Target hasn't announced any particular religious affiliation or political alliance. Meanwhile, Hobby Lobby's religious and political commitments are out in the open. The first of their core values, as stated on their webpage, is "Honoring the Lord in all we do by operating in a manner consistent with Biblical principles."[3]

So, if I were to walk into a Hobby Lobby and see a pro-life banner, regardless of whether I agree with the position, it would be consistent with what I know of the company. What if I'm an employee at one of these places? What should my expectations be then? Would it make sense for a liberal employee at Hobby Lobby or a liberal student at Hillsdale to feel that their views aren't well represented? The point in this thought exercise is simply to notice that, when it comes to political and ideological diversity, our expectations change depending on the type of institution and how it presents itself publicly.

While we've been mainly talking about businesses, the corporate world is by no means the only place where this question comes up. What are our expectations when it comes to the media? Similar to the Hobby Lobby and Target examples, it depends to some extent on the outlet. If I go to Fox News, *National Review*, or MSNBC for my news, I should be under no illusion that the information I'm presented with is the product of a politically neutral view of the world.

But what if I'm looking instead at the *New York Times* or the *Washington Post*? In such dominant outlets, failing to be clear about values and assumptions can be particularly damaging. After all, it's one thing to explicitly orient toward one political party over another, like Hobby Lobby or Hillsdale. It's another when that orientation weaves its way in via certainty. Ultimately, the impact of the more subtle influence of certainty depends on whether there's an expectation of something like neutrality.

We've said that when institutions that we expect to either remain neutral, or to welcome people of a wide range of perspectives, fail to do so, trust erodes. It's worth saying a little more about how this can work.

Let's look more closely at schools. When it comes to public schools and non-religious private schools, why does it matter if they take sides on political topics? There are a few different ways to answer this question. First, public schools are funded in part by tax dollars. And the people paying those taxes come from across the political spectrum. It follows that the children who attend public schools come from families who also span the political spectrum.

Second, one of the goals of education is ostensibly to prepare young people to become responsible, thoughtful, and participatory citizens. As such, primary and secondary school are seen as time for kids to learn socialization skills alongside math, writing, science, and social studies. Part of that means becoming comfortable interacting with people who disagree, including or especially when it comes to heated issues. This can be a hard skill to foster if the institution itself has, even unconsciously, taken a clear stand on what the "right" answer is to contentious political questions.

Third and finally, when a school takes an active stand and makes its position on an issue clear, it does so with the weight of the institution behind it. It communicates to stakeholders within that community—which might include students, teachers, parents, staff—that there's a clear good and right position and a bad and wrong one.

We gave the example earlier of Hillsdale College, an openly conservative institution of higher education. Hillsdale is unusual in its openly political orientation. For the many institutions that aim for something closer to ideological openness, what *should* the public expect when it comes to official positions and political bias? It seems clear that if the institution is trying to welcome people from a variety of backgrounds, including a variety of political backgrounds, avoiding overt political statements is important.

What's more, when it comes to large businesses anyway, there are at least two reasons why taking political positions might work against their interests. First, doing so opens them up to some risk of angering their employees who don't agree with whatever position they've taken. Second, they risk alienating part of their customer base. It is, of course, worth pointing out that *not* taking positions on certain issues (like policing, for instance) would also likely anger and alienate some of their employees and clientele.

That said, most corporations appear to prioritize, at least in principle, creating an environment that is welcoming to employees and paying customers of the widest possible range of political persuasions. But, as we'll see, certainty can make it all too easy to take a side, even when the commitment to openness across the political spectrum is sincerely held. When large corporations highlight the importance of inclusion, they create the expectation and perception that this also means being inclusive to a range of political perspectives. To the best of my knowledge, it's the rare corporation that has ever said, "We mean inclusion in every way, except political or ideological." The same can be said about institutions of higher education.

When we're talking about individuals, certainty can change how we view one another in relatively small-scale interactions, especially when those interactions play out on social media in front of large audiences. In those situations, it can lead to many of the kinds of problems we've described so far in this book—harsh judgment, demonization, and, by extension, political polarization and the like. When it comes to institutions, however, the effects of treating our knowledge as final often show up differently. In the following sections, we'll talk about what that can look like.

DEFINITIVE DECLARATIONS

One of the ways certainty shows up in the context of institutions is through the overstatement of claims. Specifically, we're talking about the kinds of statements that are presented as though they're definitive when they're not.

In order for statements to erode trust, the people listening and losing trust have to know there's overreach. So, how do people know a claim isn't definitive? In some situations, this becomes clear because institutions have to walk back a claim after new information comes to light. In this case, people who believed the initial claim may, understandably, be considerably more skeptical the next time one is made. To think this through, consider the advice on masks during the Covid-19 pandemic.

The message that they were not protective early in the pandemic was quickly followed by the stronger and more strident message that wearing a mask was the best way to protect yourself, your loved ones, and your community. This then morphed into something like this: Good people wear masks because they care about the weak and vulnerable, and bad people don't wear masks because they don't care whether they kill other people.

Ultimately, the way mask regulations were handled is an example where the uncertainty in the claim didn't get communicated when it came to the recommendations.

In early 2020, there was so much change in the CDC guidelines on masks that the *New York Times* felt compelled to publish an article about the evolution of mask recommendations.[4] In February, the Surgeon General tweeted a plea for people to stop buying masks, saying they were not effective at preventing the spread of Covid among the general public.[5] On March 15, when the CDC released a guideline recommending limiting gatherings to fifty people, there was no mention of masks. Yet, two months later, the CDC pivoted to say that masks *were* advised to all Americans outside of their homes. And by September, in a dramatic turn six months later, several public health officials were highlighting the public benefits of mask-wearing. By January 2021, President Biden put mask requirements in place in locales and buildings within federal reach.

And yet, in May 2020, mere weeks after the February tweet from the Surgeon General questioning their effectiveness, tweets like

> Why we wear the masks. The mask is a symbol. It shows we care about your safety. It shows we respect all human life. We can be infected for days without symptoms. We wear the mask to protect you! A person not wearing a mask doesn't give a damn about others. Do you wear a mask?[6]

and

> Thank you Mayor @LennyCurry and fellow hospital leaders for emphasizing the importance of wearing masks where appropriate. Masks help stop the spread and they show that we care for the health of each other and our community.[7]

were common. Given the rapidly changing advice, one might be forgiven for having a bit of whiplash. With all the flipflopping that went on, was it reasonable to conclude that the only reason someone would be resistant to wearing a mask is because they don't care about other people? Masks weren't the only topic related to Covid where certainty played a role. The politicization and moralizing were just as present when it came to shutdowns and closures.

Before we talk about Covid policies more generally, however, it's worth noting that questioning the response to Covid doesn't require concluding that what was done was wrong. It's possible to point to questions that weren't asked and weren't discussed (at least not publicly) and agree with the ultimate decision anyway. But I would argue, we'd have been better off having the discussion. Now let's dive in.

Let's start by talking about the seasonal flu. I am not making a claim about similarities or differences between it and Covid. I'm saying that a discussion about the flu is a good starting point for making our thinking explicit—in this case, our thinking about risk.

Before I had children, I don't recall ever thinking about the seasonal flu. And I certainly didn't alter my life in any way because of it. It was only when I had kids and I started taking them to get flu shots that it entered my thinking at all. To the best of my recollection, no one wore masks, and I don't recall any time since I was born when public life was altered or shut down because of the flu. And yet, I knew the flu could be deadly, especially for the old and the vulnerable. Every once in a while, a tragic tale would surface about a young, robust individual who died from the influenza virus. But in spite of this risk, I, and those around me, largely went about our lives as normal. So, the question becomes, if we didn't dramatically alter our lives for the flu, why were we doing so for Covid?

More than once, my youngest got the flu despite having the seasonal vaccine. In one particularly memorable season, he got it twice: influenza A and influenza B. Fortunately, he recovered quickly each time. So, what *was* the difference between the flu, which we'd all gotten used to living with, and Covid-19? Honestly, just writing that question makes me feel a little foolish. I can't shake the deep sense that I'm not supposed to ask. I have a general understanding that Covid is worse—it's often more severe, it has a higher mortality rate, and it's more contagious—but that's about as far as I go.

Despite my self-consciousness here, the question about how to distinguish between the two is common enough that the CDC has a webpage devoted to it.[8] Here's some of what that webpage has to say today.

It first informs the reader that the two illnesses are caused by different viruses. Covid-19 is the result of infection with SARS-CoV-2, and the flu is caused by infection with an influenza virus. I was happy to find that, in several places on its website, the CDC uses appropriately measured language. For instance, "Compared with flu, Covid-19 can cause more severe illness in some people. Compared to people with flu, people infected with Covid-19 may take longer to show symptoms and may be contagious for longer periods of time." At the end of the description, it even states, "We are learning more everyday about Covid-19 and the virus that causes it. This page compares Covid-19 and flu, given the best available information to date."

All told, the information on the website is presented (as of this writing) with a degree of modesty that seems to largely correspond to what we think we know. And yet, when the recommendations came out at the start of Covid, little of this measured language was present. What's more, any comparison between Covid and the flu, about which I still feel self-conscious, was often associated with the claim that Covid was a hoax, a view I didn't hold.

Throughout this book, I've made the point that the ability to demonize, dismiss, or judge other people harshly for holding a different opinion comes from some value, principle, or belief that's being held on to as inviolable or certain. But the right response to a description of differences between Covid and the flu wasn't obvious. Understanding that Covid was worse than the flu, the latter of which we have come to live with without much in the way of accommodations, wasn't in itself an answer to the question of what to do about it. Here's why.

If we think about the example of the flu (although this could apply to other threats as well), there is some level of ambient risk of illness and death that we've largely made our peace with. In other words, there's an amount of risk that we know is out there, but we don't alter our lives because of it.

A shared understanding that Covid-19 put us in uncharted territory doesn't answer the question of when and how to change the way we live to minimize our risk. That decision is actually a function of how we think about the answers to two other questions. The first is what *is* the level of risk of Covid? As far as I can tell, this is a question for the epidemiologists and doctors—pointing once again to why institutional trust is crucial. The second is a question that is in some ways more complicated: How much risk is tolerable and how do we weigh it against other potential adverse outcomes? We touched on this earlier when we asked whether, if the most important thing is to minimize highway deaths, we should all be driving army tanks.

To think this through, let's imagine a bar chart. On that chart, the higher you go up on the vertical axis or y-axis, the greater the risk. And the horizontal axis or x-axis would have different bars for different risks—one bar would be the flu, one would be Covid, one would be getting hit by a drunk driver, and so on and so forth. Make the unit on that y-axis any measure of risk that you want—mortality, morbidity, economic loss, etc. Let's suppose, and I'm completely making this up, that the seasonal flu gets us about one-one hundredth of the way up the y-axis, which maxes out with an apocalyptic, humanity-ending scenario.

There's probably some level of risk, some height on the y-axis, at which the vast majority of us would agree that we need to, when it comes to illness, for instance, mask up and shut down much of our public lives in order to limit transmission. In a world with a highly transmissible airborne illness with a 50 percent mortality rate (something you might see in a sci-fi movie), most of us probably wouldn't need to be told twice to stay home and hunker down. So, it stands to reason that somewhere between the risk associated with a regular flu season and the scenario I just described, we crossed a threshold.

The relevant question isn't so much whether that threshold exists as it is where it is or should be. When we fail to recognize that open discussion is the only way to talk through this—and that reasonable people could come to different answers—we set ourselves up for the kind of polarization we saw during Covid. This failure is one reason *why,* for instance, we ended up with sentiments like, either you follow these recommendations or you are callously indifferent to other people's suffering. One person thinks we're over the line, and the other thinks we're not.

There are a couple of points worth making here. One is that—and I'll just come clean—I have no idea where the line should be. I just know that wherever it is drawn needs to be the result of deliberation. If we care about avoiding the problems of certainty, wherever that line is needs to not be treated as obvious or given, and we need to bear in mind that people can and do vary in where they draw it. Another is that our public conversation about Covid tended to combine two distinct problems. One is the fact that people will disagree about where that line should be. The other is that people will also disagree over the level of risk we're actually facing.

So, does this disagreement mean that, in a situation like Covid, we just throw our hands up in the air and let things unfold as they will? Fortunately, it doesn't. The message is simply that we have to be able to talk about these things openly and without judgment. We can make decisions as a society, but we owe it to one another to make our thinking clear and to remember that people can and will arrive at different conclusions.

It's worth returning to the mask example to see what it can tell us about institutional messaging, especially given how polarized the topic became. In October 2020, a study by the Pew Research Center showed that, when asked how the pandemic had made their lives more difficult, 19 percent of Republicans and 10 percent of Democrats gave a response that included the word "mask."[9] More revealing, however, was the context in which the word was used. Among Democrats, 31 percent of the references were to express concern that other people weren't "wearing masks or taking the pandemic seriously." At the same time, 27 percent of the references to the term among Republicans were to express "skepticism about masks and/or the severity of the pandemic in general."

One of the reasons we need to be willing to question our thinking and to have it questioned is that a functional society depends on having a critical mass of people with a shared sense that we're all in this together. Ultimately, there will be times when the only reason to follow through with an action is because of some sense that it is important for the greater good. The way we get there is by building trust. The enemy of trust is certainty.

OFFICIAL STATEMENTS ON CONTENTIOUS ISSUES

When it comes to institutions and organizations, one question that often comes up is when and under what conditions leaders should try to remain neutral versus speak out and take a stand. Presumably, one would feel compelled to take a stand when the injustice is so egregious and extreme that staying silent feels like complicity. That's also when the stakes tend to feel unbearably high. And when the stakes feel high, certainty tells us that neutrality is no longer neutral. This is well captured in the famous quote by Archbishop Desmond Tutu when he said, "If you are neutral in situations of injustice, you have chosen the side of the oppressor." Those are powerful words. But, perhaps unsurprisingly at this point, they raise questions. For example, how do we know when something is the result of injustice versus some other set of causes? And how do we know who the oppressor is? Does every situation have a clear oppressor and a clear victim? Our challenge is to make clear how we get to those answers.

One of the contexts where the question of neutrality regularly plays out is in higher education. This became especially salient in the aftermath of the October 7, 2023 attacks in Israel. Largely because of its position as a center of knowledge production, debate, and dissent, higher education has been at the center of arguments about what neutrality means and whether it should even be a goal. This has been true for decades—so much so that this question was at the heart of the 1967 Kalven Report.

The Kalven Report was the product of a faculty committee at the University of Chicago. Committee members were tasked by University President George W. Beadle to prepare "a statement on the University's role in political and social action."[10] The committee's conclusions were unambiguous.

> The instrument of dissent and criticism is the individual faculty member or the individual student. The university is the home and sponsor of critics; it is not itself the critic. . . . Since the university is a community only for these limited and distinctive purposes, it is a community which cannot take collective action on the issues of the day without endangering the conditions for its existence and effectiveness.

They conclude that there is no mechanism by which it can reach a collective position without inhibiting that full freedom of dissent on which it thrives. The report continues:

> The neutrality of the university as an institution arises then not from a lack of courage nor out of indifference and insensitivity. It arises out of respect for free inquiry and the obligation to cherish a diversity of viewpoints. And this neutrality as an institution has its complement in the fullest freedom for its faculty and students as individuals to participate in political action and social protest. It finds its complement, too, in the obligation of the university to provide a forum for the most searching and candid discussion of public issues.

Ultimately, the Kalven committee, after reviewing the University of Chicago's experience with a wide range of contentious issues, determined that there was simply no way for the university to take sides on issues while also maintaining its respect for free inquiry and a diversity of viewpoints. The report made it clear that universities must maintain and sustain an "extraordinary" climate of free inquiry and political independence in order to fulfill their purpose. The importance of this document has persisted. Nearly fifty years later, the University of Chicago produced the "Report of the Committee on Freedom of Expression," which traces its intellectual roots in part to the Kalven Report.[11] This more recent report on freedom of expression, which has since become known as simply the "Chicago Principles," has been adopted by universities and colleges across the United States as they try to navigate the inevitable tension between offense and open inquiry.

While not all institutions have declared a level of commitment to open inquiry comparable to the University of Chicago, nearly all extoll values like free speech, academic freedom, and vigorous debate. And yet, despite these commitments, higher education continually finds itself on the receiving end of criticism that it's overrun with liberal bias and self-censorship—especially among conservative students—and that there's a powerful ideological orthodoxy that's run rampant.

To be sure, defenders of higher education say these concerns are little more than a tempest in a teapot and that they are largely a figment of the overactive imagination of a censorious political right. At the same time, while there are instances where the right has hand-selected examples to paint a picture of institutions lost to political correctness— for instance, the Carnegie Mellon professor who gleefully tweeted that she wished "excruciating" pain upon the dying Queen Elizabeth II—the problem is real.[12]

While there are multiple examples of situations where colleges and universities have made statements on contentious issues, one of the clearest might be after the Kyle Rittenhouse verdict. After shooting three men during civil unrest in Kenosha, Wisconsin, in August 2020, the charges against Rittenhouse included two counts of homicide, two counts of attempted homicide, and one count of reckless endangerment.[13] He was later found not guilty on all charges. When the jury reached its verdict, high-level administrators in multiple colleges and universities came out with statements condemning the verdict. As described by one article in the *Atlantic*, "Instead of using his acquittal to promote vigorous discussion, many administrators sent out statements decrying the verdict."[14]

In one example, referenced in the *Atlantic* article, the University of California at Santa Cruz Chancellor and the Interim Chief Diversity Officer together wrote, "We join in solidarity with all who are outraged by this failure of accountability." The statement continued, "We also acknowledge that this same week the prosecution and defense concluded their case in the trial of three white men charged with chasing and killing Ahmaud Arbery, a 25-year-old unarmed Black man, in February 2020, south of Brunswick, Georgia.... Trials such as these that have race-related implications can cause our BIPOC communities distress and harm. This is harm that is endured everyday through acts of racism, the pervasiveness of white supremacy and a flawed justice system."[15]

The sense that justice wasn't served in the Rittenhouse case and that the jury's decision was flawed, biased, or otherwise tainted isn't itself a problem. Nor is there a problem with being vocal, even stridently so, about one's dissatisfaction with that decision. The problem is with using the university as a platform to take a stand on an issue that's clearly controversial, heated, and contentious. If they were asked to defend their statement, the Chancellor and the Interim Diversity Officer might offer an explanation that sounds similar to what I described earlier. They might say, "We have a moral obligation to speak out against injustice. We can't just sit silent."

Of course, I'm just speculating. But I imagine this would be a plausible response to the criticism that their statement undermines a commitment to a diversity of perspectives. And yet, if they were to offer such a rationale, that reasoning would be coming from a place of certainty. But you might be wondering, where is the uncertainty in the case of Rittenhouse? I don't need to be a legal expert for questions to come to mind. They include: Was he truly acting in self-defense? Was there enough evidence to convict him in the state of Wisconsin for the crimes of which he was accused, even though the jury apparently didn't think so? Then I have questions specific to the UC Santa Cruz response, like what exactly did they mean by "the pervasiveness of white supremacy"?

You might recall that, earlier in the book, we went into some depth with the example of how people think about racism. We talked about its history and the different ways people have come to think of what the term means. Certainty on this topic lurks in the background of the UC Santa Cruz statement. After all, one of the ways you get to the sense that society is permeated with white supremacy is by either downplaying or removing the role of intent in people's positions. In other words, at every situation where racism is one of multiple possible explanations, you choose racism. To be fair, you might be right. But you also might not be.

Ultimately, the university statements that were issued after the verdict were, in all likelihood, an attempt to comfort the many people who were emotionally distressed by Rittenhouse going free. At the same time, such statements undermine the broader commitments of institutions of higher education and damage its credibility in ways that are difficult to fully measure.

It's worth pointing out that while higher education arguably occupies a unique place in our culture and society, as an institution, it's not alone in making these kinds of statements. Both the non-academic and corporate worlds have followed suit. One of the clearest examples of this was in the wake of George Floyd's murder in 2020. Organizations big and small stepped up to make it clear that they stood with Black Lives Matter and against racial injustice. They seemed to do this while paying little attention to what that meant. So, let's try to piece it apart.

If the question on the table is "Do black lives matter?," the answer is unequivocally "yes." In fact, it's so emphatically yes that it speaks to the brilliance of so naming the movement in the first place. And, consistent with my intellectual commitment to clarity, I can name the principle that leads me that conviction." All lives have equal moral value.[16]

Black Lives Matter, the movement, viewed the color of George Floyd's skin as playing a causal role in his murder. This explanation stands in contrast to alternatives, like Floyd was murdered because of bad policing. The conviction that he was killed because he was black became the thing that was being treated as certain.

To be sure, that conclusion might be exactly right. In other words, the problem isn't the suggestion that it's a viable explanation. It's the conviction that it's correct. After all, that's what justifies the judgment of anyone who disagrees. And because the issue is so contentious, that judgment tends to be both harsh and swift.

An alternative to institutional statements of solidarity might look a little different. It might, to use the Rittenhouse example, involve acknowledging people's distress, while simultaneously taking the opportunity to open up a discussion about what happened and how people might see it differently. This might include a conversation about *why* it's so heated and how people arrive at their conclusions. In other words, it could be an opportunity to dig deep rather than to dig in.

DECISIONS IN THE FACE OF VALUE CONFLICTS

In December 2020, at the University of Illinois Chicago's Law School, Professor Jason Kilborn gave an exam on civil procedure, just as he'd done for multiple years past. This time, however, would be different. In one of the routine questions on the exam, Professor Kilborn described the following hypothetical problem:

> Employer's lawyer traveled to meet the manager, who stated that she quit her job at Employer after she attended a meeting in which other managers expressed their anger at Plaintiff, calling her a "n____" and "b____" (profane expressions for African Americans and women) and vowed to get rid of her.[17]

This time, not long after the exam, students began registering their dismay about the redacted words used in the question. In short order, the Black Law Students Association (BLSA) started a petition that called for Kilborn to step down from his committee work at the law school, mandatory cultural sensitivity training, and for Kilborn to participate in an open dialogue event. The petition concluded with the following call, "We do not have time for band-aid solutions. We need surgery and this operation is not up for debate. Act now."[18] The law school offered the following response:

> The Law School recognizes the impact of this issue. Before winter break, Dean Dickerson apologized to the students who expressed hurt and distress over the examination question. The Law School acknowledges that the racial and gender references on the examination were deeply offensive. Faculty should avoid language that could cause hurt and distress to students. Those with tenure and academic freedom should always remember their position of power in our system of legal education.[19]

Let's pause for a moment. What we're seeing is another way institutions fail to rise to the challenge of being clear about their values and thinking. This leads to confusion when competing values come into conflict. One way to frame the conflicting values in this case is freedom of speech (Kilborn) and the preservation of students' feelings (BLSA). Perhaps unsurprisingly, the story didn't end with the law school's response. On January 6, 2021, the BLSA asked students to contact them if they'd been "affected by" Professor Kilborn. The following day, Professor Kilborn met on Zoom with a member of the BLSA to discuss what was happening. Kilborn described that meeting as follows:

> On Thursday, January 7, I voluntarily agreed to talk to one of the Black Law Students Association members who had advanced this petition against me. Around hour 1 or 1.5 of a 4-hour Zoom call that I endured from 5:00 pm to 9:00 pm with this young man, he asked me to speculate as to why the dean had not sent me BLSA's attack letter, and I flippantly responded, 'I suspect she's afraid if I saw the horrible things

said about me in that letter I would become homicidal.' Conversation continued without a hitch for 2.5 or 3 more hours, and we concluded amicably with a promise to talk more later.[20]

Kilborn's use of the word "homicidal" prompted the student on the Zoom call to file a complaint about feeling threatened. This decontextualized word was, apparently, all that was needed for the administration to forcibly step in. Over the course of events, Kilborn was placed on indefinite administrative leave and his classes were canceled.

While Professor Kilborn's situation may be of interest to readers for other reasons, we might ask what it has to do with certainty? The response of the BLSA to the test questions and the response of the administration demonstrates the institutional culture that often results when certainty on issues around race, identity, and intent has taken hold.

For instance, why would the BLSA conclude that redacted words used in an exam question were grounds to file a complaint? And why would the law school feel compelled to respond in a way that validated these concerns? My point in asking this isn't to suggest that the students' feelings don't matter. It's to highlight that the default assumption that feelings are or should be the ultimate arbiter of what's offensive or hurtful lacks examination. Outside the Certainty Trap, this could have unfolded differently.

It could have been an opportunity that the BLSA and the law school administration seized to enter into a conversation about language and intent and where the lines should be. After all, in a healthy culture that members want to remain open to a diversity of perspectives, such a conversation is ongoing. Yet, when conflict arose on a heated issue—in this case, who decides what's hurtful or racist—certainty led the school to be pre-committed to giving top priority to the students' feelings.

If the default in such cases is going to be to defer to the group experiencing the feeling of being offended, that decision has a series of knock-on effects that need to be acknowledged. Most importantly, it means that the community norms will always be determined by its most sensitive member. While that policy has the advantage of being clear, it is going to bump up against values like viewpoint diversity, freedom of speech, and open inquiry. A failure to engage with the competing values leads institutions to claim that they're committed to valuing diverse perspectives, while at the same time taking actions and making assumptions that suggest otherwise. And that erodes credibility and trust.

It's worth talking through one more example. This one also happens to be tied to a law school, but the question it raises is slightly different. In late January 2022, legal scholar Ilya Shapiro was poised to begin working at Georgetown Law School. The timing of his new position happened to coincide with an announcement from President Biden that the next Supreme Court nominee would be a black woman. In this context, Shapiro tweeted, "Objectively best pick for Biden is Sri Srinivasan, who is solid prog & v smart" and "Even has identity politics benefit of being first Asian (Indian) American. But alas doesn't fit into the latest intersectionality hierarchy so we'll get lesser black woman. Thank heaven for small favors?"[21]

The backlash was swift. Shapiro deleted the tweet, calling it "inartful." However, an investigation by Georgetown's Office of Institutional Diversity, Equity, and Affirmative Action was launched and Shapiro was accused of racism for his remarks.[22] The Dean of Georgetown Law School wrote:

> Mr. Shapiro's tweets are antithetical to the work that we do at Georgetown Law to build inclusion, belonging, and respect for diversity. They have been harmful to many in the Georgetown Law community and beyond.[23]

At this point in the book, we probably know that the Dean's condemnation is the result of the Fallacy of Known Intent. Let me pause for a moment to make something clear. I have no position on whether Ilya

Shapiro is racist or not. I have never met nor interacted with him. But I can imagine another way this situation might have unfolded.

Biden's ex ante declaration that he was only going to nominate a black woman raised questions that reasonable people could ask, even if they agreed with his decision. In particular, looking only at black women candidates was a way of constraining the search parameters. It was a constraint that may have been well-justified. After all, there are historical reasons why the nomination of a black woman to the Supreme Court is and was important. But it was a constraint, nonetheless. And it's conceivable that the resulting search would have yielded a different outcome than there would have been without that restriction.

It's fairly easy to see Shapiro's words as distasteful—or "inartful," as he put it. He could have been more careful about how he expressed his thoughts and concerns. But it's one thing to point to a poorly worded tweet. It's another to decry the tweet as harmful and offensive and to accuse its author of racism. Shapiro's opinion might have come from a place of racism, or it might have come from frustration about the constrained search. When we treat the opinion as damning, when we assume there's no other way to see it, we're revealing a precommitment to the idea that his intent doesn't matter.

When it comes to certainty in institutions, these kinds of scenarios—with Kilborn and Shapiro—spotlight a problem. They reveal what the institution prioritizes when tension arises between values. And sometimes, the institutional response isn't aligned with what they have been claiming to prioritize all along. For example, an observer would be understandably disoriented by an institution that claims to value freedom of expression—as both the University of Illinois Chicago and Georgetown University do—while consistently subordinating it to feelings of offense.

Here's one way to think about the incoherence I'm describing. Imagine that the University of Illinois Chicago law school set a policy that any time someone is accused of offending someone, the accused will be disciplined. Or imagine that, similarly, Georgetown Law School set a policy that, when resolving conflicts, intent doesn't matter. (Of course, this would be ironic as such policies would suggest a denial of the very due process law schools are supposed to value.)

Many people would rightly object to such a policy, but the policy itself would at least be coherent. The erosion of trust comes, at least in part, from having policies on paper that promote free inquiry and expression, making decisions that undermine them, and failing to acknowledge the tension.

Presenting Provisional Information as Definitive

One question that comes up repeatedly when people think about how institutions navigate heated issues is what the institution's goal is. For example, a commitment to understanding what's true about the world might come into conflict with a goal of advancing social progress or creating social change. In this context, many institutions in K–12 education, higher education, and journalism have, for years, declared truth as the priority. And yet, all of these institutions have found themselves awash in certainty on various heated issues. They have become places where knowledge that should be thought of as provisional is treated as final. One of the areas we can see this play out is in battles over how K–12 schools handle issues around race and identity. In particular, this means regulations around *critical race theory* (CRT).

It's not often that a theoretical framework born in academic departments generally ignored by the outside world fully jumps the rails into mainstream conversation. One minute, CRT lived a cloistered life inside the walls of academia and the next it was being discussed and argued over in every major news outlet, think tank, and talk show in the country. Much of the conversation was animated by the possibility that this framework was being woven into public school teaching . . . and taught as truth.

In the early 2020s, this issue became so politicized that it led to a spate of legislative attempts to regulate classroom instruction, specifically on issues around history, race, and identity. Defenders and advocates of CRT—largely people on the political left—felt that those who objected to it were simply unwilling to face the racism of the American past and were trying to "whitewash" history. And those with concerns about CRT—largely but not exclusively people on the political right—were convinced that its advocates were trying to convince children to hate this country.

In January 2023, Governor Sarah Huckabee Sanders of Arkansas signed an executive order stating, "As it relates to employees, contractors, and guest speakers or lecturers of the Department of Education, the Secretary is directed to review and enhance the policies that prevent prohibited indoctrination, including CRT." And "The Secretary shall ensure that no school employee or student shall be required to attend trainings or orientations based on prohibited indoctrination or CRT." The order also said that "Critical Race Theory (CRT) is antithetical to the traditional American values of neutrality, equality, and fairness. It emphasizes skin color as a person's primary characteristic, thereby resurrecting segregationist values, which America has fought so hard to reject."[24]

To be sure, it's relatively easy to get lost on this topic. And an exploration quickly leads to hard questions like who *should* decide what's taught in schools? What is the *right* way to think about the founding of the United States? How much *does* the injustice of slavery shape today's outcomes?

All of these questions warrant thorough and thoughtful discussions. And, in a healthy climate, we would be able to do just that. Instead, we find ourselves at an impasse where the Settled Question Fallacy, the Fallacy of Equal Knowledge, and the Fallacy of Known Intent have largely taken over. And instead of digging deep, we dig our heels in.

So, what *is* CRT? It might be helpful to think of it in terms of a few main tenets. Although different sources offer slight variations on how to think about these, they largely converge around four core ideas.

The first involves a rejection of the idea of colorblindness, which calls for the equal treatment of individuals no matter their race, maintains that people should be judged on their individual merits, and seeks a deemphasis on the role of race in today's society. CRT advocates believe this approach both denies and contributes to structural racism and thus often refer to the idea of colorblindness as colorblind racism. The organizing principle behind the rejection of colorblindness is that solving racial inequality requires seeing both its causes and solutions through the lens of race. Further, the thinking goes, downplaying the importance of race denies the experiences of people who have historically been marginalized *because* of that race. The quintessential expression of colorblindness is often described as someone saying, "I don't see color."

Because colorblindness infers a lack of focus on race, the argument goes, it rules out the possibility of deemphasizing race in a way that isn't institutionally or structurally racist. This points us to one question that's being treated as settled. Specifically, could we know and, if so, who would decide, if there's a scenario where downplaying the role of race *would* be the right thing to do?

One way to think about this is with a concrete example. In this case, we can look to affinity groups and organizations. Affinity groups refers to the various cultural centers or groups (African American, Latino, Asian, etc.) that often exist on college campuses and in workplaces.

When I ask students about the benefits of racial and cultural affinity groups, I'll usually get responses like they're places for students to gather with others who understand their background. Or they're places where students of color can gather and feel comfortable on a campus that's predominantly white.

Sometimes, I'll ask whether two people who share a racial, ethnic, or other type of identity background are predisposed to understand one another's life experience. What's more, I'll push, does that mean that someone who doesn't share that identity background *couldn't* understand? At this point, many will nod in agreement that there is something important that's shared among members of a racial or ethnic group.

In some ways, treating identity as both important and shared makes intuitive sense. There's a reason, for instance, that most women have close friends who are women, and most men have close friends who are men. Presumably, there's something about how you move through the world that fundamentally differs along this dimension. But this observation only raises other questions about how we think about who we are. For instance: Imagine you come from an extraordinarily wealthy family. Now, add to the scenario that your family background is Latino. Would you feel like you have more in common with a peer who is Latino but is of very modest means or with a peer who is non-Latino but who comes from a background of wealth comparable to your own?

From where I sit, there's no right or wrong way to think about this. This is a relief because, as with other examples, the goal isn't to find an answer. It's to ask the question in the first place. Here's another one to ponder: What would the world look like if people only felt like they could relate to people in their same identity group? (We'll set aside for the moment that people can fit into more than one identity group.) When asked this way, many students quickly realize that, if taken to an extreme, such a view would be divisive. If taken too far, no one would be able to communicate with anyone else. While we can hopefully agree that this isn't a viable way to build a sense of community, it does leave us wondering: If it's possible to lean too much into identity groups, how do we know when that line has been crossed? Who decides? How do we strike a balance between recognizing that identity matters while also understanding that it's not everything? And shouldn't we be talking about these things? CRT's view of an unwillingness to see the world through the lens of race as evidence of colorblind racism has made this conversation difficult to have.

The second tenet of CRT is called interest convergence. Interest convergence is the idea that members of the white majority will only support equality across groups when it suits them to do so. So, if, for instance, you observe non-Hispanic whites advocating for equal rights or for a cause viewed as supporting the black community, it can be understood as being driven by self-interest. This implies that, for instance, whites who marched with Dr. Martin Luther King Jr. did so because it benefited them in some way. Is that correct? Knowing the answer to that question would require being inside the hearts and minds of those protestors.

And yet, CRT treats the question of intent and motives as settled. It's one thing to say that someone's motives are subject to being questioned. It's quite another to declare that no member of the dominant group ever advances the cause of equality unless it's in their interest to do so.

The third and fourth tenets of CRT are similar to one another in what they're treating as settled. The third is that race and racism are inextricably intertwined. Part of what this means is that racism is normal and not an aberration. This is tied to the idea that the concept of race is created to preserve white dominance. By grouping people this way, the thinking goes, it gives cover to the broader goal of maintaining control, all while making it appear that resources in life are allocated fairly.

After all, the thinking goes, one way to get people to accept being less powerful in a society is to convince them that resources are doled out based on merit. If we all internalize the belief that merit and hard work are what get people ahead in society, then it's natural to conclude that a lack of success is a person's own fault. (Note how this harkens back to our earlier discussion of cognitive dissonance.) In this line of thinking, the notion of meritocracy is a lie that prevents people of color from rising up against the injustice in place to keep them down.

The fourth tenet associated with CRT relates to systemic racism. More specifically, it points to an unwillingness to acknowledge and recognize its full force in shaping inequality between racial groups today. It is based in the idea that racism doesn't require racial animus—it's woven into a system that produces the disparities without the actions of any individual racist.

The third and fourth tenets both treat questions of inequality as settled. They assume that racism, systemic or otherwise, is the only relevant factor when it comes to differences in outcomes across groups. And in so doing, the conclusion they lead to is that denying the role of systemic racism or advocating for or defending a meritocratic system is itself racist behavior.

Here again, the point isn't to declare that racism doesn't play a role or that the meritocracy works. Indeed, I am unprepared to make either claim. The point is to show that treating the answers to these questions as definitive and known creates the space to say that a dissenting view is, in this case, racist.

Meanwhile, the response to all this from the political right, specifically, the legislative attempts at bans, has made our ability to address this challenge worse. It's taken a real problem—the way the tenets of CRT are treated as definitive in schools—and tried to address it be countering with their categorical denial. Banning a set of ideas only distorts the mirror in a different direction.

While the question of CRT in schools shows us a glimpse of the certainty-related problems facing the educational system, there's still one more arena that deserves our attention.

Earlier, we mentioned the media in our list of institutions affected by the certainty. But it's worth sharpening that point. The challenges faced in journalism—particularly when it comes to heated issues—come largely from a broader unresolved question about what journalism's goals are.

As in the education sphere, we could ask the question of whether the primary duty of a journalist is to discover and report the truth. This was clearly the sentiment behind journalist Walter Lippmann's statement in 1920 that "[t]here can be no higher law in journalism than to tell the truth and to shame the devil."

In recent years, however, this has been called into question. In a January 2023 op-ed, former Executive Editor of the *Washington Post*, Leonard Downie, wrote, "Amid all the profound challenges and changes roiling the American news media today, newsrooms are debating whether traditional objectivity should still be the standard for news reporting." As Downie noted, "increasingly, reporters, editors and media critics argue that the concept of journalistic objectivity is a distortion of reality."[25] The thinking, as Downie described it, is "that pursuing objectivity can lead to false balance or misleading 'bothsidesism' in covering stories about race, the treatment of women, LGBTQ+ rights, income inequality, climate change and many other subjects."

In response to the article, some critics of the culture Downie described said that leaving objectivity behind would be to "destroy (what's left of) the mainstream media's credibility."[26]

So, what are newsrooms to do? One possibility is to continue to strive for objectivity. Another is to leave it behind. And a third, perhaps the worst of all, is to leave it behind while still claiming to be committed to the truth—especially if this is done without realizing it.

Downie seems to be aware of this third, and alarming, option. Which is perhaps why he writes, "Responsible news organizations need to develop core values by having candid, inclusive and open conversations. Making these values public could well forge a stronger connection between journalists and the public."

Chapter Summary

- The way institutions handle information, especially in times of crisis, can significantly affect their perceived competence and credibility.
- Institutions often face pressure to take stands on contentious issues, but this can compromise their neutrality and the trust placed in them by the public.
- The media faces a crisis regarding whether to uphold traditional ob-

jectivity or embrace a more openly subjective approach, which could impact their credibility.

- The debate around CRT in educational settings reflects a tension between certainty-based assumptions and a push for social progress. Legislative responses to CRT have further politicized the issue.

Practice Uncertainty

Look at recent communications from a school, workplace, or public figure you are familiar with. Evaluate how they present their stance on contentious issues and reflect on the impact this may have on their community. Is there a sense of certainty, or is there room for open discussion and differing viewpoints?

9

Change May Be Hard, but It's Crucial We Do It Anyway

"To counter the avoidance of intellectual challenge and responsibility, we must reduce the domination of certainty in education."

WILLIAM GLASSER

If breaking out of the Certainty Trap were easy, I probably could have summed up this book in a few short words. It would have been something like, "I don't know anything and neither do you." But there are powerful forces at play, both pulling us away from this challenge and keeping us away. What I'm asking you to do doesn't come naturally. In some ways, avoiding certainty goes against a very human need to sort information into categories in order to make sense of the world.

*Un*certainty doesn't sit well with most of us. In a sense, we tend to be uncomfortable when we feel like we're not in control of our fate. This is at least part of why it's more common to hear about people who are afraid of getting on an airplane than of driving in a car. Statistically, a car accident—even a fatal one—is far more likely than a plane crash, but for some reason, it doesn't feel that way when we're at the wheel. Compare that feeling to being a helpless passenger hurtling through the air in a metal tube 30,000 feet up.

Our need for a sense of control is part of what drives people to do things like touch wood when they've said aloud something they don't want to happen, avoid stepping on cracks in the sidewalk, and not look into cracked mirrors. It's why soccer legend Ronaldo always steps on the pitch right foot first and why Serena Williams won't wash her socks once she's on a winning streak.[1]

If trying to control outcomes is one way we try to make sense of the world, another is through pattern finding. Our tendency to seek out patterns even in the presence of random or meaningless data is so well-documented that it has a name in psychology: apophenia. It has some similarities to another known cognitive trick our minds sometimes play, called the Gambler's Fallacy. The Gambler's Fallacy is the belief that, if some event has occurred especially infrequently in the past, it's more likely to occur in the future (and the other way around—if it has occurred especially frequently in the past, it's less likely to occur in the future). However, in actuality, if the events are independent—as they are in, for instance, the roll of a die—neither of those assumptions holds.

So, what do superstitions, apophenia, the Gambler's Fallacy, and certainty have in common? They are different ways we try to make sense of and sort our surroundings. This lets us move through the world with efficiency—not having to ask ourselves, for instance, each time we see a small furry thing with pointy ears and four legs, if it's a housecat. Sorting helps us maneuver an increasingly complicated society. But it is difficult to do in a way that simultaneously keeps up with the complexity of today's world.

When much of the outside world was shut down because of Covid, one of the Netflix shows my kids convinced me to watch was *The Good Place*. It's a wonderfully funny show that, among other things, has a main character who's a moral philosophy professor. The first few seasons of the show are based on the idea that each person accumulates points during her lifetime as she does good things and loses them as she does bad things. The bigger the impact of the good thing, the more the points (and vice versa). And, when you die, the sum of all your points determines whether you get sent to the "good place" or the "bad place."

Over the course of its four seasons, the characters discover that no one's been let into the "good place" for five hundred years. As the heroes investigate why this might be the case, the first thought is that it's sabotage by the "bad place" folks. Until they learn that's not actually the case. The reason no one's gotten in is because of how complicated the world has become.

The heroes discover, for example, that if someone who lived five hundred years ago brought a basket of tomatoes to their grandmother, they got lots of points for that deed. After all, it was an unambiguously good thing. At that time, there was a good chance they grew the tomatoes themselves and hand-delivered them. They found that, today, a person doing the same action would experience a net loss of points. The reason is that, today, the tomatoes might have been picked by migrant workers who weren't paid a fair wage. Or they might have been transported in a truck spewing carbon dioxide into the atmosphere. This meant that the same good deed committed five hundred years later was now a liability. The characters realized that the world had simply become too complicated for the original point system to be meaningful.

I'm telling this story simply as a way of understanding that, while our need to sort, categorize, and pattern find is natural and helps us understand the world around us, it's not well suited to how complex that world has become. And not just because a clever TV show says so.

Forces Pushing Us Toward Certainty and Binary Thinking

When it comes to avoiding the problem of certainty, various incentives point us in the wrong direction. We're working against powerful social mechanisms that reward outrage, simplicity, and a loss of nuance. One of the main culprits, of course, is social media, a place where outrage is rewarded with more clicks, likes, shares, and retweets.[2] And yet, in order for me to justify being outraged about something, I have to be certain I am right. In other words, anything that incentivizes outrage, also incentivizes certainty.

The problems resulting from social media are well studied and include things like echo chambers and political siloes. The consequences of social media use are so well known that technology ethicist Tristan Harris has referred to the entire model as "human downgrading." Harris cofounded the Center for Humane Technology to try to stop the damage stemming from these effects.

One way to think about the Center for Humane Technology, and organizations like it, is as tackling the problems of social media from the supply side. The supply side refers to the way the platforms themselves use algorithms to manipulate users' feeds and to increase engagement—at almost any cost. In fact, on the center's website, it says, "We believe that by understanding the root causes of harmful technology, we can work together to build a more humane future."[3] To be sure, this is important work.

And yet, avoiding the Certainty Trap is a way to tackle the problems stemming from social media from the demand side. We do this by changing our susceptibility to overly simplistic claims in the first place. In this sense, we can change how we consume information and how we understand the world.

Here's another way to think about it, using a different example. If you're trying to reduce unauthorized migration, there's more than one approach you can take. You can put policies in place that make it harder or less attractive to hire migrants in the first place (demand side). Or you can try to improve conditions in the source countries so that they have less desire or need to leave (supply side). And, of course, you can do both.

We mentioned the work of Daniel Kahneman earlier, but it's worth restating here. Another reason challenging our thinking is difficult is because doing so relies heavily on what Kahneman, in his famous book

Thinking Fast and Slow, referred to as system 2 thinking. While system 1 "operates automatically and quickly, with little or no effort and no sense of voluntary control," system 2 "allocates attention to the effortful mental activities that demand it, including complex computations."[4] In other words, because leaning away from certainty means seeing the world in all its complexity, it simply takes more energy than leaning into it.

While there may be much about human nature we don't fully understand, one thing seems clear. When it comes to our need to categorize, one of the most common ways we do this is to divide the world into us and them. At a fundamental level, we view people emotionally close to us differently than people we have never met. Any time we say this person (or these people) is (are) more important to me than some other person (or people), we're making this kind of distinction. To be sure, many people would probably say that this is a completely normal and understandable line to draw. It's difficult to, for instance, imagine a world where I care about a stranger's children as much as I care about my own.

The tendency to create us and them is reinforced in too many ways to count—and not all of those ways are bad. We know, for instance, that shared experiences unify groups—and not just identity groups. For instance, there's a reason people talk about the events that shape the experiences of different generations. Whether it's the Great Depression, World War II, the moon landing, the Kennedy assassination, the *Challenger* explosion, 9/11, Covid, or some other major historical moment, there's something about going through these experiences in late adolescence that makes their effect distinct.

This is all to say that there can be little doubt that shared experiences naturally group people together. As do certain preferences and habits—think knitting clubs or the fact that there's a dating website devoted to people who love *Star Trek*. And much of the time, when we group ourselves this way, there's no harm done. If anything, these kinds of groupings can facilitate positive social interactions and connections that might not otherwise occur.

But when the tendency to draw lines between us and them is based on politics, we're in a different set of circumstances altogether. The walls are higher, the words more vitriolic, and the necessary cooperation across opponents can become impossible. That doesn't mean that there can't or shouldn't be spirited, and even heated, arguments across the aisle. It just means that, when all's said and done, we need to be able to walk away believing that the other side isn't fundamentally evil, trying to destroy the country, or in some other way acting in bad faith.

One thoughtful analysis of this very human tendency to create a sense of us and them comes from a 2014 post by Scott Alexander called "I Can Tolerate Anything except the Outgroup."[5] Drawing on Sigmund Freud's notion of the narcissism of minor differences, he argues that the designation of an outgroup emerges from "proximity plus small differences." He continues, "If you want to know who someone in former Yugoslavia hates, don't look at the Indonesians or the Zulus or the Tibetans or anyone else distant and exotic. Find the Yugoslavian ethnicity that lives closely intermingled with them and is most conspicuously similar to them, and chances are you'll find the one who they have eight hundred years of seething hatred toward."

Alexander's piece is long, but it's worth reading in its entirety. Toward the end, as he turns his gaze specifically toward the way the us and them phenomenon creates political tribalism, he writes, "The outgroup of the Red Tribe is occasionally blacks and gays and Muslims, more often the Blue Tribe. . . The Blue Tribe has performed some kind of very impressive act of alchemy, and transmuted all of its outgroup hatred to the Red Tribe." Although Alexander uses different language than this book, what drives the behavior he is observing is certainty—in this case, the raw and absolute conviction that people who see things differently are stupid and/or morally corrupt.

At this point in the book, if your first thought after reading that statement (regardless of your political orientation) is something like this: "Well, this would all be a lot easier to do if the other side weren't actually trying to destroy this country!" you might need to go back to the beginning. If your position remains, for instance, as it might have been in November 2016, that half the country is racist, you might need to interrogate your own thinking. And if you're thinking that Ron DeSantis is a knight in shining armor saving Florida from a "woke" nightmare, you probably need to do the same.

One way to interpret what I'm saying here is that we need to figure out how to compromise, how to take the best version of both sides. And while that's one possible path forward, that's not necessarily what I'm advocating for. Simply because, the "right" solution in any setting will depend on what we decide we're trying to accomplish or, as the economists say, optimize for.

In other words, nothing in this book is meant as a declaration that the answer to our problems always lies in the middle of the two political parties. Nor is it meant to suggest that we all just need to get along or hug it out. My point is to highlight the importance of examining where the tendency to judge and dismiss comes from. Realizing that the certainty driving those behaviors is simply the result of a distorted view of the world makes them a lot harder to justify.

UNCERTAINTY AND AMBIGUITY

In a 2018 article in *Nature*, cognitive scientists Marc-Lluis Vives and Oriel FeldmanHall discussed the important difference between what they call risk uncertainty and ambiguity uncertainty.[6] Risk uncertainty refers to situations where probabilities are known, while ambiguity uncertainty refers to situations where probabilities are unknown. A known probability might be something like the probability of a flipped coin landing heads up or the probability of rolling a three on a fair, six-sided die. Or the probability of winning first place in a raffle if you buy one ticket out of five thousand that are available. These kinds of uncertainties, we seem to be able to tolerate to some degree.

Yet, most of what we face in the real world are unknown probabilities. What is the probability that I'm going to get sick? What is the probability I'll trip while walking down the sidewalk? What is the probability I'll get the job I just applied for? Or what is the probability I'll fall in love? And so on and so forth.

Unknown probabilities can also include things like, what is the probability that, if I pluck at random out of all the people fired from their jobs in the last year, the person I pick was fired because of discrimination? Or what is the probability that a teenager who identifies as transgender will later regret their surgical transition? Or the probability that a low-achieving high school student would succeed academically if his school were better funded (and nothing else changed)?

Most of us struggle much more with the kinds of probabilities that are unknown than those that are. And, as you might imagine, pretty much all of the probabilities tied to the kinds of questions that animate this book fit the description of being unknown.

The lack of definitive knowledge on topics we care about doesn't mean that we have to remain silent. It just means we should be appropriately humble when it comes to how we think about them. And that, in turn, affects our interactions with people who see things differently. And yet, this book is about how, all too often, we behave and treat others in ways that fail take this into account.

Given how difficult it can be to rise to this challenge, getting a good handle on just how averse we are to *un*certainty seems important. Even though scholars have attempted to quantify people's tolerance for uncertainty, measuring it turns out to be complicated. In one protocol for making such an assessment, the Intolerance for Uncertainty Scale (IUS), respondents are asked to respond to 27 questions and rate themselves 1 (Not at all characteristic of me) to 5 (Entirely characteristic of me).[7] Sample statements include, "Uncertainty stops me from having a firm opinion," "It frustrates me not having all the information I need," "Unforeseen events upset me greatly," and "I always want to know what the future has in store for me."

One quiet Sunday afternoon, I decided to take the IUS to see how I'd score. So, I sat at the kitchen table, filled out the questionnaire, and carefully tallied my answers. Then I counted them again. The result told me that I have a remarkably low tolerance for uncertainty. I choked on my coffee and wondered if I should throw out the book I was writing (this one). How could I write a book extolling the virtues of uncertainty—something that, according to this measure, I didn't tolerate well? I thought about it for a while and realized something. When it comes to my own life, I *do* have a low tolerance for uncertainty. I like to know what's going to happen when and I like to have a plan. Not having one or both often makes me anxious. And yet, on the kinds of topics that are the focus of this book, sometimes my tolerance for uncertainty feels limitless.

Based on my own response, an obvious limitation of the IUS is that it asks the respondent about uncertainty in his own life, but we're referring here to seeing uncertainty in our understanding of the world and one another. Another conceptual difference, however, is that the IUS asks people how they feel about *not* knowing particular things. But in order for that question to even make sense, you have to recognize that there's something out there that you don't know—a "known" uncertainty. We went in some detail earlier in this book explaining how the things we take as given and don't even realize it may actually do the most damage. None of that would be captured by the IUS.

Do I Have to Open the Door to That?

Now, let's dive into what might be the scariest reason of all when it comes to a commitment to challenging our thinking. I'm referring to the quite understandable fear about what it can imply. Put another way, if there really is nothing we can be certain of, how then do we think about Holocaust deniers, flat-earthers, 9/11 truthers, QAnon followers, and people who think the moon landing was faked, to name just a few? Does it mean we need to take them all seriously now, even give them equal airtime?

One of the challenges with conspiracy theories—and what many of us see as the strange things other people believe—is that, in many instances, they *could* be true. I don't mean they are necessarily likely to be true. I just mean that it is possible that they are. In fact, in many ways, it's *because* our knowledge of the world is uncertain that they continue to thrive. One way to think about conspiracy theories is as the inevitable byproduct of the combination of doubt and our inevitably imperfect knowledge.

Let's say I think my neighbor is a Russian spy (I don't). What, if anything, could convince me that she isn't? Let's imagine a hypothetical scenario where my oh-so-patient neighbor is willing to go along with my interrogation. In my mind, if she refused, it'd probably just prove to me that she's hiding something.

Me: *Are you a Russian spy?*

Neighbor: *Um, no.*

Me: *Where were you born?*

Neighbor: *Danville, Illinois*

Me: *I don't believe you.*

Neighbor (being more than indulgent): *Here's my birth certificate.*

Me: That doesn't prove anything because Russian spy agencies can make amazing forgeries.

Neighbor: *Well, wouldn't you expect me to have an accent if I were a Russian spy?*

Me: *Of course not. They train their agents really well.*

Neighbor: *Let me introduce you to my first-grade teacher from Danville. She can vouch for me.*

Me: *Oh, that's just someone you paid to say she was your first-grade teacher.*

And so on and so forth . . .

Ultimately, there's a world where nothing she could do or say would convince me she's not a Russian spy. And here's the thing. It's theoretically possible that conspiracy-believing me would be right. Regular-me understands that the corresponding probability is so infinitesimally small that it's not really worth a lot of my time. And life is not a movie where we regularly encounter the highly improbable.[8] So, I ignore that miniscule chance, although that doesn't mean it's no longer there.

Let's take a different example. Say I believe that Covid vaccines have a 5G microchip in them. And that one of the reasons, or perhaps the main reason, the government pushed them so hard is so they can track people. Let's add to that and say I have a hunch Bill Gates has his hand in the whole project. Is there anything someone can say to convince me that's not what's going on?

At their core, conspiracy beliefs come down to what we believe when we're faced with incomplete knowledge of the world. In some ways, understanding how this works brings us back to the importance of trust in our institutions. After all, when institutions aren't viewed as trustworthy, people will seek answers elsewhere.

I need to digress for a moment. I once had a conversation with Russ Roberts, the fascinating scholar who hosts the podcast *EconTalk*. He told me about a wonderful quote a listener, Sam Thomsen, had once shared with him. It goes like this: "The Universe is full of dots. Connect the right ones and you can draw anything. The important question is not whether the dots you picked are really there, but why you chose to ignore all the others."

When trust in institutions breaks down, people stop listening to the way the leaders of those institutions tell them to make sense of the dots. They start connecting them in any which way to create all manner of different images. This brings us to an interesting point about beliefs more generally. And perhaps unsurprisingly, the ways in which what we *want* to believe plays an important role. In other words, the threshold for what we require as evidence is higher for something we don't want to believe than for something we do want to believe.

Social psychologist Thomas Gilovich captured this idea when he wrote, "For desired conclusions, we ask ourselves, 'Can I believe this?', but for unpalatable conclusions, we ask, 'Must I believe this?'"[9] The pervasiveness of uncertainty means that the answer to the first question is often yes—it's almost always *possible* to believe something. Even if an explanation is exceedingly unlikely, asking myself whether I *can* believe it is a low bar. When it comes to the second question—must I believe this?—what really meets that standard? The answer would, I imagine, be a preciously small list that would probably include things like gravity.

A 2019 *Scientific American* article dove into some of the big questions that often come up around people who believe in conspiracy theories. One of those is, should non-conspiracy theorists try to do something about them, like try to change their minds? And, if so, what should be done? Should we, as a society, care about whether people believe things that are unlikely to be true? Or should we just live and let live?

According to the article, conspiracy thinking can have two main negative effects.[10] One is that it may, ironically, lead to behavior that increases a person's feelings of powerlessness. For instance, a conspiracy theorist might be less likely to vote or, if the conspiracy theory relates to their workplace, feel less committed to their job. There can be impacts at the societal level too. Most devastatingly, conspiracy thinking can lead to the kind of dangerous and harmful behavior we saw with the horrific shooting at the Tree of Life synagogue in Pittsburgh in 2018 and the attack on the pizza restaurant Comet Ping Pong in Washington, DC, in 2016.

Given these potential consequences, we might want to understand why people believe conspiracy theories in the first place. According to the *Scientific American* article, while there are likely several factors at play, anxiety appears to play a significant role—specifically, anxiety associated with a sense of powerlessness and personal alienation. In particular, when these feelings combine with the belief that society itself is under threat, a belief in conspiracy theories can be one of the results.

With all this in mind, let's go back to our earlier question: What, if anything, can be done about conspiratorial thinking? It might seem natural to try to respond to a conspiracy theorist in a way that explains to him or her the inconsistencies in the theories, the contradictions, or simply why the theory is unlikely to be true. However, this approach hasn't proven successful, and it can even sometimes have the opposite effect.

Why might this happen? Ultimately, full leaning into conspiracy theories means seeing just about everything as evidence that supports your belief. That often means that people who try to explain why the theory doesn't make sense are "in on it" and the fact that they're trying to convince you to see things differently is simply more evidence that you're onto something important.

Scholars have come to refer to the way challenging conspiracy thinking can inadvertently entrench it as the "backfire effect." And while the evidence of its impact is mixed, there is reason to believe that the backfire effect "arise[s] most often when people are being challenged over ideas that define their worldview or sense of self."[11] In other words, the chances that challenging someone's beliefs will lead them to dig in further are most likely for precisely the kinds of topics we've been talking about in this book.

There's at least one other concern that comes up when thinking about how, in the context of uncertainty, to think about conspiracy theories. Does recognizing uncertainty in what we know about one another and about the world mean acknowledging that these views might be true? And, if it does, won't that just feed their growth?

While this concern is understandable, there are a couple of reasons that we don't need to end up in this scenario. First, as we talked about in the chapter on confidence, there's nothing about avoiding certainty that means that all explanations have an equal probability of being true. And second, realizing that our knowledge isn't definitive isn't actually a reason to lean into conspiracy theories: It's a reason to lean away from them. Here's what I mean.

Understanding that our knowledge is fundamentally uncertain means that I can't be sure the person who thinks the moon landing was faked is wrong. But it also means that that person can't be sure that I'm wrong (in thinking the moon landing is real). This presents a different way to approach and think about conspiracy theories that is both reflective of what we actually know and far less likely to lead to a backlash effect. Ultimately, conspiracy theories are incompatible with uncertainty. So, how might you get a conspiracy theorist to recognize this? The best way is by modeling it. In doing so, you'll be acknowledging the limitations of your own knowledge in a way that can encourage the other person to acknowledge the limits of theirs.

Of course, conspiracy theorists aren't the only source of concern when it comes to acknowledging doubt. What about people whose priorities compromise a desire to understand either what's true about the world or to recognize the limitations of our knowledge? For instance, what about a politician who is trying to get elected? Political campaign slogans and messages—much like tweets—tend to be definitive, oversimplified, and lacking in nuance. In such a context, delivering a message full of certainty might be exactly what the candidate needs to do to win. After all, voters often lose interest in complicated narratives and too many details. It's much easier to say, "I'm the good guy. Vote for me. He's the bad guy. Don't vote for him." Or to paint your opponent as a caricature who hasn't thought anything through or who simply doesn't care about the public.

What about news media organizations and online magazines whose entire business model is centered around clicks and traffic driven to the webpage? What kinds of stories tend to get clicked on the most? Probably not the ones with a highly measured and equivocal approach. More likely, it's the ones that make strident declarations and stake out a clear position.

While these kinds of incentives can pull people in different directions, unless they're completely abdicating a commitment to honesty, a commitment to questioning our thinking can still be a useful thing to bear in mind.

So, here's where we are. Avoiding certainty doesn't require believing conspiracy theories. And we would do well to recognize that it can be difficult to reach someone who doesn't care about understanding the world—because, for instance, they're trying to win an election. Now, there's just one more thing we're still missing.

There's a special class of topics that's worth focusing on for a moment. What about questions where acknowledging any doubt simply feels too painful to do? In some ways, this might be a subset of the conspiracy ideas we talked about earlier. For instance, if I'm committed to avoiding certainty, do I now have to engage with my Holocaust denier neighbor on the topic? Or, to bring it to one of the questions we posed as an example earlier in the book, if the question of whether George Floyd was killed because he was black is too painful for me to consider, do I still have to engage with people who want to ask it?

Ultimately, it comes down to this: We all have limits. We probably all have that one issue (or multiple issues) for which opening the door to doubt just feels like too much. And so, we want to take that issue off the table. Nothing is stopping us from doing so. But we need to do so with the understanding that, while it matters little at the individual level, the more issues more people take off the table, the worse off we are collectively. Recall that treating topics as though they can't be questioned played a big role in getting us to the point we're at now.

Despite the obstacles and concerns I've laid out here, staying out of the Certainty Trap is essential for society's growth, communication, and flourishing. Treating people as less than human—as other—lies behind many of the most heinous historical examples of things human beings have done to one another. Reducing our susceptibility to these kinds of claims can be a powerful defense against those who wish to use information for purposes other than our best interests—whether that comes in the form of a malevolent leader or whether it's in the form of a social media algorithm designed to keep us in an information silo. Leaving certainty behind can help us build the social trust we so desperately need.

CHAPTER SUMMARY

- Humans have a natural inclination to seek certainty and control as a way of making sense of the world. This is evident in behaviors like superstitions and in pattern recognition.
- Trying to debunk conspiracy theories can sometimes reinforce them (the backfire effect). We might instead model acknowledging the limits of our knowledge to foster open dialogue.
- We can always take an issue off the table for discussions. But we should bear in mind that the more things the more of us take off the table, the worse off we all are.
- People's threshold for evidence is lower for things they want to believe and higher for things they don't, leading to selective acceptance of information.
- Despite the challenges, embracing uncertainty and avoiding the Certainty Trap are essential for healthy societal discourse, growth, and resisting manipulation.

PRACTICE UNCERTAINTY

For one week, keep a journal where you note instances when you assume someone's intent or knowledge without full information. Reflect on why you made these assumptions and how they might have been influenced by your own biases or the context of the situation.

10

The Path Forward and Never Letting Up

The bad news is that avoiding the Certainty Trap, especially in the long term, can be difficult. The good news is that the skills I'm talking about can be taught, learned, and practiced. And, as with many things, with consistency, avoiding certainty will come more naturally over time. We can help ourselves along by remembering to think in terms of costs and benefits, prioritizing viewpoint diversity, consuming media from a wide range of sources, asking questions, and using the language in this book. But, perhaps more importantly, committing to avoiding the certainty means learning to recognize when we think some aspect of a heated issue is simple or obvious, and that anyone who sees it differently is ignorant or evil. *That's* the signal that you need to interrogate your thinking. There's more good news. Leaving certainty behind doesn't require anyone to admit to being wrong (maybe you're not wrong after all). It just means being a little less sure you're right. You move into the space of confidence, a space where everything can be questioned.

Avoiding certainty has specific implications for how we think and communicate with one another, especially when it comes to heated issues. When we see complexity and nuance, it becomes more difficult to judge or condemn people who disagree. You might then wonder, does this mean that we never take action, that we are destined to do nothing more than navel gaze when it comes to the world's most vexing problems?

In other words, if I'm stridently pro-choice, does a commitment to questioning and challenging my thinking mean that I can no longer in good conscience be active in my efforts to lobby for reproductive rights for women? The short answer is no. There's nothing about avoiding certainty that is incompatible with activism for any particular cause. It's entirely possible to believe strongly in something while also recognizing that it's complex. It's possible to advocate for a cause without demonizing or condemning the character of people who see it differently.

So, where did we start and where are we now when it comes to the Certainty Trap? At the beginning of the book, we introduced a mirror metaphor. Specifically, we said that we see the world almost as if reflected in a mirror—not because we're seeing our own reflection but because of another property of mirrors. The only type of mirror that perfectly reflects in proportion and distance what's in front of it is one with a flat plane of glass. Any curvature in the glass results in a distortion. Because the world is fundamentally uncertain, all certainty curves the glass. Sometimes, that curvature doesn't matter—in other words—but other times, it does. In particular, it matters when we behave as though that mirror is a window.

We talked about how the failure to question our thinking creates several problems. One is that is stops us from asking questions. This has a straightforward limiting effect on the way we accumulate knowledge. Another is that it tells us that there are no questions anyone could ask. This has the broader effect of changing social norms in a way that anyone who asks questions must either be stupid or morally deficient. And another is that it tricks us into behaving as though our values and principles don't need to be made clear or said out loud.

We defined the Settled Question Fallacy and identified some of the various forms it can take. For instance, it can involve treating our knowledge as definitive rather than provisional. It can also mean treating the path forward when it comes to contentious and complex issues as simple and obvious or as though there aren't costs and benefits to any path we choose. Identifying the assumptions that underlie our convictions, naming them to ourselves and out loud is what allows us and others to question, examine, and criticize them. We made the point that often the certainties we're not aware of do more damage than those we are aware of.

Then we turned to discussing the consequences of looking in a mirror while insisting it's a window—what we might think of as the *price* of certainty. One of those costs is that when we stop asking questions, we close ourselves off to new knowledge. Another is that behaving as though there are no questions to be asked changes social norms in a way that leads to political polarization and an inability to communicate across ideological divides. It's what leads us to both judge harshly and demonize people who disagree. And it's the indicator that we need to interrogate our thinking.

We said that when we're certain, when we've fallen into the Settled Question Fallacy, we're prone to two other fallacies. One is the Fallacy of Equal Knowledge. This is the assumption that disagreement on heated issues fundamentally stems from an asymmetry of information. When we fall into this fallacy, we're prone to think: If the other person just knew what I know, or if they just had the experiences I have had, they'd see things the way I do. When laid out in this manner, most people quickly see that it doesn't stand up to scrutiny. Then there's the Fallacy of Known Intent. Sometimes, we end up here once the person doesn't change their mind after it's been explained to them why they have the wrong opinion. When we fall into this fallacy, the assumptions we make about intent are almost always that the person is hateful in some way, often either of others or of their country.

After introducing these fallacies, we described what life looks like when we've stepped out of the Certainty Trap. We talked about the importance of trying to understand how someone arrived at their opinion or position. And the importance of going through the same exercise to understand how we arrived at our own. When it comes to other people's opinions, sometimes we can simply ask them to explain their thinking. But we can, and should, also get into the habit of figuring out all on our own how someone might have arrived at their opinion. We talked about some of the ways life without certainty can be difficult. Among other things, we have a finite amount of time in a day to devote to unpacking the thinking of other people.

We talked about how freedom from certainty is neither free nor simple. One of the key distinctions we made was between what we think of as the physical world and the abstract world. This distinction is why we can be *certain* that, for instance, 2+2=4. In an abstract world, as is the case with mathematics, the rules are entirely defined. That means that, within those confines, certainty is possible.

When we commit to questioning our knowledge, we enter a new realm, one of confidence. There's a qualitative shift that happens as we move from certainty (which we might think of as a "1" on a number line) to 0.99. That micro space of doubt we open up can make all the difference we need when it comes to our thinking on heated issues. We talked about the inherent doubt that is present when we're trying to figure out cause and effect, especially when it comes to human behavior. More generally, we raised questions like: What should and shouldn't count as evidence and who should decide?

We talked about how, as much as certainty is a problem at the individual level, it has particular consequences for institutions. Perhaps most notably, certainty, when coming from an institution, erodes trust. This is, at least in part, because we have fundamentally different expectations of institutions than we do of individuals. We don't often expect individuals to leave their political preferences aside, whereas we do for institutions. We talked about the example of critical race theory in schools and how, when it comes to the study of history in particular, the debates that surround CRT are fundamentally driven by claims of certainty about the past.

We've talked about why this challenge can be hard to commit to and why it's important that we do it anyway. There are powerful psychological forces pushing us toward binary thinking. These combine with incentive structures, many of which come through social media, that reward simplistic answers to complex problems, through things like likes and retweets. Perhaps most difficult, avoiding certainty raises questions about where we can draw the line. Do we have to open the door to any outrageous-sounding theory that comes along? The short answer is no, but it does mean we are committed to listening as much as we possibly can.

Ultimately, there are subtle but important changes we can make that would help move this transformation away from certainty along. We could build the understanding of uncertainty—including or especially when it comes to controversial and contentious topics—into our schools. This includes our K–12 schools *and* our institutions of higher education. We could transform our schools of education into places where asking questions and expressions of doubt are folded into every lesson and every topic. We could teach statistics and probability in high school. And we could pressure the mainstream media to use caution with their words and to qualify what they say in a manner that more accurately reflects what is known and makes assumptions explicit.

When it comes to remaining stuck, the costs of doing nothing are high. They include a weakening of our personal relationships, our professional spaces, and our trust in our institutions—oh, and one more thing: democracy itself. Democracy and certainty are fundamentally incompatible. A healthy democracy needs space for differing viewpoints and different views of the world. Certainty shuts down the vitality it needs to survive.

Clarifying our thinking means that we disagree differently than when we're doing so based in certainty. If you take anything away from the message of this book, it should be to try to follow these guidelines:

- Be clear and precise in our values, beliefs, goals, and principles.
- Allow those values, beliefs, goals, and principles to be questioned.
- Do not hang an argument on an assumption of hate or ignorance.
- Use language and terms in a way that your opponent would agree with.

You might find that committing to challenging your thinking in this way will change your life in multiple ways. Some may be external, in the way you relate to people, and others might be more internal. It might be how you feel when you read a news article, when you see something on social media, or when you are in conversation with someone you disagree with. While it might be exasperating at times, you can exhale knowing that you're taking an important step toward straightening the glass in the mirror in which you see the world unfold.

Acknowledgments

This book wouldn't have happened without the support, patience, and encouragement of several people. I'd like to specifically thank Kurt Volkan at Pitchstone who was willing to take a chance on me. I am grateful to my brother, Joshua Redstone, whose tireless willingness to talk through this topic deserves my unending gratitude. I would also like to thank Jessica Redstone, Ellie Avishai, Paul Redstone, and Tonia Smith for their endless encouragement. And, for their willingness to talk with me about these ideas, I would like to thank Anthony Kronman, Christian Gonzalez, Niall Ferguson, Kostas Kampourakis, Alex Small, Pamela Paresky, Chloé Valdary, Sergiu Klainerman, Joshua Katz, Bret Stephens, Carlo Rovelli, Jonathan Rauch, Michael Fertik, Oliver Traldi, Amy Wax, Kristi Williams, Chad Lakies, Aija Mayrock, Barbara Oakley, and John Horgan. Last, I am grateful to Joe Walsh for his support and willingness to write the foreword.

Appendix: FAQs

I've received a number of thoughtful questions while discussing the Certainty Trap, whether from students, colleagues, or readers. In case some readers have the same or similar questions, I thought it might be helpful to include some of them here along with my responses. The below questions are by no means an exhaustive list, but they are a useful starting point for thinking about what avoiding certainty looks like in practice.

Is the Certainty Trap a moral project?

I get where this question is coming from. Most of the book is talking about what's right, what's wrong, and how we know. But, fundamentally, the commitment to questioning what we know is an intellectual, philosophical, and empirical commitment. Sometimes I think of this work as a puzzle. I'm trying to describe how the pieces fit together.

Isn't this just another way of talking about motivated reasoning?

Motivated reasoning is indeed linked to certainty, but it's distinct in an important way. Motivated reasoning is one of the reasons why we fail to challenge our thinking—we only seek out evidence that supports our views, for instance. But it's not the only way. Earlier in the book, I talked about institutions—schools, for instance—that present information on heated issues in a way that's definitive and final. Students in that setting

232

could end up taking what they're taught as given without having engaged in any motivated reasoning whatsoever.

But we *can* be certain that there are two gametes, right?

I get this response sometimes when I suggest that there's uncertainty in the relationship between biology and gender. In some ways, the concern reminds me a little of the rabbits in the pre-Cambrian example—in the sense of who knows what scientists might find tomorrow. But let's assume that, while perhaps not certain, we can be *highly confident* that there are two gametes. Highly confident is not the same as certain. That said, there are legitimate questions to be raised about when and under what conditions established science should be challenged.

Does challenging all of our ideas mean that we have to see everything as maybe good or maybe bad?

Nope. What I am saying is that, even when it comes to something truly awful, take slavery as an example, challenging our thinking means being specific and clear about what principles or values are being violated. In that case, it's actually pretty straightforward. Maybe the principle is *I think all people have equal moral worth.* Or *I believe no person should be held captive or owned by another.* Or *I believe all people should be free to pursue their potential to its fullest.* And so on. Committing to challenging our thinking doesn't mean waffling about whether I think slavery is good or bad. It means being clear and explicit about why I've come to the position I have.

Are you saying the answer is always in the middle?

Nope. I'm saying no such thing. The problem I'm pointing to with extreme positions isn't so much the fact that they're extreme; rather, it's that they leave no room for doubt.

WHAT ABOUT QUESTIONING UNCERTAINTY?

Ahh, the thorny paradox question. Is uncertainty certain? I'm of two minds on how to think about this. Sometimes I think, yes, this is just a fundamental paradox. Uncertainty *is* certain. Like Franklin's axiom about the inevitability of only death and taxes. And leave it at that. And sometimes, if I'm feeling more reflective, it seems more appropriate to say I'm *highly confident* that uncertainty is certain.

Notes

Preface

1. I've also spent years teaching statistics and research methods, both of which come into play at various points in this book.

Chapter 1

1. Mallory Newall, "U.S. Stands Out Among 28 Countries in Perceptions of Social Tension," Ipsos, June 25, 2021, www.ipsos.com/en-us/news-polls/culture-war-around-the-world.

2. Ashley Parker, Rachael Bade, and John Wagner, "Trump Says They 'Hate Our Country.' The Democrats He Attacked Say the Country 'Belongs to Everyone,'" *Washington Post*, July 15, 2019, www.washingtonpost.com/politics/trump-calls-on-minority-congresswomen-to-apologize-after-he-said-they-should-go-back-to-their-countries/2019/07/15/897f1dd0-a6ef-11e9-a3a6-ab670962db05_story.html.

3. White House, "Biden-Harris Administration Advances Equality and Visibility for Transgender Americans," White House, fact sheet, March 31, 2022, www.whitehouse.gov/briefing-room/statements-releases/2022/03/31/fact-sheet-biden-harris-administration-advances-equality-and-visibility-for-transgender-americans/.

4. "Ex-White Supremacist Condemns Hate Groups, Tells Why He Changed," *Morning Call*, April 24, 1994, www.mcall.com/1994/04/24/ex-white-supremacist-condemns-hate-groups-tells-why-he-changed/.

5. "Former Member of the Aryan Nations Floyd Cochran," *Fresh Air with Terry Gross*, March 21, 1994, freshairarchive.org/segments/former-member-aryan-nations-floyd-cochran.

6. See, for example, Florida House of Representatives, CS/CS/HB 1557, 2022 Legislature, www.flsenate.gov/Session/Bill/2022/1557/BillText/er/PDF; and Commonwealth of Virginia Office of the Governor, "Ending the Use of Inherently Divisive Concepts Including Critical Race Theory, and Restoring Excellence in K-12 Public Education in the Commonwealth," executive order, 2022, www.governor.virginia.gov/media/governorvirginiagov/governor-of-virginia/pdf/74---eo/74---eo/EO-1---ENDING-THE-USE-OF-INHERENT-LY-DIVISIVE-CONCEPTS,-INCLUDING-CRITICAL-RACE-THEO-RY,-AND-RESTORING-EXCELLEN.pdf.

7. Zack Stanton, "How the 'Culture War' Could Break Democracy," *Politico*, May 20, 2021, www.politico.com/news/magazine/2021/05/20/culture-war-politics-2021-democracy-analysis-489900.

8. Zogby Analytics, "Will the US Have Another Civil War? Zogby Analytics," Zogby Poll, February 4, 2021, zogbyanalytics.com/news/997-the-zogby-poll-will-the-us-have-another-civil-war.

CHAPTER 2

1. Hart Research Associates/Public Opinion Strategies, "NBC News Survey," Study 220699, October 2022, s3.documentcloud.org/documents/23171526/220699-nbc-news-october-poll-v3.pdf.

2. Pew Research Center, "As Partisan Hostility Grows, Signs of Frustration with the Two-Party System," August 9, 2022, www.pewresearch.org/politics/2022/08/09/as-partisan-hostility-grows-signs-of-frustration-with-the-two-party-system/.

3. Department of Philosophy, "Red Herring," Texas State University, www.txst.edu/philosophy/resources/fallacy-definitions/Red-Herring.html (accessed February 2, 2023).

4. Some scholars and activists will point out that we don't have to simply throw our hands up in the air if the difference is rooted in biology. An alternative remedy would be to rebuild or reshape the labor market in such a way that rewards, or at least doesn't penalize, women for these patterns. In other words, there's an argument to be made that the differential, even if biologically rooted, is a function of distortions in the kinds of traits that are valued and that may be changeable, even if the trait itself is genetic. Nothing I'm saying here refutes that point. It's simply a taller order that calls for more revolutionary, and therefore more difficult, change.

5. We'll talk about this in more detail when we discuss the importance of moving from certainty to confidence.

6. School of Public Affairs, "What Is Civil Discourse?" American University, www.american.edu/spa/civildiscourse/what-is-civil-discourse.cfm (accessed February 2, 2023).

7. Sarah Stanley, "Facebook Posts: Says Fred Trump Was Arrested for 'Participating in KKK Riot' in 1927," *Politifact*, March 28, 2019, www.politifact.com/factchecks/2019/mar/28/facebook-posts/heres-whats-known-about-fred-trumps-arrest-after-k/.

8. Gabor David Kelen and Lisa Maragakis, "COVID-19 Vaccines: Myth Versus Fact," Johns Hopkins Medicine, March 10, 2022 (updated), www.hopkinsmedicine.org/health/conditions-and-diseases/coronavirus/covid-19-vaccines-myth-versus-fact.

9. Mayo Clinic Staff, "COVID-19 Vaccines: Get the Facts," Mayo Clinic, May 1, 2024, www.mayoclinic.org/diseases-conditions/coronavirus/in-depth/coronavirus-vaccine/art-20484859.

10. It's not "equality" in the strictest sense, given Vonnegut doesn't talk in the story about what happens to people who were below average.

CHAPTER 3

1. Steven J. Pearlman, *America's Critical Thinking Crisis: The Failure and Promise of Education* (Steven Pearlman, 2020); Steven J. Pearlman and David Carillo, "As the U.S. Innovation Ranking Falls, Real Critical Thinking Is Needed," *Hill*, February 18, 2021, thehill.com/changing-america/opinion/539404-as-the-us-innovation-ranking-falls-real-critical-thinking-is-needed/.

2. We'll talk about a twist on this claim when we talk about abstract worlds in chapter 6.

3. Some evidence suggests this might, in fact, be the case. Many theories have suggested that echo chambers are the driving factor in the way social media increases political polarization. But a 2022 *Proceedings of the National Academy of Sciences* paper found the opposite. It found that it's, in fact, contact with opposing views that pushes people to more extreme positions. One possible explanation for this is that the contact with opposing views makes people want to close ranks with like-minded folks to clearly establish who's on which side. But it's also consistent with the idea that contact with opposing ideas brings people in contact with others who judge them, and that judgment also pushes people to extremes. Petter Törnberg, "How Digital Media Drive Affective Polarization through Partisan Sorting," *Proceedings of the National Academy of Sciences (PNAS)* 119, no. 42 (October 10, 2022), doi.org/10.1073/pnas.220715911.

4. Pew Research Center, "Political Polarization in the American Public," June 12, 2014, www.pewresearch.org/politics/2014/06/12/political-polarization-in-the-american-public/.

5. Scott Adams, "Good Example of Our Two-Movie Reality," *Scott Adams Says*, February 12, 2017, www.scottadamssays.com/good-example-of-our-two-movie-reality/.

6. Anthony N. Washburn and Linda J. Skitka, "Science Denial across the Political Divide: Liberals and Conservatives Are Similarly Motivated to Deny Attitude-Inconsistent Science," *Social Psychological and Personality Science* 9, no. 8 (2017), doi.org/10.1177/1948550617731.

7. Peter H. Ditto and David F. Lopez, "Motivated Skepticism: Use of Differential Decision Criteria for Preferred and Nonpreferred Conclusions," *Journal of Personality and Social Psychology* 63, no. 4 (1992): 568–84, doi.org/10.1037//0022-3514.63.4.568

8. David G. Myers and Helmut Lamm, "The Group Polarization Phenomenon," *Psychological Bulletin* 83, no. 4 (July 1976): 602–27, https://doi.org/10.1037/0033-2909.83.4.602.

9. Ibid.

10. Marija A. Bekafigo et al., "The Effect of Group Polarization on Opposition to Donald Trump," *Political Psychology* 40, no. 5 (October 1, 2019): 1163–78, doi.org/10.1111/POPS.12584.

11. Jennifer McCoy and Benjamin Press, "What Happens When Democracies Become Perniciously Polarized?," Carnegie Endowment for International Peace, January 18, 2022, carnegieendowment.org/2022/01/18/what-happens-when-democracies-become-perniciously-polarized-pub-86190.

12. Karen Nussbaum, "We Can Move Beyond Political Polarization Through a Working-Class Economic Agenda," *Jacobin*, February 13, 2022, jacobin.com/2022/02/working-america-canvassing-us-working-class-voters-polarization.

13. Stephanie Forrest and Joshua Daymude, "Reducing Extreme Polarization Is Key to Stabilizing Democracy," Brookings Institution, January 26, 2022, www.brookings.edu/blog/techtank/2022/01/26/reducing-extreme-polarization-is-key-to-stabilizing-democracy/.

14. Gene Healy and Caleb O. Brown, "Partisanship, Polarization, and Polit-

ical Hatred," Cato Daily Podcast, December 20, 2021, www.cato.org/multime-dia/cato-daily-podcast/partisanship-polarization-political-hatred.

15. Yuval Levin, "The Irony Of Our Polarized Age," *National Review*, December 20, 2021, www.nationalreview.com/corner/the-irony-of-our-polarized-age/.

16. David Blankenhorn, "The Top 14 Causes of Political Polarization," *American Interest*, May 16, 2018, www.the-american-interest.com/2018/05/16/the-top-14-causes-of-political-polarization/.

17. Christopher Ingraham, "Members of Congress Are Physically Walking across the Aisle Less Often, According to 'the Largest Collection of C-SPAN Videos Ever Compiled,'" *Washington Post*, November 21, 2018, www.washing-tonpost.com/business/2018/11/21/members-congress-are-physically-walking-across-aisle-less-often-according-largest-collection-c-span-videos-ever-com-piled/.

18. Valerie Strauss, "No Systemic Racism? Look at Student Achievement Gaps in Reading," *Washington Post*, June 19, 2021, www.washingtonpost.com/education/2021/06/19/systemic-racism-reading-scores/.

19. Törnberg, "How Digital Media Drive Affective Polarization."

20. Nick Bilton, "An Average American Consumes 34 Gigabytes a Day, Study Says," *New York Times*, December 9, 2009, www.nytimes.com/2009/12/10/technology/10data.html.

21. Shelly Chaiken and Alison Ledgerwood, "A Theory of Heuristic and Systematic Information Processing," in *Handbook of Theories of Social Psychology: Volume 1*, ed. Paul A. M. Van Lange, Arie W. Kruglanski, and E. Tory Higgins (SAGE Publications Ltd, 2012): 246–66, doi.org/10.4135/9781446249215. N13; Kyle Hill, "This Is Your Brain on the Internet (Maybe)," *Scientific American*, September 11, 2012, blogs.scientificamerican.com/guest-blog/this-is-your-brain-on-the-internet-maybe/.

22. Nicholas Carr, "Is Google Making Us Stupid?" *Atlantic* (July 2008), www.theatlantic.com/magazine/archive/2008/07/is-google-making-us-stu-pid/306868/.

CHAPTER 4

1. A friend once pointed out to me that there's at least one other reason as well. That is, I might think the person who disagrees is disconnected from reality, delusional, or in some way crazy. While that is certainly a possibility, I don't focus on it here because my sense is that it's a far smaller fraction of people who are viewed this way, relative to those who are viewed as uneducated or hateful.

2. Other reasons, as we'll discuss later on, include differences in what counts as evidence and a lack of trust in the researchers and institutions that produce the research.

3. Tomohiko Ukai et al., "Habitual Tub Bathing and Risks of Incident Coronary Heart Disease and Stroke," *Heart* 106, no. 10 (May 2020): 732–37, doi.org/10.1136/HEARTJNL-2019-315752.

4. Curtis Bunn, "Report: Black People Are Still Killed by Police at a Higher Rate than Other Groups," *NBC News*, March 3, 2022, www.nbcnews.com/news/nbcblk/report-black-people-are-still-killed-police-higher-rate-groups-rcna17169.

5. Roland Fryer Jr., "An Empirical Analysis of Racial Differences in Police Use of Force," *Journal of Political Economy* 127, no. 3 (June 2019), doi.org/10.1086/701423.

6. Maria Krysan and S. Moberg, "Tracking Trends in Racial Attitudes," Institute of Government and Public Affairs, University of Illinois System, 2021, igpa.uillinois.edu/programs/racial_attitudes_2021.

7. P. J. Henry and David O. Sears, "The Symbolic Racism 2000 Scale," *Political Psychology* 23, no. 2 (June 1, 2002): 253–83, doi.org/10.1111/0162-895X.00281.

8. Ibid.

9. Bart de Langhe and Philip Fernbach, "The Dangers of Categorical Thinking," *Harvard Business Review* (September–October 2019), hbr.org/2019/09/the-dangers-of-categorical-thinking.

10. Kelly McLaughlin, "Colorado State University Students Were Pictured in Blackface," *Insider*, September 13, 2019, www.insider.com/colorado-state-university-students-pictured-in-blackface-2019-9.

CHAPTER 5

1. Kwame Anthony Appiah, "Is It OK That My Co-Worker Keeps Her Anti-Abortion Views on the Down Low?," *New York Times Magazine*, August 23, 2022, www.nytimes.com/2022/08/23/magazine/abortion-views-work-ethics.html.

2. Walter MacMurdo, "Kooks Serves Pop-Up Breakfast Burritos with Handmade Tortillas Out of a Food Cart on Cesar Chavez," *Willamette Week*,

May 16, 2017, www.wweek.com/uncategorized/2017/05/16/kooks-serves-pop-up-breakfast-burritos-with-handmade-tortillas-out-of-a-food-cart-on-cesar-chavez/.

3. Jamilah King, "These White Cooks Bragged about Bringing Back Recipes from Mexico to Start a Business," *Mic.com*, May 19, 2017, www.mic.com/articles/177642/these-white-cooks-bragged-about-stealing-tortilla-recipes-from-mexico-to-start-a-portland#.SiLNqfePz.

4. Priya Sridhar, "SDG&E Worker Fired Over Alleged Racist Gesture Says He Was Cracking Knuckles," *NBC San Diego*, June 15, 2020, www.nbcsandiego.com/news/local/sdge-worker-fired-over-alleged-racist-gesture-says-he-was-cracking-knuckles/2347414/.

5. Michael Powell, "Sundance Liked Her Documentary, 'Jihad Rehab,' until Muslim Critics Didn't," *New York Times*, September 25, 2022, www.nytimes.com/2022/09/25/us/sundance-jihad-rehab-meg-smaker.html.

6. Sometimes, it can be easy to recognize that people interpret their experiences differently, but there might be a question of, well, what do most people in a particular group think? In the Free Black Thought case, the argument might be something like, well, of course, there's variation in opinion in the black community, but the vast majority of people in this community have a shared view of the world. While this is a reasonable point, it only raises more questions—such as, does certainty become defensible if a majority of people share a particular view? The short answer to that question is no.

7. Bernie Lucht, ed., *Ideas: Brilliant Thinkers Speak Their Minds* (Goose Lane, 2005).

CHAPTER 6

1. For a transcript and audio of the speech, see "This Is Water by David Foster Wallace" (Full Transcript and Audio)," *Farnam Street*, fs.blog/david-foster-wallace-this-is-water/

2. Hans Rosling, Ola Rosling, and Anna Rosling Rönnlund, *Factfulness: Ten Reasons We're Wrong about the World—and Why Things Are Better than You Think* (Flatiron, 2018).

3. Anthony Tommasini, "To Make Orchestras More Diverse, End Blind Auditions," *New York Times*, July 16, 2021, www.nytimes.com/2020/07/16/arts/music/blind-auditions-orchestras-race.html.

4. Bret Stephens, "Climate of Complete Certainty," *New York Times*, April 28, 2017, www.nytimes.com/2017/04/28/opinion/climate-of-complete-certainty.html.

5. Editor in Chief, "We Respond to the Historians Who Critiqued The 1619 Project," *New York Times*, January 19, 2021 (updated), www.nytimes.com/2019/12/20/magazine/we-respond-to-the-historians-who-critiqued-the-1619-project.html.

6. Leslie M. Harris, "I Helped Fact-Check the 1619 Project. The Times Ignored Me," *Politico*, March 6, 2020, www.politico.com/news/magazine/2020/03/06/1619-project-new-york-times-mistake-122248.

7. Arun Venugopal, "'1619 Project' Journalist Says Black People Shouldn't Be an Asterisk in U.S. History," *NPR*, November 17, 2021, www.npr.org/2021/11/17/1056404654/nikole-hannah-jones-1619-project.

8. Robert George (@McCormickProf), in a post on Twitter, July 1, 2020, twitter.com/mccormickprof/status/1278529694355292161.

9. Executive Office of the President, "Establishing the President's Advisory 1776 Commission," *Federal Register*, Executive Order 13958, November 2, 2020, www.federalregister.gov/documents/2020/11/05/2020-24793/establishing-the-presidents-advisory-1776-commission.

10. Edmund L. Gettier, "Is Justified True Belief Knowledge?," *Analysis* 23, no. 6 (June 1963): 121–23, doi.org/10.1093/ANALYS/23.6.121.

11. Alvin I. Goldman, "Discrimination and Perceptual Knowledge," *Journal of Philosophy* 73, no. 20 (August 1977): 771–91, doi.org/10.2307/2025679.

12. Ursula K. Le Guin, "The Ones Who Walk Away from Omelas," in *New Dimensions*, ed. Robert Silverberg (Nelson Doubleday, 1973).

13. "Moral Machine," moralmachine.net (accessed February 4, 2023).

14. It turns out, researchers have shown, that those cars can be pretty easy to fool. For instance, by using tape to write the words "love" and "hate" on a stop sign, the cars misread it as a 45-mph sign. By modifying a right-turn arrow from its usual shade of black to a pixelated grey-white, the car treated it as a stop sign. By placing a piece of black tape across the middle of the "3," researchers tricked the car into reading a 35-mph sign as an 85-mph sign. The programs can get things wrong. See Matt Kimberley, "Self-Driving Cars Could Be Fooled into Dangerous Manoeuvres by Anyone with a Handful of Stickers," *Car Throttle*, August 8, 2017, www.carthrottle.com/news/self-driving-cars-could-be-fooled-dangerous-manoeuvres-anyone-handful-stickers; Kate Gibson, "Tesla Tricked into Speeding by Researchers Using Simple Electrical Tape," *CBS News*, February 19, 2020, www.cbsnews.com/news/tesla-tricked-into-speeding-by-re-searchers-using-electrical-tape/.

CHAPTER 7

1. Marianne Bertrand and Sendhil Mullainathan, "Are Emily and Greg More Employable Than Lakisha and Jamal? A Field Experiment on Labor Market Discrimination," *American Economic Review* 94, no. 4 (August 2004): 991–1013, doi.org/10.1257/0002828042002561

2. Patrick Boyle, "What Is Gender-Affirming Care? Your Questions Answered," Association of American Medical Colleges, April 12, 2022, www.aamc.org/news-insights/what-gender-affirming-care-your-questions-answered.

3. Jamuna Prasad, "The Psychology of Rumour: A Study Relating to the Great Indian Earthquake of 1934," *British Journal of Psychology* 26 (1935): 1–15.

4. Leon Festinger, *A Theory of Cognitive Dissonance* (Stanford University Press, 1957).

5. Melvin J. Lerner and Carolyn H. Simmons, "Observer's Reaction to the 'Innocent Victim': Compassion or Rejection?," *Journal of Personality and Social Psychology* 4, no. 2 (August 1966): 203–10, doi.org/10.1037/H0023562.

6. Arielle Pardes, "Does Cocaine Have Any Potential as an Antidepressant?," *Vice*, February 11, 2015, www.vice.com/en/article/3b7g8v/can-cocaine-cure-grief-210; Barbara Bronson Gray, "A Brief History of Ulcer Treatments," *Los Angeles Times*, April 22, 1994, www.latimes.com/archives/la-xpm-1994-04-22-va-48924-story.html; Walter Sneader, "The Discovery of Heroin," *Lancet* 352, no. 9141 (November 1998): 1697–99, doi.org/10.1016/S0140-6736(98)07115-3.

CHAPTER 8

1. Pete Buttigieg, *Trust: America's Best Chance* (Liveright, 2020).

2. To be clear, in the current context, we're focused on social norms and context, not the legal framework.

3. Hobby Lobby, "Our Story," newsroom.hobbylobby.com/corporate-background (accessed February 4, 2023).

4. Marie Fazio, "How Mask Guidelines Have Changed," *New York Times*,

April 27, 2021, www.nytimes.com/2021/04/27/science/face-mask-guidelines-timeline.html.

5. Maria Cramer and Knvul Sheikh, "Surgeon General Urges the Public to Stop Buying Face Masks," *New York Times*, February 29, 2020, www.nytimes.com/2020/02/29/health/coronavirus-n95-face-masks.html.

6. K Lloyd Parker (@kalpha7), in a post on Twitter, May 26, 2020, twitter.com/kalpha7/status/1265220225894690817.

7. Kent Thielen (@KentThielen), in a post on Twitter, May 28, 2020, twitter.com/KentThielen/status/1266136517673652224.

8. Centers for Disease Control and Prevention, "Similarities and Differences between Flu and COVID-19," March 20, 2024 (last reviewed), www.cdc.gov/flu/symptoms/flu-vs-covid19.htm.

9. Patrick Van Kessel and Dennis Quinn, "Republicans, Democrats Differ on Why Masks Are a Downside of COVID-19," Pew Research Center, October 29, 2020, www.pewresearch.org/fact-tank/2020/10/29/both-republicans-and-democrats-cite-masks-as-a-negative-effect-of-covid-19-but-for-very-different-reasons/.

10. Harry Kalven, Jr., et al., "Kalven Committee: Report on the University's Role in Political and Social Action," University of Chicago, November 1967, provost.uchicago.edu/sites/default/files/documents/reports/KalvenRprt_0.pdf.

11. Geoffrey R. Stone et al.,, "Report of the Committee on Freedom of Expression," University of Chicago, January 2015, provost.uchicago.edu/sites/default/files/documents/reports/FOECommitteeReport.pdf.

12. Andrew Lawrence, "Uju Anya on the Queen, Jeff Bezos and the Family History behind Her Tweet," *Guardian*, September 14, 2022, www.theguardian.com/uk-news/2022/sep/14/uju-anya-queen-nigeria-colonialism-empire.

13. Todd Richmond, "These Are the Charges Kyle Rittenhouse Faces in Kenosha Shooting," *PBS News Hour*, November 2, 2021, www.pbs.org/newshour/nation/ap-explainer-what-charges-does-kyle-rittenhouse-face.

14. Conor Friedersdorf, "Universities Try to Force a Consensus About the Kyle Rittenhouse Verdict," *Atlantic*, November 26, 2021, www.theatlantic.com/ideas/archive/2021/11/universities-forced-consensus-kyle-rittenhouse/620809/.

15. Cynthia Larive and Judith Estrada, "Statement on Not Guilty Verdict in Rittenhouse Trial," UC Santa Cruz, November 19, 2021, news.ucsc.edu/2021/11/statement-rittenhouse.html.

16. Of course, this claim, as with all claims, is subject to challenge.

17. Eugene Volokh, "The Law School Acknowledges That the Racial and Gender References on the Examination Were Deeply Offensive," *Volokh Conspiracy*, January 15, 2021, reason.com/volokh/2021/01/15/tenured-law-prof-apparently-suspended-for-racial-harassment-lawsuit-problem-on-a-civil-procedure-exam/.

18. Collective Committee, "Call to Action: Insensitive and Racist Content on UIC John Marshall Law School Exam!," Change.org, December 2020, www.change.org/p/dean-dickerson-and-chancellor-michael-amiridis-insensitive-and-racist-content-on-uic-john-marshall-law-school-exam

19. Kathryn Rubino, "Law School N-Word Controversy Is More Complicated Than It Appears at First Glance," *Above the Law*, January 13, 2021, abovethelaw.com/2021/01/law-school-n-word-controversy-is-more-complicated-than-it-appears-at-first-glance/.

20. Andrew Koppelman, "Is This Law Professor Really a Homicidal Threat?," *Chronicle of Higher Education*, January 19, 2021, www.chronicle.com/article/is-this-law-professor-really-a-homicidal-threat?cid=gen_sign_in-&cid2=gen_login_refresh.

21. Anemona Hartocollis, "Ilya Shapiro Quits Georgetown's Law School Amid Free Speech Fight," *New York Times*, June 6, 2022, www.nytimes.com/2022/06/06/us/georgetown-ilya-shapiro.html.

22. Lauren Lumpkin, "Ilya Shapiro Apologizes for 'Appalling' Tweets Ahead of Georgetown Law Appointment," *Washington Post*, January 27, 2022, www.washingtonpost.com/education/2022/01/27/georgetown-law-ilya-shapiro-tweets/.

23. William M. Treanor, "Dean's Statement Re Ilya Shapiro," Georgetown Law School, June 2, 2022, www.law.georgetown.edu/deans-statement-re-ilya-shapiro/.

24. Executive Department, "Proclamation," EO-23-05, State of Arkansas, January 10, 2023, governor.arkansas.gov/wp-content/uploads/EO-23-05-Prohibit-Indoctrination.pdf.

25. Leonard Downie Jr., "Newsrooms That Move beyond 'Objectivity' Can Build Trust," *Washington Post*, January 30, 2023, www.washingtonpost.com/opinions/2023/01/30/newsrooms-news-reporting-objectivity-diversity/.

26. Bret Stephens, "How to Destroy (What's Left of) the Mainstream Media's Credibility," *New York Times*, February 9, 2023, www.nytimes.com/2023/02/09/opinion/mainstream-media-credibility-objectivity-journalism.html.

CHAPTER 9

1. Robert Duff, "7 Most Famous Sports Superstitions," *Sports Betting Dime*, March 5, 2021, www.sportsbettingdime.com/guides/articles/famous-sports-su-perstitions/.

2. Kristen Senz, "Outrage Spreads Faster on Twitter: Evidence from 44 News Outlets," Harvard Business School, Working Knowledge, July 13, 2021, hbswk.hbs.edu/item/hate-spreads-faster-on-twitter-evidence-from-44-news-outlets.

3. Center for Humane Technology, "Who We Are," Center for Humane Technology, www.humanetech.com/who-we-are (last accessed March 4, 2023).

4. Daniel Kahneman, *Thinking Fast and Slow* (Farrar, Strous and Giroux, 2011).

5. Scott Alexander, "I Can Tolerate Anything Except The Outgroup," *Slate Star Codex*, September 30, 2014, slatestarcodex.com/2014/09/30/i-can-toler-ate-anything-except-the-outgroup/.

6. Marc Lluís Vives and Oriel Feldmanhall, "Tolerance to Ambiguous Uncertainty Predicts Prosocial Behavior," *Nature Communications* 9, no. 1 (June 2018): 1–9, doi.org/10.1038/s41467-018-04631-9.

7. Kristin Buhr and Michel J. Dugas, "The Intolerance of Uncertainty Scale: Psychometric Properties of the English Version," *Behaviour Research and Therapy* 40, no. 8 (2002): 931–45, doi.org/10.1016/S0005-7967(01)00092-4.

8. John Navin, "Why Coincidences, Miracles And Rare Events Happen Every Day," *Forbes*, February 18, 2014, www.forbes.com/sites/john-navin/2014/02/18/why-coincidences-miracles-and-rare-events-happen-every-day/?sh=51d5813c1f1b.

9. Thomas Gilovich, *How We Know What Isn't So: The Fallibility of Human Reason in Everyday Life* (Free Press, 1991).

10. Melinda Wenner Moyer, "People Drawn to Conspiracy Theories Share a Cluster of Psychological Features," *Scientific American*, March 1, 2019, www.scientificamerican.com/article/people-drawn-to-conspiracy-theo-ries-share-a-cluster-of-psychological-features/.

11. Ibid.

About the Author

Ilana Redstone is a professor of sociology at the University of Illinois at Urbana-Champaign. She can be found on X @irakresh and more of her work is available at www.ilanaredstone.com.